MW00964308

Musical Understanding
Perspectives in Theory and Practice

Betty Hanley & Thomas W. Goolsby, Eds.

© 2002 The Canadian Music Educators Association

All rights reserved. No part of this work may be reproduced or used in any form or by any means, electronic or mechanical, including photocopying, recording, or any information storage or retrieval system, without the prior written permission of the Canadian Music Educators Association.

Cover Design by Zamage Digital Imaging, Inc.
Cover Image by William Zuk and Paul Marcano
Book Design by Betty Hanley
Cartoons by Robert Dalton
Printed and bound in Canada by Friesens

Canadian Cataloguing in Publication Data

Main entry under title:

Musical Understanding

Perspectives in Theory and Practice
Includes bibliographical references.
ISBN 0-920630-10-3

1.Music—Understanding—Teaching and learning—Schools. 2. Education—Curriculum.
I. Hanley, Betty, 1942– II. Goolsby, Thomas W., 1953– III. Canadian Music Educators Association.

Contents

Introduction
Down the Rabbit's Hole

Betty Hanley

> *It is the desire to understand, to find meaning, that distinguishes Homo sapiens from the rest of the animal kingdom, that defines the species.* (Wade Roland, *Ockham's Razor*, p. 189)

Where does a book begin? It could begin with a question, an idea, a story you want to tell, a need for dialogue. This book began with questions. What is musical understanding? How do or could music educators teach for musical understanding? What does musical understanding look like? How can music teachers evaluate student understanding? Although this book began with questions, within its pages can be found many stories, paths, and perspectives.

Developing understanding in students has been a long-standing, if elusive, goal of music education. The precursor to this book, the *Symposium on Musical Understanding* held in Victoria, February 22–23, 2001, grew out of questions and concerns arising from my reading about Harvard University's Teaching for Understanding (TfU) (Wiske, 1998). Unlike Harvard's original Project Zero (Cf., Gardner & Perkins, 1988) and Arts PROPEL (Cf., Davidson, et al., 1992), which focused on the arts as important domains, TfU, with its intriguing pedagogy, has largely neglected music in its publications (Blythe & Associates, 1998; Veenema, Hetland, & Chalfen, 1997; Wiske, 1998). I was perplexed. Why was music excluded in an enterprise that should have equal import for music education? My concern did not stop there.

Over the past few years, in courses addressing pedagogy and curriculum, my graduate students (experienced music teachers) had been encountering rather formidable barriers when asked to identify generative topics in music (as opposed to rehearsing, listening, or composing) and conceptualize what teaching for musical understanding would look like. Why was this the case? While it would be irresponsible of me to generalize solely on the basis of my experience, there seems to be some evidence that teacher education programs have not been preparing teachers to conceive of teaching music as something beyond skill development and knowledge deployment (Younker, 2000).

Reading Swanwick's (1997, 1999) and Swanwick and Franca's (1999) work on musical understanding further increased my resolve to better understand musical understanding. My interest in the topic was piqued yet again when I listened to Renate Zenker present an overview of her dissertation on musical understanding at a research session of the 2000 British Columbia Music Educators' Conference. I decided that it was crucial and timely to bring together music educators who shared an interest in musical understanding so they could engage in a dialogue whose purpose was to shed light on a central issue in music education.[1]

In an international call for papers, music educators were invited to address musical understanding and its role in music classrooms from both theoretical and practical perspectives. The focus questions were:

(1) What is musical understanding? What are the issues surrounding musical understanding?

(2) How can musical understanding be nurtured in the music classroom? How do we know when it has been achieved?

In identifying these two areas, I did not intend to perpetuate the false dichotomy between theory and practice that has plagued education and pitted scholars and practitioners against each other. Indeed, in the "Reconceptualized" view of curriculum that currently dominates the field (Hanley & Montgomery, 2002; Pinar, Reynolds, Slattery, & Taubman, 1995), the relationship between theory and practice is seen to be symbiotic: "Our view is that contemporary scholars are simultaneously closer to both 'practice' and closer to 'theory'" (Pinar, 1995, p. 40). Although the chapters in this book are placed in either Part 1

---

[1] The Symposium would not have taken place without the support and generous assistance of the University of Victoria, the British Columbia Music Educators Association, and the Canadian Music Educators Association.

(Theoretical Perspectives) or Part 2 (Perspectives in Practice), they do not fit exclusively in either location; indeed, they largely bridge the theory/practice divide. Contributors agreed with R. Wiggins, one of the participant-observers, who stated: "I can't separate theory from what I do and I can't stop theorizing in my practice." A convergence of practice and theory is, thus, evident throughout this book.

The thirteen papers selected by referees for delivery at the Victoria *Symposium* and subsequently transformed into the chapters in this book range from philosophical analysis (Chapter 2), critical theory (Chapter 5), constructivist theory (Chapters 3, 4, 9, and 12), teaching for understanding (Chapters 8 and 14), to Gordon's theory of audiation (Chapter 6). Only one chapter is new: Thomas Goolsby agreed to provide a historical background for the other chapters (Chapter 1). Chapters 2 through 14 address a number of issues: the role of the body in music education (Chapters 7 and 13), listening to music (Chapters 7 and 11), performance-based music education (Chapter 12), the interrelated role of cognition and culture (Chapter 4), assessment in music education (Chapter 14), multicultural music education (Chapter 4 and 11), and curriculum (Chapters 8, 9, 10, and 12). There is also a range of research methodologies (qualitative, reviews of the literature, analytical, biographical, historical, and descriptive). The variety of perspectives contributes to a rich and colorful tapestry.

The *Symposium* was organized to foster dialogue. One of its unique features was an opportunity for "second thoughts." Presenters were encouraged to comment on (and even revise) their papers in view of the on-going dialogue. A number of presenters chose to incorporate second thoughts as part of their presentations and, later, in their chapters. The authors are commended for their willingness to listen, consider other views, and revise their thinking when necessary. This book is, consequently, not a typical proceedings but a set of papers that have been revised and, in many cases, re-worked on the basis of the *Symposium* and subsequent dialogue.

In addition to the presenters whose names appear as authors in this book, a number of participant-observers contributed valuable input to the dialogue: Tammy Duggan and Beth Pineo, music educators from Nova Scotia; Dr. Robert Wiggins, Oakland University, Michigan; Dr.

Gerald King, Dr. Moira Szabo, and Sheila Sim, University of Victoria, British Columbia; and Karen Lee, University of British Columbia. Dr. Antoinette Oberg, University of Victoria, served as the dialogue facilitator.

We are grateful to Dr. Robert Dalton for the whimsical cartoons that introduce each part of the book, to Dr. William Zuk and Paul Marcano for a digital cover image that symbolizes the potential of understanding, and Scott Donatelli of Zamage Digital Imaging for a cover design that artistically conveys the tone of the book.

The Dialogue

Dialogue was very important to the *Symposium*, but not all the ideas discussed over the two days are addressed in the chapters of this book. I have selected three issues that appear in the transcription of the deliberations as examples of the way dialogue challenged those in attendance to rethink their positions. The selected issues are: listening to music, multicultural music education, and Gordon's audiation theory. No consensus on the issues was expected in such a brief encounter; none was reached.

Listening to Music

Not surprisingly, listening to music was a topic that generated considerable interest. Is listening to music passive or active? Is listening to music a qualitatively different experience for performers and non-performers? How do we listen to music of other cultures? Can listening be taught?

Shively, coming from an instrumental performance background, asked whether listeners might have different ways of using musical knowledge—different from those of performers and conductors. That is, is there a distinct way that listeners use knowledge when they have no background as performers, conductors, etc.? This question speaks to the structure and value of music listening for non-performers and performers and the possible need for more informed listening by performers.

The discussion about listening was closely related to the nature of musical experience and the degree to which education should impose on or shape this experience. Richardson explained her view: "I have enjoyed the opportunity to stop at the 'because,' just to be in the moment. The music experience is powerful, always right there. You can't talk about it.

We don't give ourselves credit for this experience, or our students." Bush responded: "Students can experience some really great things in my classroom but, if I don't ask them to think and feel it and analyze it and step back and look into it, they are missing a whole level." There was a clear disagreement between hermeneutic and cognitive perspectives (Walker, 2000).

Researchers tell us there is a difference between untrained and trained listeners (Davies, 1994; Geringer, 1995; Hare, 1977; Smith, 1997). Furthermore, the way many people use music in their lives (De Nora, 2000) seems contrary to the disinterested, analytical listening traditionally fostered by music educators. Szabo (2001), too, supports the importance of the emotional responses of untrained listeners in her study of gramophiles (avid listeners and collectors of Western art music). Shively's question may have originated in his concern about performance-based instrumental programs at the secondary level and a neglect of the musical growth of students who opt out of such programs.

Meanwhile, Fiske, building on what he calls a constructionist theory and reinforcing the generally constructivist orientation of the group, proposed that music educators make the mistake of thinking there really is a piece of music out there. Instead, he suggested they should realize there is no piece out there, just "air molecules bouncing back and forth. There is no melody, no harmony, no aesthetics, no meaning [out there]. We construct the piece." If this is the case, then listening experiences and teaching strategies should be reconceived, recognizing what learners bring rather than only imposing expert knowledge (Hanley, 1997; Wiggins, 2001).

Multicultural Music Education

Multicultural music education was another complex issue frequently revisited during the *Symposium*. Do we need to perform a culture's music to understand it? How is music experienced by people in other cultures? The role of ritual, visual appeal, and cultural perspective were addressed in the following transcription.

> *[Zenker] There are many approaches to multicultural music. Some say you have to be a performer in a culture's music to understand it. Others disagree. These issues are not resolved. The debate is whether to use perform-*

ance or to talk about the culture. How strictly do we have to adhere to a cultural context? How close to the performance style? Do we do composition with a type of music that is not written down? We need to remain as culturally true as possible.

[R. Wiggins] We neglect how close music is to ritual in many cultures. "What role does music play in your culture?" is a ridiculous question for many people. Music is not separate thing for them. Music in the West at one time was connected to everyday life and slowly got separated into performance. Now? For the young, there is no music that is not also visual and has no text. But schools of music still promote that view of music.

[Zenker] Why not use visuals? For program music?

[R. Wiggins] I'm thinking of something deeper than that. The fact is that, in a lot of popular music, listening includes movement, a video. Thirty or forty years ago, the idea of going to a popular music concert was exciting, but the musicians stood still and sounded very much like what came over the phonograph speakers. Now, performance is different—costumes, lighting, fireworks.... What is the visual imagery they see? Maybe they can't just listen? Maybe when the visual is not there, there is something missing from the experience. In many culture music by itself isn't important; it's what they're doing while the music is happening that is important.

J. Wiggins addressed the need to begin with our students' values and concerns rather than our own.

This argument about what's appropriate... If we are supposed to be helping children use their frames to understand the rest of the world, everything has to start from their perspective, not ours. Music from other cultures must be taught respectfully and as authentically as possible, but they [students] should build on the tools they already have. They can't necessarily be taught in the same way as other cultures (e.g., the use/non-use of notation). Constructivism brings a different perspective.

Bartel considers how we mistakenly characterize music of other cultures as static: "We think of the music of other cultures as traditional/primitive (stuck in the past). In fact, the music of Zaire, for example, is in a state of fusion. The traditional music may exist in places but...." What music should be taught? When do we know enough? How can we keep up with a changing/evolving understanding of music from other cultures?

Gordon's Theory of Audiation

One of the most contentious issues at the *Symposium* (other than the definition of musical understanding itself) arose during Gerhardstein's presentation of the historical antecedents of Edwin Gordon's theory of audiation and its connection to musical understanding. The issues surrounded the merits of the theory and were grounded in a clash between constructivist (Brooks & Brooks, 1993; Duckworth, 1996; Fosnot, 1996), behaviorist, and expressionist perspectives.

> *[R. Wiggins] I would like to challenge Gordon's thesis that to audiate music is to understand it. Consider a comparison with language. You can decode words without understanding their meaning. The same applies in music. Musical understanding involves more than the recognition of tonal and rhythmic patterns and the reproduction of these patterns internally or externally. I see this in classes; students don't go the next step to musical understanding. Consider for example the first and last movements of Beethoven's* Fifth Symphony. *The tonal/rhythmic patterns heard in the first movement are different from those in the last movement. Yet, as a musician, I understand that those two are connected and somehow reflect back to the first movement.*

> *[Gerhardstein] Gordon has been criticized for being atomistic. He wouldn't agree with the description above. He did attempt to determine the sequence of learning patterns. Still there is a leap that must be made between the tonal and rhythmic patterns and musical understanding.*

> *[J. Wiggins] There is a disconnection between what Gordon proposes in terms of outcome and the practice he suggests—a bottom-up approach measuring little tid-bits. He did not rely on Vygotsky. Musical understanding and audiation should be linked.*

> *[Bartel] What the mind does is recognize, compare, and classify patterns. That is the essence of what you are saying. But, does pattern recognition, etc., constitute musical understanding? If so, how? It sounds like the simple graphic phonemic level of language processing, which we know is far from understanding, For example, Muslims are taught to read the Koran. They read, say, pronounce but have no idea of what they are reading. Music education research needs to learn from language processing as it applies to meaning making and apply what is learned. For example, music educators think that a misstep on violin or piano is a mistake. It is not considered a miscue. When music students make mistakes, these are not simply missteps but cognitive predictions. Did Gordon address "mistakes"?*

> *[Zenker] I can understand audiation as a process. Understanding is an outcome, not a process—an outcome of doing processes. Audiation is a*

process towards understanding. The problem with Gordon is that he attempts to mix process and outcome. He talks of activities. Performance is not understanding; it is a process, a part of what we do to achieve musical understanding....

[Gerhardstein] Gordon would not say that audiation is just a process. He would not say that audiation is just the doing, it is also the end.

[R. Wiggins] I'm not comfortable with the statement that understanding is the result, the outcome. Outcome has such a final sound to it. To me understanding is something that is continuous; it constantly feeds back. What Gardner, [J.] Wiggins, and I would say about understanding is in relation to doing—doing something is evidence that you have understanding. But even in the process of doing something you are gaining additional understanding/perception. Even with all the words in the English language, we still don't have enough words to differentiate some of these things: new understanding, new points of view about something, new perceptions that come as a result of doing something that assumes you have some understanding to begin with. To say that understanding is the outcome of doing something is not accurate. I think there is a circle.... One part of Vygotsky that I can't align with Gordon is that with Vygotsky there is so much a sense of engaging in the process as part of developing understanding, the whole cognitive apprenticeship notion and the zone of proximal development that we mentioned yesterday and the support of knowledgeable others. Learning is a process that happens with someone else. Whenever I've seen Gordon, it appears as if "I'll show you what to do," "do it." "now you understand what I asked you to do." That's very inconsistent with Vygotsky.

Once again, perspectives collided (in a collegial way). The task now is to consider each perspective thoughtfully in order to determine its merit and consider how each might deepen our own understanding.

Chasing the Rabbit

Can musical understanding be taught? How can we help students listen to music with understanding? How can we engage students in the music of other cultures at more than a superficial level when the music of other cultures is also evolving? Is understanding a noun or a verb? An outcome or a recursive process? What is musical understanding? Is a definition needed? How do we know when students understand? The authors in this book provide a number of intriguing and potentially useful perspectives and their answers to some of these and other questions.

Does this book provide all the answers—everything you ever needed to know about musical understanding? Of course not. Do I now have a better understanding of musical understanding. Yes. Do I have *the* final answer? Not likely, but I do have an answer—a basis for making practical decisions that impact on my students. I could divulge my answers to the questions raised in this book, but that's not what this book is about. As Bartel put it:

> *It is a challenge for us to do research presentations that are herme-neutically open—for us not to interpret all for the person rather than to trust the meaning making of the audience. [This trust] will be a long time in coming, especially in music. We have spent the past 20 years practising repetitive music making by ourselves. We're in education and like to control the curriculum and what students learn. We're in research that likes to control. To give up control is nearly impossible.*

Well, it's time to begin. Each of you will weigh the merits of the answers provided by the authors. It is our collective hope that that you will find your own answers as you enter the dialogue.

Down the rabbit's hole...

References

Blythe, T., & Associates. (1998). *The teaching for understanding guide.* San Francisco, CA: Jossey-Bass Publishers.

Brooks, J. G., & Brooks, M. G. (1993). *The case for constructivist classrooms: In search of understanding.* Alexandria, VA: Association for Supervision and Curriculum development.

Davidson, L., Myford, C., Plasket, D., Scripps, L., Swinton, S., Torff, B., et al. (1992). *Arts PROPEL: A handbook for music.* Cambridge, MA: Harvard Project Zero & Educational Testing Service.

Davies, S. (1994). *Musical meaning.* New York: Cornell University Press.

De Nora, T. (2000). *Music in everyday life.* Cambridge, UK: Cambridge University Press.

Duckworth, E. (1996). *"The having of wonderful ideas" and other essays on teaching and learning* (2nd ed.). New York: Teachers College Press.

Fosnot, C. T. (Ed). (1996). *Constructivism: Theory, perspectives, and practice.* New York: Teachers College Press.

Gardner, H., & Perkins, D. (Eds.). (1988). *Art, mind & education: Research from Project Zero.* Urbana, IL: University of Illinois.

Geringer, J. M. (1995). Continuous loudness judgments of dynamics in recorded music excerpts. *Journal of Research in Music Education, 43* (1), 22–35.

Hanley, B. (1997). An integrated listening model. *Canadian Music Educator, 38* (3), 37–41.

Hanley, B., & Montgomery, J. (2002). Contemporary curriculum practices and their theoretical bases. In R. J. Colwell & C. Richardson (Eds.), *The new handbook of research on music teaching and learning* (pp. 113–143). New York: Oxford University Press.

Hare, F. G. (1977). Dimensions of music perception. *Scientific Aesthetics, 1,* 171–180.

Pinar, W. F. (1995). An introduction. In W. F. Pinar, W. M. Reynolds, P. Slatter, & P. M. Taubman (Eds.), *Understanding curriculum: An introduction to the study of historical and contemporary curriculum discourses* (pp. 3–65). New York: Peter Lang.

Pinar, W. F., Reynolds, W. M., Slatter, P., & Taubman, P. M. (1995). *Understanding curriculum: An introduction to the study of historical and contemporary curriculum discourses.* New York: Peter Lang.

Smith, J. D. (1997). The place of musical novices in music science. *Music Perception, 14* (3), 227–262.

Swanwick, K. (1997). Assessing musical quality in the national curriculum. *British Journal of Music education, 14* (3), 205–215.

Swanwick, K. (1999). *Teaching music musically.* London: Routledge.

Swanwick, K., & Franca, C. C. (1999). Composing, performing and audience-listening as indicators of musical understanding. *British Journal of Music Education, 16* (1), 5–19.

Szabo, M. (2001). *For the love of music: Avenues of entry into the world of Western art music.* Unpublished doctoral dissertation, University of Washington, Seattle.

Veenema, S., Hetland, L., & Chalfen, K. (1997). *The Project Zero classroom: New approaches to thinking and understanding.* Cambridge, MA: Project Zero.

Walker, M. E. (2000). Movement and metaphor: Toward an embodied theory of music cognition and hermeneutics. *Bulletin of the Council for Research in Music Education, 145,* 27–42.

Wiggins, J. (2001). *Teaching for musical understanding.* New York: McGraw-Hill.

Wiske, M. S. (Ed.). (1998). *Teaching for understanding.* San Francisco, CA: Jossey-Bass Publishers.

Younker, B. A. (2000). The role of musical thinking in selected Canadian elementary music curricula: Evidence of success and ideas for consideration. In B. Hanley & B. A. Roberts (Eds.), *Looking forward: Challenges to Canadian music education* (pp. 169–192). Victoria, BC: Canadian Music Educators Association.

Part 1

Theoretical Perspectives

Thought and theory

Historical Perspectives on Musical Understanding

Thomas W. Goolsby

Musical Understanding and Musical Meaning

A primary challenge in writing an historical essay is determining where in history to begin. This chapter is made even more challenging by the need to provide an historical context for a series of chapters that address a difficult and complex psychological construct: "musical understanding."

If the collective authors had addressed "music meaning," the task would have been easier as the literature abounds with articles, monographs, and books dealing with musical meaning. The position taken, however, is that musical understanding is a distinct construct and that developing musical understanding can serve to enhance musical meaning. The implications for music education are many and of considerable import.

On the basis of the music produced by Bach, Mozart, Beethoven, Wynton Marsalis and jazz player, Milt Hinton (who appears on more 20th century recordings than anyone), to list a few, we must assume that musical understanding exists. We can also safely assume that, over the centuries, thousands of listeners have understood and continue to understand music. Most of us would agree that Handel, Haydn, and Brahms understood music but we have little evidence concerning how they attained their musical understanding other than it would have been dependent on their genetic, social, economic, educational, and political environments (which would have differed dramatically for each).

The working definition of understanding for this chapter is borrowed from Leonhard (1972):

3

> Knowledge refers to any body of facts gathered by study, investigation, or observation. Understanding applies to the comprehension of [these] facts and the ability to apply knowledge in a problem-solving situation. These definitions imply that knowledge alone has little value and that it can be put to use only when accompanied by understanding. (p. 19)

This definition encompasses Bloom's Taxonomy for Cognitive Knowledge (Bloom, Krathwohl, & Masia, 1964), Krathwohl's Taxonomy for the Affective Domain (Krathwohl, Bloom, & Masia, 1964), and Harrow's Taxonomy of the Psychomotor Domain (1972). But as we explore musical understanding, we find an "ill-structured domain" (Spiro, Feltovich, Jaconsen & Coulson, 1995). Musical understanding is not only an amalgamation of the three recognized taxonomies but also includes non-traditional types of knowledge such as intuition, perception, and others.

Early Twentieth Century

It was not until the turn of the last century, when certain philosophers began to ask *why* questions about individual thought processes, that psychology emerged as a new discipline. Further, it was not until the first three decades of the 20th century that psychologists pursued the idea of "understanding" through learning theory and another three decades before instructional theory was seriously studied.

Music's unique combination of temporal and tonal properties is taken for granted by most listeners. For music teachers, much knowledge is delivered, but as Leonhard suggests, this knowledge can (and should) go one step further for the student; it is first learned then applied in problem-solving situations so as to produce and refine understanding. Successful music education programs are generally evaluated by ensemble performance, and a few conscientious teachers may even administer achievement tests on factual knowledge. But true musical understanding is elusive and a construct that many teachers have ignored or perhaps never considered. Clearly, far too few teachers provide opportunities to apply knowledge to problem-solving situations in music classes.

Psychology became an established discipline around the turn of the last century. Psychologists are devoted to searching beyond a description of mental constructs in order to develop theories that attempt to provide in-depth explanations of the processes that lead to the development of knowledge, application, and understanding. In the area of educational psychology, theories assist in identifying appropriate methods. The mysteries associated with music as a unique art form attracted many of the best psychologists of the 20th century. In this chapter, the work of selected psychologists who have attempted to explore musical understanding in innovative ways will be examined, beginning with Carl Seashore.

Seashore (1866-1949)

Carl Seashore, in writing *The Psychology of Musical Talent* (1919) was the first psychologist to devote much of his career to setting up a basis for musical understanding. His focus on musical understanding made Seashore something of a maverick among his contemporaries. He investigated musical talent, a term he used for the construct "musical aptitude." Clearly, Seashore also included musical training as part of music education. In Seashore's day, training would have been limited to chorus in schools and private lessons for instrumental music; the first four-year degree in music education was initiated in 1922. He attempted, however, to describe and explain the musical mind through the processes of recognition and analysis of structural elements, genetic history, physiological conditions (race and ethnic descent were fashionable during his day), and laws of behaviour. Many of his research results related to what Leonhard would later call "knowledge," but by adding laws of behaviour and later elaborations along with his development of the *Measure of Musical Talent* (1919) in which students were expected to apply their knowledge, he was the first to explore "musical understanding" systematically.

Seashore, as a basic researcher, could not avoid including acoustics in his studies. He consequently viewed the musical mind as perceiving the attributes of sound (pitch, intensity, duration, and extensity) and the traits of the human mind that apprehend and express the attributes of sound, specifically "the hearing of tones, the production of tones, the representation of tones in memory and imagination, musical thought, and musical feeling" (p. 7). He claimed that his purpose in researching musical properties was to gain systematic knowledge of what comprises musical understanding and to interpret the cultural aspects of life. He sought to comprehend the basis for understanding ourselves and our pupils as musicians so as to provide improved procedure in musical training.

By identifying these traits (representation of music in memory and thought) as components of the musical mind, Seashore was moving closer to what we presently call musical understanding. Further, he criticised previous proponents of faculty psychology as failing to recognize the inherent unity and intricate interweaving of mental powers. He observed that thought was inseparable from feeling and action, just as action is inseparable from feeling and thought, and feeling cannot exist without thought and action. He addressed musical listening as another complex structure of mental processes: listening requires imagination and action, and feeling draws from instinct and memory. Here Seashore's work became even more in-line with our working definition of musical understanding as he alluded to students' knowledge base, their ability to explain or reflect (thought and action), their ability to interpret (thought, feeling, imagination, and memory) and their application (based on their knowledge—the attributes of sound in representational form in the mind).

Seashore remained for the most part somewhat sceptical of the strong behaviourist movement initiated by J. B. Watson ("The Founder of Behaviourism") and B. F. Skinner. Seashore never abandoned the traditional "introspective method" used by psychologist during the very earliest years and again much later in 20th century theory.

Mursell (1893-1963)

Building on the ideas of Seashore and others, that "understanding music" is far different from understanding other art forms, Mursell recognized in his *The Psychology of Music* (1937) the uniqueness of music. That is, while one's normal expectation is that a painting may be of something and a poem about something, music by nature is non-representational.

> Walter Peter's famous dictum that "all the arts bend towards the condition of music," which we take to mean that all the arts tend to center

upon the values of pure design, may indeed be true. But of them all, music alone naturally and completely arrives. (p. 18)

Mursell nevertheless recognized that the art of his day (1920s–1930s) reflected a tendency toward abstraction.

Mursell reviewed a tremendous body of psychological literature written during the 1910s to 1930s and concluded that emotional arousal is independent of types of music and there is no correlation between physiological changes and the types or styles of music. Sharing a broad cultural feature (Western tonality) allows music to carry a tremendous wealth of emotion without the baggage of representation or symbolism that accompany other "thoughts" that trigger emotions. Mursell provided evidence that tonal patterns yield their effects not only because of the structure of patterns but because they are diatonic; Western tonality and Western music's unique psychological characteristics can be enjoyed without formal musical training. Music, he thought, allows one to enjoy the music for its own sake, without concern for reference or symbolism.

For Mursell, listening is the primary musical activity. Clearly, the composer listens in the mind's ear as he composes, and the performer develops her craft through listening. Listening to music is a selective response in which certain elements in the total complex of the musical experiences become controlling while others are subordinate. Certainly, a basic error would be to assume that the listener has a response to all aspects of the music, just as it would also be a mistake to assume that listeners hear the same thing during a performance. Music can be heard and enjoyed with respect to any one of the many elements that together comprise the complete musical experience. Individuals are limited by their knowledge base or prefer different elements. Further, each listener may be influenced by different elements in the music at different times.

Mursell proposed that a major task of music educators is to assist students to attend to a broader range of musical elements and the way these are interwoven to create the musical complex. Further, it may be that young listeners, as well as the most experienced listeners, can never hear the whole. Teaching individuals to attend to what is important in the work and how to select its salient features is, therefore, critical. As everyone brings something to the listening experience, when listeners are asked to describe what they hear, they are likely to use a variety of indefinite terms whose connotations differ for each person.

Mursell recognized components in the music that become the listener's focus and can determine the nature of his musical understanding.

1. The lowest level of musical understanding occurs when the listener's attention is focused on shifting dynamics and qualities of tone; there is little or no awareness of musical structure or design.

2. One step upward is the sequencing of tonal patterns into melodies, perhaps the most common center of interest and pleasure in listening. Melody will be the primary focus in consciousness and the determining start of musical understanding.

3. The perception of rhythm is the next step toward musical understanding.

4. Harmonic content of music is an advanced component essential to musical understanding (although in Mursell's day, due to lack of music education programs, such understanding was rarely achieved by listeners).

5. Mursell's final intrinsic factor that leads to musical understanding is what he labeled the "general architectonic design of the music" (p. 215). Until listeners master the previous four factors, comprehend form, and immerse themselves in the design of the music, they can never fully understand music or appreciate its aesthetic significance.

Mursell wrote a landmark text, *Psychology for Modern Education* (1952), in which he addressed the major issues confronting school teachers. Among these issues was how we learn, which in part laid the foundation for current cognitive psychology on music learning theory and instructional theory. Mursell recognized three ways of learning:

- learning by understanding,
- learning by thinking, and
- learning by grouping organized relationships.

These are not considered by Mursell to be three different processes but the same process of insight, gained through different types of circumstances.

In this chapter, only Mursell's ideas of learning by understanding will be explored. Here is an example to clarify what he meant by learning by understanding. A group of elementary school children is to "learn" about the Provinces and Territories of Canada. One class uses a geography book, memorizing names of Provinces, major rivers and lakes, capitals, islands, borders, and so forth. Perhaps students look at a map or draw an outline with a few salient features. Then they are given a test and do fairly well. In another class, the children are allowed to spread sand on a large table and construct a model of Canada. They work together, discussing, checking resources, deriving ways to demarcate boundaries and rivers (such as colored yarn) and make frequent adjustments. This approach is less tidy and less convenient than the textbook approach; it is time consuming, with perhaps some wasted time; probably fewer facts are addressed. Nevertheless, which class is likely to emerge with the most useful and lasting knowledge of Canada? The difference is significant—the second class did activities that encourage understanding while the first class acquired facts. Mursell would support the second example as developing understanding.

Mursell's dictum that to understand is to learn (1952, p. 152) is similar to Leonard's definition that application of knowledge results in understanding. In Mursell's view, learning is enhanced, and the results of learning are improved when understanding is the goal [which today might translate to teaching with a variety of learning modalities and learning styles and seeking deeper meaning than mere factual knowledge].

Today, music teachers realize that insight sometimes occurs in a flash—the "aha" moment that teachers strive for. As Mursell observed, most understanding and insight come more slowly; the primary reason for Mursell's suggestions for understanding the educational process and teaching procedures is to reduce the students' toil and the labor of learning. Much learning results from experimentation, from searching for a solution, from problem-solving, and critical thinking—from trying to understand. Music teachers must realize that mistakes are not fatal, and those who simply correct errors for them do their students an injustice. Consistent formative and diagnostic evaluation are necessary for identifying the source of errors and assisting students in learning how to correct their own mistakes (Colwell & Goolsby, 2002).

Like Seashore, Mursell did not follow the mainstream behaviorist movement that was so popular during the first half of the century. His ideas of student-centered education, "psychological focus," and problem solving were ahead of his time.

∞⌘

The next psychologist in this chapter had more of a music background than training in psychology. In 1958, Gordon completed his doctorate at the University of Iowa, where Seashore had spent most of his professional life. After a number of years playing string bass with some of the most famous names in jazz history, he began a career of pursuing a research agenda investigating musical aptitude; he is the only researcher to date to develop and refine a theory of music learning.

Gordon (1927-)

Edwin Gordon has earned the admiration of the international music education profession for pursuing the meaning of a single, important construct for 40 years: musical aptitude. A prolific author of books, articles, and tests, Gordon earned even greater distinction at the MENC 2000 National Conference in Washington, DC when he concluded his speech at the Measurement and Evaluation session by commenting that perhaps musical aptitude does not exist at all.

Gordon's theory of "musical understanding" is dependent on the listener's (or student's) ability to first audiate music. Having spent several decades refining his controversial theory of "musical understanding" and his definition of audiation he wrote:

> audiation takes place when we hear *and comprehend* music for which sound is no longer or may have never been physically present. In contrast, aural perception takes place when we simply hear sound that is physically present. *Sound is not comprehended as music until it is audiated after it is heard.* (Gordon, 1993, p. 13, Gordon's emphasis)

Gordon never defines comprehension but dances well around it.

By 1997, he had altered his definition of audiation by borrowing ideas of popular cognitive psychologists and comparing music to something closer to language:

audiation takes place when we assimilate and comprehend in our minds music that we have just heard performed or heard performed in the past. Sound becomes music only through audiation, when, as with language, you translate the sounds in your mind to give them meaning. (pp. 4–5)

By 1997, his definition of audiation for musical understanding abandoned the idea that audiation could occur even when music "may never have been present." This significant change has implications for composition, score reading, and other major musical activities in that audiation is no longer necessary for score reading or improvisation.

Borrowing from music theorists such as Sloboda (see below), Gordon compared music and speech. Gordon proposed that, just as we listen to language and give meaning to what was just said by recalling what we have heard earlier, we simultaneously anticipate what we will hear while thinking/processing what was just said. He expanded this notion to suggest that, while listening to a performance, we assign meaning to what was just heard by recalling what we have heard on earlier occasions and by anticipating what we will hear next as we audiate what was just (or is being) performed. In audiating we summarize and generalize what we have just heard and are hearing and we anticipate what will follow.

Continuing to use language as an analogy for musical processing Gordon stated:

language is a result of the need to communicate, while speech is how communication takes place, and thought is what is communicated.... Compared to music this translates to music is a result of the need to communicate, while performance is how communication takes place, and audiation is what is communicated. (1993, p. 14)

From this analogy he determined that "music is a literature." He supports Sloboda's claims (below) that music is not a language because it has no grammar, but it does have syntax—the orderly arrangement of sounds.

Gordon finally addressed "musical understanding" in terms of comparing it to musical appreciation. For Gordon, appreciation means to evaluate highly or approve warmly, often with expressions or tokens of liking; understanding means "to group the meaning of." He recognized that musical understanding "as a purpose of music education is gaining acceptance, but that understanding is a step toward appreciation; all but possibly the purely emotional reactions to timbre and dynamics in music depend on understanding" (1993, p. 35).

Ideas like placing "understanding" as a step toward "appreciation" have made Gordon's writings controversial for more than 30 years. For example, an individual might be a true connoisseur of good food—that is, hold a very deep appreciation of food—yet not understand how it is prepared, what the ingredients are, or even care about either consideration.

Addressing "musical understanding" separately from appreciation, Gordon established six consecutive stages: Stage 1 involves hearing sound. In Stage 2 we unconsciously hear series of pitches and durations in the music; we consciously organize through audiation the collective series of pitches and durations into tonal patterns of essential pitches and rhythm patterns of essential durations. This process leads to future recognition and identification of tonal and rhythmic patterns.

Stage 3 results from the ability to recognize tonal and rhythmic patterns, but at this stage we "consciously" establish the tonality and meter of music from the patterns. Stages 2 and 3 occur virtually simultaneously—continuous interactions of organizing tonal and rhythmic patterns to determine tonality and meter, then verify our hypotheses. In Stage 4 we verify tonality, keyality, meter, tempo, and use this knowledge to recognize and identify "sequence, repetition, form, style, timbre, dynamics and other relevant factors that enable us to give meaning to music" (p. 25).

Stage 5 is further growth toward musical understanding—with Stages 1-4 still occurring simultaneously. Here we consciously recall tonal and rhythmic patterns organized and audiated in other pieces of music. We accomplish this recall by recognizing similarities and differences from those present in the music we are currently hearing. Each new musical piece may alter all that we have organized, recognized, and mostly processed in the previous stages.

The more music we hear, the larger our vocabulary of tonal and rhythmic patterns in various tonalities and meters. When the music we hear is familiar, the audiation process becomes relatively simple; but when we hear unfamiliar music, the audiation process is more complex.

In Stage 6 we understand music to the extent that we can predict what will occur next in the music. The more accurate our predictions, the greater our "musical understanding." If our predictions are inaccurate, we have difficulty understanding the music; if only a few predictions are inaccurate, we may go through Stages 4 through 6. If we are grossly incorrect, we may revert to stage 1 and possibly stay there. Not all students are able to advance beyond Stage 1. This inability to progress further is source of Gordon's idea of aptitude.

Late Twentieth Century

During the last few decades of the 20th century there was widespread recognition that behaviorists encountered difficulty in identifying overt behaviors demonstrating musical understanding. Behaviorism has been gradually replaced by cognitive psychology; "musical understanding" is from this newer framework. Unlike behaviorists, cognitive psychologists studying "music understanding" also recognize the importance of intuition.

In 1985, John A. Sloboda characterized the new psychology as the emergence of a cautious experimental mentalism, showing that it was possible to study complex processes such as attention and recognition in more realistic settings than rigorous laboratory investigations and still maintain reliability and control. Unlike in behavioral psychology, in cognitive psychology, subjects introspect on complex processes and perform tasks from whose accuracy or speed of execution something about the internal structure of the [mental] system controlling these tasks can he inferred. By the 1970s, when Sloboda had published his first experiments in the music processing of pianists, the field of cognitive psychology had broadened in several directions. One direction was a greater interest in higher cognitive processes and the control of complex behavior coupled with an interest in the organization of knowledge and the deployment of cognitive skills. An important outcome was a renewed interest in problem solving that had been much neglected since Mursell's early career.

A second major development in the growing discipline of cognitive psychology during the last two decades of the 20th century was the attempt to study cognitive skills in situations more closely resembling real life rather than artificial laboratory conditions. Thus, unlike experiments associated with behavioral psychology, cognitive psychology focuses on how people deal with extended and meaningful material rather than on fragmented, meaningless stimuli.

John S. Sloboda was the first significant cognitive psychologist to address musical understanding. While only his first book is addressed in this historical overview, his work has expanded and matured to establish him as one of the major leaders in the field today.

Sloboda (1950-)

John Sloboda's work focused on what people do with music rather than on what they say they do. Since the 1980s he has studied musicians on "their turf" rather than in artificially constructed laboratory conditions:

> I try to give as much prominence to output skill (e.g., performing) and higher cognitive functioning (e.g., composition) as I do input skill (e.g., listening). Finally, my criterion for selecting empirical studies to describe is that they should have a particular theoretical or practical importance. (1985, p. 9)

One premise of cognitive psychology is that most of our affective responses to music are learned (culture specific). A second premise is that musical responses cannot be explained in terms of conditioning. For example, listeners within the same musical culture generally agree on the emotional character of a given musical selection even if they have never heard it previously. A behaviorist interpretation would rely on prior "conditioning" and predict wide response differences according to the circumstances of listening. Furthermore, the experienced emotional character of a piece of music is not unchanging; rather, veteran listeners identify a web of differing emotions that are evoked by the detailed sequence of events in many types of music and continue to become refined the better the music is known. Behaviorists, on the other hand, would propose that conditioning would lead a listener always to respond to the generalized emotional response acquired at the original conditioning.

Sloboda uses an excellent analogy to explain the role of cognitive psychology in the study of "musical understanding." When you hear a joke, you must perceive and identify the words, recognize them as sentences, form a mental image of the propositions that the words reveal, and then determine the nature of the incongruity, double meaning, or whatever is needed to "make" the joke. In short to "get" the joke, you require a large set of cognitive processes drawn from your knowledge of language and knowledge of the world. Next, you then process what you understand to determine your affective response. The cognitive stage is a prerequisite of the affective response. We do not find a joke funny unless we understand it. Sloboda is quick to observe that the affective stage does not necessarily follow the cognitive stage. A person may very well understand the music he hears without being moved by it: "If he *is* moved by it then he must have passed through the cognitive stage, which involves forming an abstract or symbolic *internal representation* of the music" (1985, p. 3). It is this internal representation, what Gordon labeled audiation, that is the focus of the cognitive psychology of music.

The way people represent music to themselves determines how well they can remember and perform it. Composition and improvisation require the generation of such representation while perception (listening) involves constructing them. Because such representations are learned, they may be viewed as skilled behaviors. While we all agree that composing and performing are complex skills, the abilities to hum or whistle a familiar melody or hear a wrong note in a performance are also complex skills that can shed light on the internal representations of music and how they are constructed—especially when comparing untrained and trained listeners.

Most mental representations of music are constructed by remembering chunks, or groups of musical material. Most musical material is constructed of patterns and structures (e.g., chords, scales, and arpeggios), and most individuals exposed to such music will become familiar with them. On a larger scale, thematic repetition, and certain harmonic progressions are common. An untrained person using these basic structures can identify or hum common melodies such as "For He's A Jolly Good Fellow," regardless of the key, speed, or instrumentation. This simple example illustrates how melodic memory is an abstraction from the physical stimulus.

The primary difference between trained and untrained listeners is the number and complexity of the structural features that the listener is able to abstract. Most "ordinary" listeners are limited to the awareness of the music's foreground—small or short patterns made up of a few adjacent notes. Musical training assists in acquiring a larger vocabulary of terms used to describe musical structure. Training in hearing and identifying cadences, tonic chords, passing notes, and so forth often helps extend memory capacity. Formal training does not necessarily mean that the untrained musician does not process these structures, but the trained musician relies on explicit knowledge rather than the implicit knowledge that characterizes untrained musicians.

This combination of "natural," implicit knowledge plus the external training and the *application* of explicit knowledge enhances "musical understanding." There are, of course, those born gifted, such as Mozart and the jazz bass player, Milt Hinton, but, for the majority, of us, "musical understanding" requires training and guidance.

Serafine (1945–)

Mary Louise Serafine, in *Music As Cognition* (1988), was among the first to publish a definition of music cognition. For her, "musical understanding" included a simple construct in which untrained individuals can distinguish between different types of music and recognize familiar melodies (even when embedded in a larger work, such as "Going Home" in Dvorak's *New World Symphony*). A slightly more advanced level of "musical understanding" occurs when one can determine if two selections are different or similar in global features such as mood, dynamics, meter, tempo, timbre, number of instruments, and perhaps melodic-structural characteristics. These same individuals seem to know intuitively if a phrase is in progress, is about to end, or is definitely ending. This type of "musical understanding" is culture specific.

Serafine recognized that music teachers, especially instrumental teachers, teach many performance skills, but youngsters already know the subtle aspects of music that may have never been formally taught: order in music, what features should be attended to, what makes melodies similar and different (meter, length, rhythm, tempo, etc.), what aural property makes a tune end, and more. These "intuitions" grow without formal training, just as would occur with language.

Serafine defined music as "thinking in or with sound"; this conceptualization was the basis for music cognition. In exploring "musical understanding" she emphasized music's organization in an ongoing temporal context, separating it from all other art and from mere "sound": "The temporality of music is its defining feature, and the role of specific pitch, duration, loudness, and timbrel characteristics of sound events is of only secondary importance" (1988, p. 69). She viewed music as movement in time that explores simultaneous and successive events that embody points of arrival and status, points of departure and continuation, and a strain of event-to-event similarities, transformations, and differences. To avoid dealing with acoustical properties, like Mursell, she viewed music as subjective construction: "it leans to the side of the subject insofar as it locates the organization of musical events...in the mind, not with the piece" (p. 70). Using this definition she was able to avoid labeling the score or an unplayed musical composition as music.

Her definition emphasizes aural-cognitive activity and excludes all non-aural material. Here she parted sharply with much of what Gordon proposed. She did recognize the tendency to use words to describe pitch, chords, melody, harmony, rhythm, and meter to make it easier to communicate *about* music, but not as a requisite for "musical understanding."

Deutsch (1937–)

In editing the second edition of *The Psychology of Music* (1999), Diana Deutsch drew from many sources including her own experiments to investigate the tasks our auditory system uses to analyze the complex, constantly changing acoustic spectrum from many different sound sources during musical performance. When people listen to music, their auditory system groups elements together according to rules based on frequency, amplitude, temporal position, spatial locations, or some multidimensional attribute such as timbre. Any of these rules can be used for grouping, but the conditions that determine what to group are complex. This conceptualization broadens the boundaries of recognition of tonal patterns (cf., Mursell) and recognition of tonal and rhythmic structures (cf., Gordon) to include a number of mental processes that create components used to construct a whole.

Early Gestalt psychologists proposed that grouping elements into configurations is based on various rules. One rule is proximity—closer elements are more likely to be grouped than are elements further apart. Another rule is that we tend to group elements that are similar (e.g., sounds that are similar probably originate from the same instrument while different instruments may produce dissimilar sounds). A third rule consists of grouping elements that tend to follow each other to form a line or curve. For example, in listening, a sequence that changes smoothly in frequency is likely have been generated by a single source while an abrupt change in frequency may reflect the presence of a new source. A fourth rule, what Deutsch calls "common fate," is that elements that change in the same way are perceptually linked together. In music, components of a complex spectrum that arise in synchrony (for example, timbre) are likely to emanate from the same source, while the sudden addition of a new component may signal the emergence/change of a new source. A fifth principle is that we tend to group things that are familiar to us. Overall, visually and aurally grouping by conformity allows us to interpret our environment most effectively. These principles are evident in the way we hear music.

Deutsch was among the first to study groupings of multiple streams of tones that arise from different regions in space, such as in the seating arrangement of an orchestra or band. This approach raises questions about groupings by pitch, amplitude, or timbre, or whether spatial location is a valid means of grouping. Results indicated that when tones emanate from different locations, temporal relationships have important impact on how they are perceived. When the tones arrive to the listener simultaneously, they are organized sequentially based on pitch proximity. When the tones are heard separated by time, grouping by spatial location is so powerful that it becomes impossible for the listener to integrate them into a single melodic stream. It may be of interest that Berlioz addressed this very phenomenon in his *Grande traité d'instrumentation et d'orchestration modernes* (1844).

Interestingly, many of the groupings and integration of sounds discovered by Deutsch and others resemble the rules that appear in theory and harmony books (e.g., the one mentioned by Berlioz). For example, most students are taught to construct melodies. Another example is the rule of counterpoint that prevents voices from crossing, which correlates with the need to maintain distance between lines so that listeners will hear separate sequences of tones. One final point Deutsch addressed is the advent of computer music, a kind of music in which the composer is no longer bound by the restrictions of acoustic instruments or seating arrangements but instead is faced with an infinite number of compositional techniques. As a result of computer music, understanding certain basic perceptual phenomena has become of critical importance. For example, it is important to identify the factors of timbre that help us group musical sequences and the factors that help us separate components in order to perceive multiple sound images.

In short, Deutsch replicated much of the previous work of researchers but developed an emergent synthesis. The result is five principles that seem obvious but have been substantiated by 50 years of research and form a basis for "musical understanding." Her anticipation of the mounting interest in computer composition may well give new meaning to, or at least a broader conceptualization of "musical understanding."

Dowling (1935–)

Jay Dowling has investigated music perception and cognition for the past quarter century. Dowling recognized that "musical understanding" requires a sub-conscious analysis, as there is no time for reflection on each detail of a performance as the music progresses. Like Sloboda and Deutsch, he used language as an analogy: a listener does not dwell on each word or inflection but perceives the entire sentence and understands the overall meaning.

Emphasis should be placed on the ease and speed with which adults' process cognitive tasks in the domain of speech and music that is familiar to them and the degree to which that ability depends on and improves with experience and training. For example, when listening to a melody that has been complicated by the temporal interweaving of distraction tones, listeners are more accurate in judging pitches that match familiar, culturally determined norms than those pitches that do not.

The only music psychologist included in this chapter who investigated developmental "musical understanding," Dowling found that infants already possess many of the traits used to understand the music of their birth culture, and these develop either informally or formally through adulthood.

> The perceptual learning with the music of a culture provides the listener with a fund of implicit knowledge of the structural patterns of that music, and this implicit knowledge serves to facilitate the cogni-

tive processing of music conforming to those patterns. (Dowling, 1999, p. 604)

Dowling used the term "implicit," as did Deutsch, for the knowledge collected through perceptual learning as it is not always available to conscious thought. Further, neither the knowledge base in its entirety nor the cognitive processes through which knowledge is applied is always available to consciousness. Listeners engage in far more complex cognitive behaviors than they realize. There is evidence, for example, that listeners with a low degree of "musical understanding" and with only moderate training encode scale steps to the notes of the melodies they hear; most do not realize that they are capable of doing so, much less that they do it whenever encountering a new melody. Implicit knowledge of the Western musical scale structure has become so imbedded over years of experience that the knowledge is applied automatically whenever adults listen to music. The degree of knowledge determines the degree of "musical understanding."

As one would imagine, young children do not demonstrate any preference for the Western major scale. Toddlers recognize specific melodies (e.g., the theme song to *Sesame Street*) and begin singing spontaneously around age one. Most of this singing occurs during play and appears to be toddlers' exploration of their voices, but by age 2 through kindergarten, children are able to sing brief phrases of songs repeatedly. The contour of these songs appears to be constant, but the pitch may vary. The rhythm of these early songs is often consistent and appears to resemble speech patterns.

Melodic contour appears to be perceived and reproduced consistently at a later age. A number of experiments created by Dowling also indicate that 2- to 4-year olds are able to perceive and recognize the same versions or short passages whether they are tonal or atonal: "It was not until ages 7 and 8 that tonality began to be a factor...and only by ages 9 or 10 [that] a difference appeared between recognizing familiar versions and the same-contour imitations" (the adult pattern perception) (1999, p. 614).

Dowling cited other studies that indicate perception and memory lock into a stable scale structure by age 5 (e.g., in songs like "Twinkle, Twinkle" and "Happy Birthday"). During later childhood, by age 12, evidence also indicates a stable memory for short atonal sequences of tones. These results were supported by a number of investigations that included music instruction in atonal and tonal music. Children who experienced training in both appeared to have broader perceptual ability and memories/knowledge (or "musical understanding") that allowed them to reproduce both tonal and atonal melodies.

Overall, development of rhythmic organization is a multilevel structure appearing early and, by age 5, the child demonstrates sophisticated perception and the ability to process and organize rhythms. There is some development during the school-age years, but Dowling provided evidence that the rhythmic perception and cognitive processes used by children to organize patterns are not so different from those of adult non-musicians.

Lipscomb (1959-)

Although Scott Lipscomb chronologically belongs before Deutsch, I have reserved him for last as he differs from the others in significant aspects of music cognition. Drawing on prior research in the second edition of the *Handbook of Music Psychology,* Lipscomb (1996) developed a new theory that may be labelled an "emergent synthesis," as it draws from Gestalt psychology (or description) and constructivism for pedagogical implications. He views the cognitive psychology of music as the study of how aural stimuli are recorded, organized, and stored in memory in a new and different form from their acoustical properties in order to achieve "musical understanding." The listener's musical training plays a significant role in this process. Thus, Lipscomb's view of music cognition involves more than the simple perception of pitch, dynamics, timbre, and rhythmic characteristics of the stimulus.

Lipscomb pointed out the blurred distinction between sensation, perception, and cognition throughout the history of cognitive psychology; writers have been reluctant to state where each of these processes begins and ends and the next stage takes over. In general, says Liscomb, sensory information is required for perception, and cognitive processes act upon the knowledge gained through perception. Both are required for "musical understanding."

Sensation involves the transfer of information to any of our five senses, serving as the catalyst for the interaction between an individual and his environment. This information is held in sensory memories—an echoic memory for auditory stimuli and an iconic memory for visual stimuli.

Perception utilizes sensory information to formulate an understanding of our world. During this stage of processing, important elements of the incoming data stream are filtered out for further processing, while less important information is discarded. Attention plays an essential role during this stage; focused attention results in the recognition of objects (visual or auditory) and patterns that will be subsequently integrated into the perceiver's ordered interpretation of the environment (p. 134).

Cognition finally involves the acquisition, storage, retrieval, and use of knowledge obtained through the senses and perceptual systems. This assimilation and interpretation of new ideas based on past experiences is labelled "apperception." Music differs from many data sources due to its temporal nature, which requires the perceiver to be an active participant in the musical experience, constantly generating expectations based on past experience and interpreting auditory information on the basis of immediately preceding sounds.

Variation of perception due to a person's past experience is a natural consequence of one's culture. Difficulties arise when listening to music of other cultures—both at low levels (e.g., tonality and pitch patterns), and high levels of processing (e.g., the overall structure of musical sounds within a piece of music). As proposed by Serafine to explain the acquisition of musical understanding, Lipscomb also views music as communication between composer, performer, and listener. In Western music, the composer communicates musical information (his cognitive ideas) to the performer through notation; these symbols are then interpreted as perceived by the performer into acoustical signals that reach the listener through the data stream. The listener, then, recodes the data into musical structures in the mind.

In order for this co-operative communication to be successful, the composer, performer, and listener must share certain common knowledge—either implicitly (intuition for example) or explicitly. Explicit knowledge is that which can be expressed verbally. Private lessons are excellent examples of situations where both explicit and implicit knowledge are used for instruction. Attempting to get a student to play with a "warmer" sound, for example, usually defies verbal description and is best communicated by modelling. "Training and education frequently involve a process of transferring implicit knowledge into explicit knowledge" (p. 136).

When listening to music, we constantly redirect our attention to selective features of the data stream. This focus of attention is guided by our pre-existing knowledge of structures, or schemata, developed through past experience. These schemata lead us to expect what will occur next in the music and influence which features or elements will be our focus (and which elements we will remember).

In theorizing now, musical schemata are created; a model of brainlike systems consists of nodes that represent objects or features of the world. Connections between nodes (associations) become stronger in proportion to the number of times they are activated simultaneously. The degree to which any node is activated at any moment is determined by the number of connections currently active in response to a given musical event. That is, musical understanding is in direct proportion to the number of nodes that are associated with other nodes. Musical stimuli can directly activate one or more nodes that are associated ("attached") to other nodes, resulting in indirect activation of additional nodes within the neural web.

This idea of neural nodes comprising a schemata of music cognition also explains how individuals "fill in" elements in perception that do not exist in the physical world. For example, listeners can fill in a missing root of a chord while hearing a chord that actually does not contain the root. Or when a dominant seventh chord follows a subdominant chord, the representational image of the tonic chord of the key will be strongly activated.

Cognitive psychology in music is still new and remains a new application. Most studies still continue to use a reductionist approach of short isolated sequences of tones or rhythms, trading reliability for validity. Lipscomb calls for more studies that incorporate musical contexts more closely resembling genuine musical situations.

Summary

This chapter has presented the work of eight 20th century researchers in music education: Seachore, Mursell, Gordon, Sloboda, Serafine, Deutsch, Dowling, and Lipscomb. These researchers were selected based on their efforts to investigate musical understanding using approaches that, at the time of their publication, were new to the field. Two forthcoming major handbooks will address the psychology of music in greater depth: *The New Handbook of Research on Music Teaching and Learning* (Colwell & Richardson, 2002) and *The Science and Psychology of Music Performance: Creative Strategies for Teaching and Learning* (Parncutt & McPherson, 2002).

The development of technology and multimedia devices should enhance our ability to study musical understanding with greater validity while maintaining greater control and reliability. Using a variety of means to study musical understanding will enhance reliability as well as allow for comparison of research methodologies. The process of musical investigation would be greatly enhanced by collaboration among musicians, teachers, psychologists, neurologists, and music theorists.

One of the purposes of this book is to assist teachers with conceiving musical instruction that transcends performance only training, didactic teaching, and trite creativity exercises—that is, to teach for musical understanding. If this book serves to establish or motivate some individual to develop an acceptable theory of musical understanding, or even of music education—then all the better.

No credible theory of music education could be sustained, however, without the insightful mental analytical processes of the musical phenomenon addressed by psychologists; nor could it be limited to formal musical training. Listening to music and recognition of patterns and structures, and developing anticipation or expectations are essential to the human experience within such a theory. Such a theory, or even description requires objective, subjective, and intuitive aspects. "No sensitive practice of music education can take place without at least an intuitive grasp of the qualitative nature of the human response" (Swanwick, 1988, p. 3).

Karl Popper has written much on the notion of theories and provides additional insight into our dilemma of establishing a theory of musical understanding. Popper's (1979) idea of human knowing or understanding is divided into three distinct entities. The first entity is the objective world (tangible objects and observable events); the second is the mental state (our constantly changing subjective experience and interpretation our environment). The third is an entity of ideas, "of theories in themselves, and their logical relations; of arguments in themselves; and of problem situations in themselves" (Popper, 1979, p. 154). In this third entity, we all contribute something but receive more than we give.

The psychologists reviewed in this chapter delved deeply into this world of ideas, human thinking, and imaginative speculation. They have devoted their careers to searching for systematic, logical explanations and seeking the organising principles that characterise musical listening and allow us to define musical understanding. All recognise that music is somehow processed through patterns, or sequences, or structures that the mind connects as a single strand or flow, moving toward closure. All at least imply that the greater one's musical vocabulary, the greater, or keener, or quicker one will achieve musical understanding through the application of knowledge.

During the last third of the 20th century, it would appear that music educators in North American colleges and universities (despite the "old guard" in music theory programs) have shifted the focus of music education—as first advocated by Seashore—toward student-centred music programs in schools. Composing and listening are growing in emphasis in many programs even though most still remain performance-oriented. Programs (including those performance-oriented programs) that provide students with the opportunities to think critically, solve problems, and make musical decisions are moving toward supporting the development of musical understanding.

References

Bloom, B. S., Krathwohl, D. R., & Masia, B. B. (1964). *Taxonomy of education objectives: The classification of educational goals.* New York: Longman.

Colwell, R. J., & Richardson, C. (Eds.). (2002). *The new handbook of research on music teaching and learning.* New York: Oxford University Press.

Colwell, R. J., & Goolsby, T. W. (2002). *The teaching of instrumental music* (3rd ed.). Upper Saddle River, NJ: Prentice Hall.

Deutsch, D. (Ed.). (1999). *The psychology of music* (2nd ed.). San Diego: Academic Press.

Dowling, W. J. (1999). The development of music perception and cognition. In D. Deutsch (Ed.), *The psychology of music* (2nd ed.) (pp. 603–625). San Diego: Academic Press.

Gordon, E. E. (1993). *Learning sequences in music: Skill, content and patterns.* Chicago, IL: GIA. Publications.

Gordon, E. E. (1997). *Learning sequences in music: Skill, content, and patterns* (Rev. Ed.). Chicago, IL GIA Publications.

Harrow, A. J. (1972). *Taxonomy of the psychomotor domain: A guide for developing behavioural objectives.* New York: D. McKay Company.

Krathwohl, D. R., Bloom, B. S., & Masia, B. B. (1964). *Taxonomy of educational objectives: The classification of educational goals. Handbook 2: Affective domain.* New York: D. McKay Company.

Leonhard, C., & House, R. W. (1972). *Foundations and principles of music education* (2nd ed.). New York: McGraw-Hill.

Lipscomb, S. D. (1996). The cognitive organization of musical Sound. In D. A. Hodges (Ed.), *Handbook of music psychology* (2nd ed.) (pp. 133–175). San Antonio, TX: IMR Press.

Mursell, J. L. (1937). *The psychology of music.* New York: W.W. Norton.

Mursell, J. L. (1952). *Psychology for modern education.* New York: W.W. Norton.

Parncutt, R., & McPherson, G. (Eds.). (2002). *The science and psychology of music performance: Creative strategies for teaching and learning.* New York: Oxford University Press.

Popper, K. (1979). *Objective knowledge* (new ed.). Oxford: Clarendon Press.

Seashore, C. E. (1919). *The psychology of musical talent.* New York: Silver Burdett.

Seashore, C. E. (1919). *Measures of musical talent* (Manual of instructions and interpretations and 78 rpm recording). New York: Columbia Gramophone Company.

Serafine, M. L. (1988). *Music as cognition: The development of thought in sound.* New York: Oxford University Press.

Sloboda, J. (1985). *The musical mind: The cognitive psychology of music.* New York: Oxford University Press.

Spiro, R. J., P. J., Feltovich, Jaconsen, M. J., & Coulson, R. L. (1995). In L. Steffe, & J. Gale, (Eds.), *Constructivism in education* (pp. 85–108). Hillsdale, NJ: Erlbaum.

Swanwick, K. (1988). *Music, mind, and education.* New York: Routledge, Chapman and Hall.

The Dynamic and Complex Nature of Musical Understanding[1]

Renate Zenker

Introduction

The nature of musical understanding is dynamic and complex because it involves questions concerning the role that performance, culture, concepts, personal experiences, listening, creativity, kinesthetics, personal meaning, and comprehension play in it. Indeed the nature of musical understanding is so complex that a discussion of only one of these considerations would be sufficient to generate a substantial work. Yet, despite the multifaceted nature of musical understanding, it can be all too easy to assume that, as music educators, we somehow intuitively know what it is and develop our music curriculum accordingly. The past and current crisis in music education, with consistent budget cuts at all school levels and the search for a rationale for music education in our technologically product-driven society, has caused us to re-examine music education curricula. At the root of music education are the questions "What is musical understanding?" and "How should we teach for it?"

My purpose here is to contribute to the clarification of the nature of musical understanding through an examination of many of the characteristics of "understanding" itself and a discussion of how these characteristics are evident in musical understanding. As I show in this chapter, there is much that a discussion of "understanding" can tell us about musical under-

---

[1] This chapter was developed from sections of chapters 1, 4, and 5 of my Ph.D. dissertation, *Understanding Music Cross-Culturally: A Philosophical Examination,* (University of British Columbia, Vancouver, BC, 2000). It has been revised in response to the dialogue that took place at the Victoria Symposium on Musical Understanding, February 22–23, 2001.

standing and its place in the development of school music curricula. Understanding has a number of characteristics:

1. The word understanding is ambiguous in that it has different senses. That is, when we say "We understand X," the statement has more than one possible meaning.
2. Understanding, as a verb, belongs to a class of verbs that indicate an upshot or outcome, not an activity; we cannot "do it"; it results from us doing many activities. Understanding as a noun is primarily a capacity to see connections and notice things that others do not, which results from having had many understanding "upshots."
3. Understanding involves concepts and perception recipes.
4. We can talk about internal/external understanding.
5. Understanding is the basis of appreciation.
6. Understanding is a matter of degree; different levels of sophistication are possible.
7. Understanding has a "dynamic" quality; our understanding changes as our knowledge base and experiences change.

I will explore each of these characteristics of understanding in this chapter.

Understanding Has Different Meanings

Baily (1996), in the opening to his criticism of Walker's (1996) essay "Open Peer Commentary: Can We Understand the Music of Another Culture?" points out the ambiguity surrounding the term "understand" in reference to music. Walker defines musical understanding as a product of the way the mind works when it engages in musical behaviour: "Implicit in the title is a discussion about what different human groups might share in the way of commonalties in the way minds work and therefore in their products where music behaviour is concerned" (p. 103). Baily questions Walker's assumption concerning the nature of musical understanding:

> Is he [Walker] asking whether we can successfully analyze the music of another culture, in terms of its underlying principles, its "grammar," its relationship to the social structures and cultural systems in which it is embedded? Or is he asking whether we can *perceive* the music of another culture "correctly," i.e., can we hear it in the same way that a culture-

bearing member of that society in question does? Or is he asking whether we can learn to *perform* music other than our "own"? (pp. 114–115)

I think that in pointing out the different senses of musical understanding, Baily (1996) has found the root of the problem of the meaning of understanding with regard to music. We cannot assume what musical understanding is or that it means only one thing.[2] I begin with this example from the debate in the literature on the nature of cross-cultural musical understanding as an introduction to the ambiguous nature of understanding and musical understanding.

We use understanding in a variety of ways in our everyday language: "I understand science." "I understand how you feel." "I understand why you will be late." "I understand the story." Each of these uses of understanding results in a slightly different sense of the word and involves different criteria by which we assess our understanding. If we are speaking of understanding science, we mean that we have knowledge of it as a subject. "I understand how you feel" results in a more empathetic sense of understanding—that a person can imagine, feel, be sensitive to another person. To understand why you will be late is to grasp an explanation. Or to understand a story is to have the ability to read and grasp the meaning of words according to linguistic conventions.

Martin (1970) points out that the verb "understand" takes a variety of indirect questions which are implied according to the object(s) of understanding and the context in which this understanding is to occur. As she notes, when we say we understand a person we can have various implied meanings: one can understand *what* a person is saying, or understand *that* a person is lying, or understand *why* a person is saying something or understand *how* a person knows what s/he is saying. Her point is that with regard to a particular discipline, there is not one and only one characteristic question that can be asked. Similarly in understanding music, we can understand *what* makes one piece of music different from another, understand

---

[2] It is important to recognize the ambiguous nature of "understanding" for all types of music research. For example, an empirical study assessing musical understanding may be assessing one aspect of musical understanding (such as rhythm recognition) whereas an ethnomusicological study may assess another aspect of musical understanding (such as the cultural significance of a piece of music). We may need to combine various types of research to develop a complete picture of musical understanding.

that one rhythm is different than another, understand *why* one genre of music is different from another, and understand *how* the musics of various cultures differ.

Davies (1994b) makes a similar argument, giving extensive musical examples to support his thesis, that knowing *how* the music is put together is not sufficient for understanding. Knowing *why* it is put together as it is and what the subtle differences are compared to other works of its kind is important to music education. When discussing how a listener comes to understand a piece of music he writes:

> She needs to ask not just "how are these works put together?" but "why are they put together as they are?" This latter question, asked as one about function involves a consideration of how the particular work differs from others of its kind, and in turn requires a grasp of what it is that distinguishes one musical kind from another.... If the work is a concerto, knowing how it is put together will tell her next to nothing about whether it succeeds as a concerto unless she has some idea of what concertos are supposed to be for and what difficulties are presented to the composer in meeting that function within the broad confines of a sonata form framework. (p. 70) [3]

This discussion of understanding concerning why, how, what, and that, is what makes the statement "I understand X" more complicated than originally thought. Different types of understanding of the same thing or same group of things are possible, and this understanding varies also according to context.

There are, it seems to me, six paradigm uses of understanding:

1. The general comprehension use means "to comprehend; to apprehend the meaning or import of; to grasp the idea of" (*The Oxford English Dictionary*, 1989, p. 984). This sense of understanding implies the recognition of the character and constituent parts of something, for example, "I understand the school system," and "I understand the parts of a song." This sense includes discrimination between two things or

---

[3] Understanding music, does not, however, exhaust itself in the how and the why of its structure. If we understand how a particular piece of music is put together as it is and why, what about understanding the experience we have when we listen to it. In order to recognize that we are hearing music when we hear it we have already recognized that there is more to it than the perception of a succession of sounds.

among a group of things, for example, "I understand that you are coming to the party, but John is not," and "I understand the differences between an oboe and a clarinet."

2. The language use has as its objects words, sentences, or signs. In this sense, to understand means to grasp or "get a handle on" the meaning of something as in "to apprehend the meaning or idea by knowing what is conveyed by the words or signs used: [understand] Russian, [understand] a message in code, [understand] a wink" (*Webster's 3rd New International Dictionary*, 1976, p. 2490). If we consider Western music notation to be a type of written language made up of signs, or consider the tonal syllables "do, re, mi...," we can include this sense of understanding when we talk about understanding music.

3. Another use of understanding addresses the question of how to do something such as a task or job. This sense of understanding means having knowledge in the practice of something, being able to carry out a task or a skill. This use of understanding would apply to the child understanding how to play baseball, or somebody understanding how to fix a car, or understanding how to write all the inversions of a dominant seventh chord.

4. The personal character use of understanding is "to apprehend clearly the character or nature of (a person)" (*The Oxford English Dictionary*, 1989, p. 984). When we say that we understand a person we cannot mean that we simply recognise a person, but mean that we are aware intimately of what another person is like so that we understand why that person acts in certain ways. In other words, we know the person's character. For example, "We better understand Beethoven's music when we understand Beethoven."[4]

---

[4] See for example Davies (1994a):

The analogy between understanding music and understanding a person can be taken further. To understand an individual as a person with a character, a self-structured life, is to presuppose a natural and social history for human beings—a form of life. Our understanding of music

5. The empathetic use of understanding is defined as "to show a sympathetic or tolerant or indulgent attitude toward something" (*Webster's 3rd New International Dictionary*, 1976, p. 2490), for example, "Helen is an understanding person." This use of understanding assumes the necessity of personal experience, a delicacy of perception and being critically, sensitively, and emotionally aware of subtleties. This use stems from the doctrine of "*Verstehen*" (Martin, 1970). The thrust of this doctrine is that by putting ourselves in another person's position, or having been in the same position ourselves, we come to know their way of living, acting, behaving and we can come to see things or feel as the other person does.[5]

6. The interpretation use of the term understanding, involves investigation, categorisation, and an examination of the deeper meaning of something. It is

> to regard in a particular way or with a particular meaning in mind; interpret in a single one of a number of possible ways; the power to make experience intelligible by bringing perceived particulars under appropriate concepts; the capacity to formulate and apply to experience concepts and categories, to judge, and to draw logical inferences. (*Webster's 3rd New International Dictionary*, 1971, p. 2490)

This sense presupposes some knowledge base in that we cannot regard in a particular way, interpret, achieve mental grasp of the causal/nature of something unless we have the appropriate information. An example of this type of understanding would be of a very specific nature such as: "Do you understand why this music composition is an excellent example of the Romantic period?" This type of understanding involves knowledge of previous categories.

It seems clear that there are many different senses of understanding and that all of them are applicable in a musical context.

---

is similar. Musical works must be seen as belonging within a history of styles and traditions of composition and performance. (p. 369)

Understanding as an Upshot: Task-Achievement Analysis

We have seen that educational terms such as understanding tend to be very difficult to classify clearly as they are most often ambiguous. When we attempt to organise and classify educational terms such as teach, learn, train, understand, appreciate, and even educate itself, we are dealing with interesting philosophical problems in Rylean task-achievement analysis (1959) that are centrally important to the classification of these terms. This type of analysis provides distinctions between verbs that express actions or tasks (e.g., racing, hunting, reasoning, listening) and those verbs that pair with them and express the outcomes or upshots of these actions or tasks (e.g., winning, finding, concluding, and hearing, respectively), which Ryle calls achievement concepts. To recognize what Ryle is saying, it is helpful to consider the definition of a verb as "any of a large class of words in a language that serve to indicate the occurrence of performance or an action, the existence of a state or condition, etc." (*Collins Dictionary of the English Language*, 1986, p. 1683). This definition goes beyond the definition of a verb as an "action word" that most of us learned in school. In other words, not all verbs are action words. As Ryle points out, some verbs are tasks or "action words" and some others are upshots or "serve to indicate the existence of a condition." Ryle's main point is that certain words represent the successful outcome of the tasks in question and are not tasks in themselves. For example, winning the race is not a task in itself but is the result of running the race. Winning is the upshot of running the race, just as finding a lost key is not a task in itself, but is the upshot or result of hunting for the key.

White (1967) distinguishes a subset of action verbs in which the action consists centrally of paying attention to something (listening, watching, looking). The verbs that pick out the upshots of attention verbs White called "reception" verbs (hearing, noticing, seeing). White explains: "What we receive, comes to us provided we have been appropriately prepared. We do not produce it or gain it, secure it or bring it off" (p. 69), and "to be struck by something in the sense of noticing...is to receive knowledge of it, to be able to tell what it is" (p. 70). According to White's concept of "re-

---

5 Scruton (1983) provides an interesting discussion of the possibility of some type of empathy being involved in understanding the expressive elements of music (pp. 94–99).

ception" or "noticing" verbs, we hear, notice, or see people or things around us based on concepts we acquire or through perception recipes, as I discuss below. And according to White, noticing is not something we *do*; it *happens*—but only if we are appropriately prepared.[6]

Understanding falls into yet another special category of achievement words that I label multi-faceted reception concepts and Scheffler (1965) calls "attainments." According to Scheffler, some educational terms, such as "appreciate" and "understand," outstrip very general uses and definitions of "to believe, know, learn, and teach" and are difficult to classify and define. These attainments have an element of Ryle's achievements in that they are upshots rather than activities and have an element of White's reception concepts as we must be appropriately prepared. They move beyond achievements and reception concepts in that they do not have strictly associated single techniques or tasks, but groups or sets of techniques or tasks. Scheffler, therefore, concludes that there is no such a thing as "understanding know-how."

> One who understands quantum theory knows how to read and one who appreciates music knows how to listen. But these bits of know-how are not strictly associated; they are not equivalent to knowing how to "understand" and knowing how to "appreciate" respectively. Understanding and appreciation cannot, it would seem, readily be said to be exercises of technique or know-how, as swimming might be said to be an exercise of swimming know-how. For there seems to be no such thing as "understanding know-how" or an "appreciating know-how." Much less can learning to understand or to appreciate be suggested to reduce to mere acquisition of such know-how. (p. 19)[7]

As with other reception concepts, understanding, as we use the word in normal language usage, is not something in which you can engage. Since understanding as a verb is not an "action word" or an activity, it is an outcome. For example we find the sentence, "I was too busy understanding to answer the phone," quite odd because understanding is not something that we can do, but is rather a result, upshot, or outcome of the completion of other activities. Understanding is something that may happen to you when

---

[6] Daniels (1996) provides a very interesting discussion of two views of mind-doing and noticing.

[7] I discuss the relationship between understanding and appreciation in a later section.

you have thought, studied, or completed various tasks. This is not to say that understanding happens with no effort, although at times it may appear to, but that understanding itself is not a task; rather we have to complete various tasks in order to understand. There is no single technique or task associated with understanding. Instead, there are sets or groups of techniques or tasks depending on the object of the understanding.

Thus, when we talk about people having a good understanding of something (understanding as a noun) we mean that they have had a lot of upshots or outcomes through their engagement in various activities. They have developed the capacity to see connections and "get it right." In this sense, understanding is an epistemological state persons achieve when they can see things that other people might miss.

Musical understanding is very closely tied to the nature of understanding itself. To develop musical understanding we must engage in a wide variety of musical activities such as playing, singing, listening, composing, performing, improvising, reading music, and learning musical concepts. There is no single type of "understanding-music-know-how," as Scheffler might have suggested had he extended his concept of their being no "understanding-know-how" to music.

Musical understanding logically develops from personal experiences with music. People who can be said to have a "music understanding" have had a lot of upshots or outcomes in the sense that they have engaged in many musical activities and had many musical experiences that have lead to understanding the music. People with musical understanding have developed the capacity to make connections in music and notice what they have been trained to notice through various musical activities. Musical understanding in this sense is an epistemological state that individuals achieve so they can hear things in the music that other people lacking the same level of musical understanding would miss.[8]

Understanding, Concepts, and Perception Recipes

When we talk about musical understanding we invariably begin to talk about musical concepts. There are several points about understanding and

---

[8] I discuss levels of understanding later in this essay.

concepts that, when clarified, can tell us about the role concepts play in musical understanding.

In music education we talk about the musical "elements" of rhythm, harmony, and melody and how we describe the difference between hearing sounds and hearing these musical elements. But these musical "elements" are in fact concepts or simply ideas that help us understand and talk about music. A rhythm is a musical element but it is also a concept differentiated from melody, for example, by sub-concepts (pitched versus unpitched sounds, tune) and from other rhythms by sub-concepts (pulse, metre, simple time, compound time).

An important point about concepts for understanding music is that we can have a concept or an "idea" of an apple, a bed, or a rhythm without having a formalized definition of the object or even a term for the object. We may think and hear music through musical concepts we have gained by experience without having the specific musical terminology or definitions. Thus when we say a person (P) has a concept of rhythm, the meaning is ambiguous. We can mean:

1. P possesses the ability to recognize rhythm in music but does not know it is called "rhythm." P may also be able to recognize, but not name, the sub-concepts of rhythm. P may be able to describe rhythm and the sub-concepts of rhythm in his or her own words.

2. P can recognize and name the concepts and or sub-concepts of rhythm.

3. As Budd (1985) points out, P may possess the concept necessary for recognizing rhythm, but fail to do so:

> The possession of a concept that applies to musical events is not the same as the ability to classify musical events on the basis of their sounds by using the concept: someone can possess a musical concept and yet be quite unable to apply the concept to music as he listens to the music. (p. 246)

For education, this distinction between having concepts and not being able to name them and having concepts and being able to name them is important. I have previously written about what I called "an intuitive/organic conceptual apparatus" (Zenker, 1994) that helps to explain how we develop concepts. The term "conceptual apparatus," often used by philosophers, is sometimes a place holder or a metaphor for a person's system of concepts already in place or to be acquired.

> In discovering our musical conceptual apparatuses, we can distinguish two extremes of a continuum: an intuitive/organic apparatus and a reflective apparatus. An intuitive/organic conceptual apparatus evolves from a person experiencing and getting used to a certain genre of music from an early age. For example, a person brought up in North America may unintentionally develop a framework of categories into which s/he can fit the music of the day (or even the musics of the day) based in his/her experience of listening to Western music(s). This person may or may not be aware of this framework, or the use s/he makes of it in listening to music. This organic apparatus will determine what sounds "normal" and what sounds "odd" and in the absence of education or training, will also have significant impact on what the person likes or dislikes. By studying, teaching, modelling, etc., this unreflective apparatus can be modified—it can become more complex, sophisticated and varied. Having a reflective conceptual apparatus means that a person has developed a conceptual apparatus different from the (intuitive) organic one which s/he previously possessed. (p. 40)

To teach for understanding we can make students aware of the concepts (ideas or general notions) they already possess and raise these to a reflective level. We can teach students the appropriate musical terminology for the concepts they possess so that they can demonstrate that they understand by giving the correct music terminology for sounds they hear. This points to another aspect of understanding—that it involves being able to give evidence or demonstrate that we do in fact understand. It is also possible that a person needs a more sophisticated vocabulary to come to a more sophisticated understanding of music.

As Budd (1985), Levinson (1990), Ryle (1959/1949), and Kivy (1990) have explained, it is important to recognize, however, as with my description of an intuitive/organic apparatus, that not all the ways in which we understand music have to do with concepts,

According to Ryle's (1959/1949) notion of perception recipes, through our experiences in the world, we learn to recognize many things by the way they appear to us through our experiences with them, rather than through abstract concepts. For example, as a child, we learn to recognize a plane in flight without having any abstract concepts of physics, aerodynamics, or engineering. Even though we may see a wide variety of different types of planes we "perceive" them under the "recipe" of the "machine that flies in the sky" in the sense that we are simply accustomed to what planes look like and how they sound.

In the case of music and the function of perception recipes in it, Ryle provides the example of a tune. We may understand a tune we have heard before, without having a concept of a tune, but through thinking, in the sense of "following the tune" according to the "recipe of the tune" that we have acquired through hearing it repeatedly.

> In short, he is now recognising or following the tune, if, knowing how it goes, he is now using that knowledge; and he uses that knowledge not just by hearing the tune, but hearing it is a special frame of mind, the frame of mind of being ready to hear both what he is not hearing and what he will hear, or would be about to hear, if the pianist continues playing it and is playing it correctly. He knows how it goes and he now hears the notes as the progress of that tune. He hears them according the recipe of the tune, in the sense that what he hears is what he is listening for. (p. 226)

Hearing the music according to the "recipe" of the tune, means that rather than having an abstract concept of a "tune," we simply know "how it goes" so that we can differentiate one tune from another.

Levinson (1990) agrees that we can understand a piece of music by "hearing it in an appropriate way" and that the relevant background knowledge we need to do so is largely "tacit" and "intuitive":

> A musically literate listener in the sense under consideration—that is, listening literacy—need never have digested a formal definition of concerto or a fugue, need never have grasped the least fundamental of harmonic theory, need not know how many octaves and fractions thereof each orchestral instrument spans, need not be able to tick off the characteristics of Baroque style. He need only have an implicit grasp of things—in his bones and ears, so to speak. His literacy ultimately is a set of experientially induced, context-sensitive dispositions to respond appropriately to musical events in specific settings, and not in terms of recoverable information in a mental dictionary of musical matters. (pp. 24–25)

Budd (1985) supports Levinson's claim that we understand much about what is "going on" in the music without explicit knowledge of all musical concepts.

> It is often not required that someone should recognize something as an instance of a certain concept under which it falls, or even that he should

possess the concept, if he is to be aware of that phenomenon in a work of art and understand its role within the work. (p. 246)

Kivy (1990) writes that we develop "perceptions" of "rightness" or "wrongness" in music through our listening experiences. According to Kivy we also have an "innate" ability to describe music in our own words, without a formalized musical vocabulary, although we may have difficulty with verbalizing these "internal" descriptions.

To conclude this section, we do not need explicit knowledge of concepts to understand music in the sense of "knowing how to follow" the music. Although we may be unaware of it, however, we may initially develop concepts, often without explicit musical words, by experiencing the music we hear around us in our particular culture. It is important for educators to make students aware of their "perception recipes" or their "intuitive/organic apparatuses," which we can consider to be different terms for the same thing, to prepare them for more sophisticated levels of understanding.

Internal and External Understanding

A characteristic of understanding is that, when we attempt to understand something, we tend to compare one part of the object of our understanding to another part or we compare the object of our understanding to something else.

Martin (1970) discusses two different, though related, types of understanding that are very useful for a discussion of understanding music. She calls these types external and internal understanding.

> There are in general two different sorts of connections that may be involved in understanding, depending on the way the thing is to be understood, X, is treated. On the one hand, X may be treated as a whole, a unity, and may be connected or related to something else, something apart from it: let us call connections of relations of this sort external. On the other hand, X may be taken in isolation—that is to say, without relating it to other things-treated as a composite, and parts or aspects of it may be connected or related; let us call connections or relations of this sort internal.... Let us call the sort of understanding that takes something X as a unity and relates it to something else as external understanding and let us call the sort of understanding that takes X as a composite, singles out parts or aspects of X, and discovers relationships internal understanding. (p. 154)

According to Martin, when we have an internal understanding of something, we understand it under some description in relation to itself and understand there are various types of internal descriptions possible. Martin gives the example of a sonata, which can be understood internally in different ways; it can be understood in terms of its larger "parts" or "movements" and it can be understood in terms other smaller parts such as rhythm, melody, and harmony. Her point is that internal understanding of a sonata can vary from person to person according to the connections they hear and the descriptions that they have in mind. She states: "It may be the case that the parts of a given thing are in fact related in more than one way—the movements of a sonata, for example, may be related temporally and tonally" (p. 154). Thus Person 1 could understand a sonata temporally, in terms of which movements, slow or fast, occurred in which order and which musical theme occurred at which points and when they were repeated. Person 2 could understand the same sonata tonally in terms of the key of the sonata and the various chord progressions throughout it.

According to Martin, when we have an external understanding of something, we classify the object of our understanding in relation to something else; we "understand something under some description as bearing some relation to something else which is itself under some description" (p. 159). Within an external understanding of art, music, or literature, Martin includes such factors as the life and times of the creator and the social conditions of the times. This means we can understand a sonata externally by not only comparing it to other sonatas but also by situating it in the composer's life and times.

Other examples of internal and external understanding are of a novel and a painting. We can discuss the novel under a description of its internal parts, such as plot, character development, suspense, etc. We can also discuss the novel externally in terms of how it compares to other novels, the historical period in which it was written, and the novelist's life. We can understand an impressionist painting internally in terms of its style, colours, and subject matter, but we can also relate the painting to others of its genre as well as to paintings outside its genre.

Martin makes the point that external understanding often involves classifying either an object, person, or idea. The skill we develop to classify a particular musical work as a sonata, for example, means that we gain understanding of it once it has been put into a certain category. External understanding involves being able to categorize the object, person, or idea in question.

> In understanding by classifying, one's primary interest is in the way X fits in with other things and not in the parts of X as such at all. The redescription or classification does rest on them, and they may have to be invoked in justifying that classification; furthermore, the classification itself may well bring to our attention parts of X hitherto unnoticed.... If a person knows nothing about the impressionist movement, it will be of no avail to redescribe something he knows to be a painting as an impressionist work. (p. 159)

It seems to me that Martin's notion of a distinction between internal understanding (considering a piece of music in relation to itself and/or its parts and subparts) and external understanding (considering a piece of music in relation to other pieces of the same type and other external factors such as information about the composer and his or her life and times) is useful and interesting in a discussion of understanding music, but can be an artificial distinction. There is certainly "give and take" between internal and external understanding of a piece of music. For example, Campbell (2000) has made use of the same terminology as Martin in his discussion of the music of J. S. Bach. How we determine the character and speed of his keyboard music so that we understand how to perform it, depends on both internal and external clues. Internally, we can listen to the choice of mode and the shape of the melodic line to determine the character and speed of the music. Externally, we can play the melody and compare it to a vocal piece with a similar melody and examine the text to help determine the expression of the piece.

Understanding and Appreciating

The relationship between understanding and appreciating music is important for a discussion of musical understanding. As I will discuss below, understanding is the basis of appreciation, and understanding may also imply appreciation. It is a relationship that is complicated to explain, due to the ambiguity of both the terms involved.

There is a tendency in the literature written from the Western art music perspective, to sometimes use "understanding" music interchangeably with "appreciating" music as in the example below, where Goldman

(1995) begins by talking about "understanding" but ends up talking about "appreciation."

> In regard to the types of affective states aroused, debate centres on whether these are ordinary garden-variety emotions or feelings peculiar to the experience of listening to music. No one disputes that the latter feelings are crucial to listening to music with understanding. Musical forms, as these combine harmonic, rhythmic, and melodic elements, are heard and often identified through developmental affect. Formal developments that are not yet complete—for example harmonic progression from tonic to subdominant to dominant or regularly rising melodic patterns—create expectations for further development and resolution. These expectations are felt as tensions, and the affective effect is heightened by delay or prolongation of the fulfilment of expectation and closure. Those who appreciate music do not listen passively and passionlessly. They actively listen for what is to come in light of what has been foretold, pointed ahead by the unfolding progressions. (p. 51)

In some other cases, "appreciate" is used in regard to music, where understanding is used for other subjects, suggesting that "appreciate" is a more appropriate approach to discussing music. For example, in the quotation on page 34, Scheffler (1965) writes about "understanding" quantum theory, but about "appreciating" music. (This may, however, just be an older style and choice of vocabulary in writing about music.)

Although the concept of appreciation is a formidable topic in itself (Hare, 1985; Zenker, 1994), as is understanding, here I can outline several important aspects of appreciation. The central sense of "appreciation" is the estimation of value that may or may not imply positive evaluation or "liking." Appreciation is ambiguous and, for the purpose of my discussion here, has three main senses:

1. a subjective liking sense: It can mean "liking" in the sense that a person simply likes something but has no reasons why, except for a positive, subjective, emotional response.

> Appreciation can mean that we have the appropriate knowledge and understanding to make objective judgements about something.

2. a judgemental sense: Appreciation can mean that we have the appropriate knowledge and understanding to make objective judgements about something. This is the central sense of appreciation.

3. an objective liking sense: It can mean liking in a sophisticated sense; we like something because we use a set of objective conditions (Bergman, 1994) to ascribe a level of artistic value to the music and we value it based on our understanding of it.

Although appreciation does not require "liking" more so than understanding, it implies liking or favouring and is made more robust with liking. Pedagogically speaking, it is important to be able to give reasons for liking music. Important for education is that appreciation presupposes understanding—we can only assign value to the music once we understand it. We cannot appreciate music, except in the subjective liking sense, unless we understand it.

Understanding is the basis of appreciation, but there is also a sense in which understanding implies appreciation. If we understand the structure of a piece of music and can recognize the expressive elements of the music, we tend to evaluate it. We make judgements about the worth, quality, structural and expressive elements, significance, affectiveness, effectiveness, goodness, complexity, and simplicity of a piece of music. These are all value judgements based on the musical concepts we have learned.

In a sense, appreciation is the "end stage" of understanding music. Appreciation moves beyond understanding in that it involves the estimation of value when the object of our understanding is something to which we usually ascribe value such as in literature, music, and visual art. If we appreciate a piece of music we would naturally also have taken the necessary steps to understand it. If we understand a piece of music internally (how the various parts fit together to create the whole) and externally (compared to other pieces of music), we also tend to evaluate it. We also make judgements concerning artistry involving how well the performer has captured the style of the piece of music as well as the technical skill displayed.

If we understand a piece of music beyond the most basic level, it would be odd not to appreciate it in some or all of the ways I have outlined above. And conversely if we "like" a piece of music, in the subjective liking sense of appreciation, it is pedagogically important to learn to give reasons for this liking.

Levels of Understanding

The discussion of understanding music to this point (including various senses of understanding, understanding as an upshot, elements, concepts, internal/external understanding, intuitive/organic and reflective conceptual apparatuses, and perception recipes) suggests that there are a variety of considerations involved in understanding music and that different levels of understanding are possible.[9] Budd (1985) and Tanner (1985) have described levels and types of understanding music based on the notion that understanding music, like understanding many other things, is a matter of degree. Reimer (1996) has also suggested that "understanding exists on a continuum of possibilities" (p. 84). Davies (1994a) writes that "an understanding and appreciation of music, like understanding in general, can be both partial and a matter of degree" (p. 378). When we talk about understanding something in normal language usage, we talk about all sorts of understanding. We talk about a person's understanding being "initial," "limited," "shallow," "better," and "more or less sophisticated." These different types and levels of understanding are certainly possible in understanding music.

As I outlined in the section on the senses of understanding, understanding can be equated with comprehension but it can also mean more than comprehension: reflection and analysis and profound realization of the significance of something. It is difficult to outline what exactly various degrees of sophistication of musical understanding may include, but it seems that, beyond the level at which understanding is associated with comprehension, the more sophisticated the musical understanding, the more a variety of considerations must be taken into account.

Indeed, there are an the increasing number of considerations taken into account in Tanner's (1985) levels of understanding:

> Level one is a matter of sensing the nature of the thematic material.... Understanding music at this basic level consists in the ability to follow how the themes in the music unfold, to be able to hear the basic structure of the music.... Level 2 is the level at which one begins to explain how the music works by talking of modulations, inversions, counterpoints and

---

[9] Discussion of conceptual apparatus and perception recipes points to the fact that by the time children reach school they are not musical "blank slates" but have an implicit grasp of the music that they have heard around them.

the rest.... This level moves beyond level one in that it explains how the music is written and what changes are made so the themes and structure of the music unfold as they do.... Level 3 takes us from the realm of the technical—which naturally involves a certain amount of theory—into that of the explicitly theoretical. (p. 230)

This third level involves reconciling what Tanner calls the "background" and "foreground" of the music.

The background consists of the common stock of rules and idioms in which the music of the time is written, and is presupposed by the piece which will inevitably employ these rules extensively. The foreground is what the piece actually consists in (1985, p. 230). A full understanding of such a piece will involve seeing what the precise balance of background and foreground is, and in exploring the relationship between the two. (p. 231)

It seems that Tanner's Level 1 is the same as the comprehension sense of understanding music, "following the music," which is also similar to Ryle's (1959/1949) notion of perception (sound) recipes. According to Tanner's levels, as our understanding becomes more sophisticated, we become aware of the "foreground" (internal) and the "background" (external) elements of the music.

Of course this notion of levels is just one possible description of how understanding becomes more sophisticated. Budd (1985) proposes that a person's level of sophistication of understanding can be assessed under four different dimensions:

Someone's understanding of a musical work can be said to be superficial if although he can follow a performance of the work without feeling lost, he fails to hear much of the significant detail or structure of the work. His understanding of a musical work can be said to be inaccurate (or imprecise) if, although he can follow a performance of a work well, he has mistaken (or only a rather indefinite) conception of how the music should sound, and so how it should be performed. The third category of understanding is this: someone's understanding of music can be said to be narrow if it covers few kinds of styles of music, either in the sense that he is not able to follow most forms of music or in the sense that he is not able to appreciate most forms of music i.e., to see what value there is in them. Finally, someone's understanding of music can be said to be primitive if he can respond only to the simplest musical relations and structures. (p. 234)

Budd's dimensions of understanding, as he describes them, are actually the negation of what we want to happen in understanding for education. Understanding means that we have "got it right" and that we can tie together knowledge and see connections. For education, we want students to change and *improve* in their understanding so that they see, or in the case of music, hear things that others who have not achieved the same level of understanding, do not. We want a person's understanding, in contrast to Budd's description, to deepen, to become more accurate, to broaden and to become more sophisticated. Musical understanding is a matter of degree in that it exists on a continuum of possibilities of becoming more sophisticated and refined, which leads to a discussion of the dynamic nature of understanding.

Dynamic Characteristic of Understanding

Although the objects of our understanding may differ as well as the criteria by which we judge our understanding, it is important to consider the general nature or underlying meaning that serves to connect the various uses of understanding. Scheffler (1965) suggests that understanding

> involves something analogous to perception: seeing the point. Or it might be construed to include having explained or paraphrased the doctrine in question in special terms, initially intelligible to the person. Or again, it might be thought to require a certain degree of experience or maturity (as in understanding Shakespeare's plays). However we interpret it, it seems *not* to reduce to the subject use of *know*. (p. 18)

When we understand, there is a change in our capacities that may affect how we behave, think about something, or our purpose or outlook on life. In this sense, the changes that occur in us because we understand are dynamic;[10] as we understand more, we see more connections so that our understanding constantly changes and grows; it is never static or complete.

Understanding seems to connote a dynamic quality existing between the knowledge to be learned and how the learning is accomplished, i.e., the learner's interaction with the subject matter. Both Daniels (1986) and Barrow and Milburn (1990) consider the concept of understanding to have

---

[10] When we are talking about understanding being dynamic we have to be careful not to confuse change with action.

properties like a combination of "learn" and "know" that encompasses both the agent (the learner) and the subject matter.

> It [understanding] is like know in its epistemological role, particularly in the fact that we must satisfy something analogous to an evidence condition—even when we are talking about our own U [understanding]. It is like learn in that "learn" serves to tell ourselves and others that our abilities, dispositions, etc. have been relatively permanently altered. To come to understand is likewise to change our abilities—to see, do, realize, appreciate, etc. (Daniels, 1986, p. 285)

> In the first place the connotations of "knowledge" and "understanding" are rather different. The former may suggest the acquisition or possession of information in an inert form. While the latter necessarily implies that the information in question is imbibed in such a way that it cannot lie inert. Secondarily, by concentration on knowledge and learning we have to some extent kept the two distinct: while philosophers consider the nature of knowledge in the abstract, psychologists study the mechanics of learning, without paying much attention to what is being learned. But what is of prime interest to us as educators is precisely the experience or act of understanding that encompasses both the agent and the subject matter. (Barrow & Milburn, 1990, p. 320)

The dynamic aspect of understanding can be described in many ways and using many different frameworks. We can say that understanding is not a "one-way" street between the knowledge to be learned and the learner, but that the learner interacts with the subject matter by forming more questions, testing hypotheses, having expectations about what is to be learned, comparing one type of knowledge with another, predicting what will happen in a given situation, explaining and analyzing, and beginning the process all over again. In other words musical understanding is not something "out there" that we can grasp or a muscle that we can flex. Rather we construct our musical understanding based on our interaction with music and our acquisition of musical knowledge.

> We construct our musical understanding based on our interaction with music and our acquisition of musical knowledge.

We react to and interact with music based on patterns we recognize in the music and the social/cultural context of the music mingled with our personal musical history, experiences, and theoretical knowledge.

Conclusion

As has been shown, there is a great deal that can be discovered about what may be involved in musical understanding through an examination of the nature of "understanding" itself. An analysis of the complex nature of this concept provides a framework for musical understanding as well as confirms its complexity. At the same time an analysis of understanding exposes assumptions and presuppositions as to what constitutes musical understanding. As I see it, this type of analysis of understanding and musical understanding is the first and necessary step to the creation of a complete theory of musical understanding. A complete theory of musical understanding would require interdisciplinary studies of what the interrelationships of theories of the concept of mind, psychology of music, ethnomusicology, and neuroscience can tell us about the complex nature of, and the many factors involved in, musical understanding.

The most important characteristics of musical understanding derived from the characteristics of understanding I have discussed in this essay are:

1. There is no single type of "music-understanding-know-how," but a wide variety of musical activities in which one must engage.
2. Musical understanding as a capacity to make connections in music results from *many* activities and experiences with music and recognizing relationships among musical activities and experiences (i.e., a person has had a lot of musical upshots or outcomes).
3. Musical understanding is the basis of music appreciation.
4. There is not some type of "musical understanding" "out there" that we can grasp, but it is constructed and created by each individual according to the activities in which that person engages and his/her experiences.
5. Musical understanding is polymorphous. That is, we pass through many different stages and levels of musical understanding depending on the musical context.

To address musical understanding as I have in this essay may indeed make many music educators uncomfortable with their own philosophies of music education. They may also realize that they may have taught music for many years without really examining the concept of musical understanding. But as music educators at all levels of the curriculum know, music education has been in crisis and continues to be removed from the school curriculum. The need to make changes in the way we teach music in the traditionally performance-driven band, choral, and orchestral programs setting has existed for far too long. We need to question why we continue to educate "musicians" in the highly-practised perfectionist sense rather than teaching for various levels of musical understanding in which performance plays only a part. We, as music educators, need to constantly and consistently evaluate and re-evaluate the complex and dynamic nature of musical understanding as our musical environment changes and grows or we may miseducate by not teaching some important aspects of music.

I hope my examination of musical understanding will contribute to the dialogue needed to make important changes in the ways we teach music in school and to inform the ways musical understanding can be included in the variety of educational contexts in which music is studied.

References

Baily, J. (1996). Commentary. In R. Walker, Open peer commentary: Can we understand the music of other cultures? *Psychology of Music, 24*, 114–117.

Barrow, R., & Milburn, G. (1990). *A critical dictionary of educational concepts* (2nd ed.). New York: Teachers College Press.

Bergman, S. (1994). An objective aesthetics? Implications for arts education. *Paiduesis: Journal of the Canadian Philosophy of Education Society, 8* (1), 17–28.

Budd, M. (1985). Understanding music. *Proceedings of the Aristotelian Society. 59* (Suppl. Vol.), 233–248.

Campbell, M. (2000, May). *TEXT, urTEXT, conTEXT: Focus on J. S. Bach.* Paper presented at Tom Lee Music, Vancouver, Canada.

Collins Dictionary of the English Language. (1986). London: Collins.

Daniels, L. B. (1986). Response to Richmond on understanding and aesthetics. *Proceedings of the Philosophy of Education Society (Forty-second Annual Meeting)*, 281–285.

Daniels, L. B. (1996). Eisenberg's Heisenberg: The indeterminacies of rationality. *Curriculum Inquiry, 26* (2), 181–192.

Davies, S. (1994a). *Musical meaning and expression.* Ithaca, NY: Cornell University Press.

Davies, S. (1994b). Musical understanding and musical kinds. *Journal of Aesthetics and Art Criticism, 51* (2), 69–81.

Goldman, A. H. (1995). *Aesthetic value.* Boulder, CO: Westview Press.

Hare, W. (1985). *Controversies in teaching.* London, ON: Althouse Press.

Kivy, P. (1990). *Music alone: Philosophical reflections on the purely musical experience.* Ithaca, NY: Cornell University Press.

Levinson J. (1990). Musical literacy. *Journal of Aesthetic Education, 24* (1), 17–30.

Martin, J. R. (1970). *Explaining, understanding and teaching.* New York: McGraw-Hill.

Reimer, B. (1996). David Elliott's "new" philosophy of music education: Music for performers only. *Bulletin of the Council of Research in Music Education, 128,* 59–89.

Ryle, G. (1959). *The concept of mind.* London, UK: Penguin Classics. (Original work published 1949)

Scheffler, I. (1965). *Conditions of knowledge: An introduction to epistemology and education.* Chicago, IL: University of Chicago Press.

Scruton R. (1983). *The aesthetic understanding: Essays in the philosophy of art and culture.* Manchester: Carcanet New Press.

Tanner, M. (1985). Understanding music. *Proceedings of the Aristotelian Society. 59* (Suppl. Vol.), 215–232.

The Oxford English dictionary (1989). Oxford: Clarendon Press.

Walker, R. (1996). Open peer commentary: Can we understand the music of another culture? *Psychology of Music, 24,* 103–114.

Webster's 3rd new international dictionary of the English language (unabriged). (1976). Springfield, MA: G & C Merriam.

White, A. R. (1967). *Philosophy of mind.* New York: Random House.

Zenker, R. (1994). Music appreciation and education. *Canadian Music Educator, 36* (2), 7–11.

Zenker, R. (2000). *Understanding music cross-culturally: A philosophical examination.* Unpublished doctoral dissertation, University of British Columbia, Vancouver, BC.

Meaning and Understanding in Music
The Role of Complex Constructs
Lee Bartel

Situating Myself

Knowledge is personal. Therefore, my knowledge about meaning and understanding in music is personal and connected to personal experiences. A number of experiences have contributed to shaping my personal knowledge. My dissertation work on cognitive-affective response to music led me to define response to music as constructed by the percipient, "as an accumulation of a series of individual perceptions or registration" (Bartel, 1988). Another experience was my observation of how my daughter Melanie's mind worked—which I would characterize as "Nine, ten, big chicken." Her attempts to memorize things like "One, two, buckle my shoe...nine, ten, big fat hen" revealed comprehension rather than verbatim memory. She often formed the "concept" (big chicken) but lost the specific word "label" (big fat hen) for it. In my son Lucas I observed almost the opposite phenomenon. When he was in grade 9 he was diagnosed with Aspergers Disorder and revealed an amazing vocabulary but difficulty in processing meaning from discourse. His mind seemed to hold individual meaning concepts as word labels, but he had difficulty with the connections among them.

As a research team member at the Bloorview Macmillan Centre, I studied attention in head-injured adolescents and observed that executive management of the mind's data stock is crucial to functional knowledge. My recent work with EEG neurotherapy, brain response to sound, and the difference between sound as music and music as sound have placed "knowledge" and understanding in a new cognitive context for me (Bartel, 2000).

51

Most recently, my work on a chapter on trends in research for *The New Handbook of Research on Music Teaching and Learning* (Colwell & Richardson, 2002) has led me to contemplate things like complexity theory, constructivism, data mining, and knowledge development in databases. As I present my thinking on meaning and understanding in music in this chapter, many of these experiences may become evident.

I admit that when I approach musical meaning and understanding I have specific interest in the "educating process" rather than "music performed." I am not simply referring to constructs related specifically to processing performed music but to the development of understanding of music encountered in the classroom. Music learning is integral to music understanding.

Defining Key Ideas

The ideas, "meaning," "knowledge," and "understanding," have been a constant preoccupation of philosophy, epistemology, or metaphysics for over 2000 years, and definition of terms is often the focus. In common use we often do not differentiate clearly among the ideas and possibly confuse the terms by exchanging them. For example, we might say, "Do you know the meaning?" or "Do you understand the meaning?" or "Does this knowledge mean anything to you?"

Although "know" and "understand" are often used interchangeably, "meaning" is a more differentiated construct. "Meaning" can be what something signifies, what something represents (denotes), or the connections one makes to something (connotation). These three meaning-functions operate whether meaning is believed to reside externally or objectively "in the music" or whether meaning is believed to be a personal internal construct.

In the "external" view, meaning is an objective property of the music. In the most extreme form of this view, the contemplative tradition, music is believed to have meaning properties that independently "act on" the listener and create their "aesthetic" effect.

The "internal" view is premised on the belief that there is no reality apart from representations of it, with the implication that music only exists once we construct it. Musical meaning cannot be "in" the music, adhere to the music, or be objectively coded in sound, or "in" the communication—we construct our personal meaning from the sound waves bombarding our ears.

I prefer a more moderate realist view, where potential for meaning is believed to adhere to the properties music presents to the listener's mind but the listener is assumed to engage in a constructivist process of assigning meaning, making connections, and developing associations that functions as the meaning-complex for experienced sound. In this view, reality is believed to exist apart from personal representations of it. I hold that meaning is the pattern of associations one establishes among sense data, whether internal or external in origin. Music is someone's external representation of inner meaning and, therefore, it must represent that meaning somehow. This perspective still sees some meaning "in" the music.

Although often used interchangeably, "knowledge" and "understanding" do have different meanings. "Knowledge" can be taken to be the sum or range of what has been perceived while "understanding" refers to a comprehension of the significance of what has been perceived. Using a modern analogy, "knowledge" is the basic content of a web page, while "understanding" is a pattern of association among web pages.

> "Knowledge" can be taken to be the sum or range of what has been perceived while "understanding" refers to a comprehension of the significance of what has been perceived.

The mind works with "bits" of knowledge. Often we equate these with linguistic labels—words. In music, for example, our knowledge of "melody" is considered equivalent to the word label, and the characteristics of melodies to other word labels. We realize, however, as musicians that our knowledge of "melody" and specific "melodies" is much richer than dictionary definitions of specific words. In the struggle to recognize this richness, we have developed various terms to denote a "bit" of knowledge. For example, we talk of representation, meme, idea, notion, thought, schema, percept, or concept.

What is the best word for the basic level of knowledge? "Representation" captures the function of "image" of reality, distance from reality, agency inherent in knowledge but seems to distort knowledge by its strong "image" orientation. "Meme" was created by Richard Dawkins

(1980) as an equivalent to "gene" and seems primarily applicable to foundational concepts rather than specific word denotations or image memories. The "schema" advocates do not seem to clarify fundamental knowledge. Rather they focus on the "theory" relationships among knowledge bits. The "constructivists" do not explain what is constructed but emphasize the individual role in the creation of knowledge. Those who talk about "percepts" seem to imply these are transferred whole. Words like "concept," "thought," or "idea" are in such common use their meanings lack specificity.

I have decided to use the word "construct" to refer to "bits of knowledge" because of its use in the research vocabulary as a created definition, its meaning in Kelly's (1955) Personal Construct Psychology as an anticipatory structure, and its close tie to constructivism. Perhaps the word in common usage most closely aligned with "construct" is "concept." Fiske (1996) states "concepts—not words—are in charge of thinking. Language does not direct thought, and ideas expressed by words are not equal to the words themselves. That is, words are not ideas and ideas do not require words" (p. 148). I argue that our knowledge exists as constructs. The content of constructs is not shaped by words. Rather the meaning of words is shaped by constructs.

Some Caveats

Although a discussion of fundamental knowledge and meaning easily moves to the neural network level, I will leave that discussion to Harold Fiske. Also, I am not interested here in what specific EEG pattern responds with activity. Nor will I discuss how, neurologically, constructs come into being. Rather I take a pragmatic approach and draw a leaf from Complexity Theory—there is simplicity inherent in what looks complex, and complexity in the simple. "When life seems to be the most complicated, a simple order may be just around the corner. And when things appear simple, we should be on the lookout for the hidden nuance or subtlety" (Briggs & Peat, 1999, p. 89). I will try to make simple what is complex and probably create some confusion about what may really be simple.

A Review of Some Views

Since understanding and meaning are at the core of any philosophy, a thorough analysis of the ideas of some of the contributors to music education philosophy would take much more time and space than I have here. I will, therefore, comment briefly on the work of four individuals whose views directly or indirectly "muddied the waters" of music education in relation to the role of understanding.

David Elliott

To say "Elliott" today is essentially to say "praxial," and to say "praxial" is to touch a sensitive nerve in many music educators. Praxial music education seems to be something you must be for or against. On this topic I feel a bit like Keith Swanwick (1998) who said:

> Although it has been interesting and at times fun to participate in and follow the twists and turns of MayDay thinking, I do feel diffident about producing a paper.... I also worry about the theorising, not in principle...but the kind of mind set that seems to dominate much music education in the USA. Here I agreed with Bob Walker: we need to get outside this incestuous circle.

Let me clarify a few points at the outset: (1) "praxial" is not equivalent to constructivist, and neither Elliott nor anyone else holds the "rights" to a particular view of knowledge; and (2) a constructivist view of knowledge does not determine the phenomenological nature of musical experience.

While the term "musical meaning" is basically absent from Elliott's (1995) book, musical knowing (formal, informal, impressionistic, supervisory, and procedural) is given considerable attention. Elliott argues that "knowledge is the key to enjoyment and control" (p. 117); he refers presumably to the knowledge developed through music education. One might then conclude that more knowledge would equal more enjoyment and that little knowledge would equal little enjoyment. The question this raises for me is how can young children enjoy music? And why is it then that people's peak experiences with music tend to happen in early years? (Gabrielsson, 1989, 1991). Why is it that the study of music often reduces pure "musical" enjoyment and increases the enjoyment of criticism and the enjoyment of problem solving?

Elliott argues further that "musicianship" is the coming together of the five forms of knowledge, that musicianship equals understanding, and that, "my musicianship [understanding] lies in the quality of my music making, in what I get done as a performer (improviser, composer, arranger, or conductor)" (p. 57). Note Elliott does not include listener in his list here. Earlier Elliott seems to argue that you can only know what you do (not that doing merely gives evidence of knowing). If this were true, then musical understanding could never proceed beyond one's ability to perform. What does a conductor, composer, or arranger perform? When does understanding music depart from physical "music making" and develop inside the mind? And does it not develop from listening—beyond what one can actually do on an instrument? How much "performing" is enough for you to proceed in your mind? Is there no place for "imagination" or fantasy? Interestingly, Elliott never defines performing but bases his assertions on performing, not on musicing (e.g., p. 57). In my opinion, Elliott's view of knowledge, learning, and musical experience assumes too slow an ascent, is too linear in progress, and ascribes too little learning from early exposure and none from inherent structure.

One common interest in relation to music is how people respond to music or how they experience music. My definition (Bartel, 1988) of response as a meaning-construct created from registrations points to a constructivist approach to addressing "emotional" response and consequently emotional knowledge and understanding. In his clear emphasis on "thinking" cognition, Elliott gathers "emotional" matters into impressionistic knowledge but gives no place at all to emotional response and essentially disregards the phenomenological experience of music. What phenomenological aspects there are seem focused on "artistic decision making" rather than on aspects of feeling or responding. This position may be a result of the priority Elliott gives to performing over listening. He (1995) states: "[M]usic programs geared to recorded music do not provide the proper conditions for developing the several kinds of knowledge required for intelligent listening because recordings place the student as listener outside the artistic decision making process" (1995, p. 99). Is intelligent listening different from feelingful listening? Elliott says further that "educating competent, proficient, and expert listeners...depends on the progressive education of competent, proficient, and artistic music makers in the present" (p. 99). I grant that music making is a special form of connecting constructs (developing understanding)—but not the only one. Understanding cannot be limited to the extent of physical performing ability—or else one must conclude that the vast majority of people who fill concert venues, purchase recordings, and listen to the radio derive some benefit from something they simply do not understand.

Howard Gardner

Gardner emphasizes performance in relation to understanding. He (1999b) explains: "An individual understands a concept, skill, theory, or domain of knowledge to the extent that he or she can apply it appropriately in a new situation" (p. 119). Gardner, however, does not argue that understanding is developed through the process of performing but rather that it is only *observable* in some outward "performance." His claim is easily misinterpreted by musicians who inevitably see performing as "music performing" rather than simply "an outward doing." But Gardner uses performance to refer to the broad sense of observable behaviour. Where Elliott seems to believe you must perform to understand, Gardner emphasizes that a student must "perform" for understanding to be assessed.

Gardner acknowledges the difference between the real nature of knowledge and understanding as a process of mental representation and the utilitarian assessment demands of schooling today. In addition he seems to differentiate between knowing (as the physical event of the mind capturing information) and understanding (now defined as the ability to provide evidence of knowledge to satisfy testers). He does have some problem with his current strong association between understanding and performance but seems to opt for a view that will satisfy the testing climate.

In *Disciplined Mind* (1999b) he states:

Talk of a "performance of understanding" may seem a bit oxymoronic, since we usually think of understanding as an internal event, one that occurs in mental representations, between the ears. And we have no reason to doubt that much is occurring between the ears, as inadequate representations are being challenged and—should teaching and learning prove successful—more adequate ones are being constructed. Still the focus on understanding as a performance proves salutary. (p. 129)

In *Intelligence Reframed* (1999a) he states:

[F]olk wisdom and contemporary psychology convince us that understanding is an event or process that occurs between the ears—in the mind or brain.... I underscore the importance of processes of mental representation that occur in the assimilation and transformation of knowledge...but the physical events that occur in the mind or brain...are irrelevant to their educational missions. Instead, when it comes to understanding, the emphasis falls properly on performances that can be observed, critiqued, and improved. (p. 160)

Despite Gardner's re-interpretation of understanding to fit the current test-driven educational mind-set in North America, honest test makers and interpreters know and always assume that the person being tested knows and understands more than can be tested or "performed" since the context created for such performance brings with it many constraining features.

Gardner's current perform-it-for-the-test approach to understanding is brought into further dissonance given his long-standing commitment to multiple intelligences. Multiple intelligences mean multiple representations, and real understanding would therefore be in multiple representations; however, most performances draw only on one form of representation and consequently do not provide adequate evidence of understanding. Gardner is forced then to pursue the nearly impossible, stating that "one may believe that this 'mental representation' offers the optimal way to convey that particular topic" (1999b, p. 202). In contrast, I argue that the best representations are multiple. And so our search should be for the family of representations that can convey the core ideas in a multiplicity of ways at once accurate and complementary.

Gardner's contribution to education has been substantial and significant. He has done a great service for education in music by identifying music as an intelligence. His theory and pedagogical contribution, however, has been focused on the "intellectual" or "subject discipline" aspect of knowledge. It has had a strong traditional flavour about it (maybe that is why it has been so acceptable). He has, for example, shied away from identifying as "an intelligence" engagement with spiritual phenomena. He has also pursued one of the errors of modern cognitive psychology in essentially ignoring everything in the body but the cortex. The cognitivists basically ignore the emotive and conative aspects of experience and, hence, their place in learning. In one of his latest books he does finally acknowledge this critically important aspect of learning.

> The role of emotions in learning has undergone renewed scrutiny.... Creating an educational environment in which pleasure, stimulation, and challenge flourish is an important mission. Also, students are more likely to learn, remember, and make subsequent use of those experiences with respect to which they had strong—and, one hopes, positive—emotional reactions.... if one wants some things to be attended to, mastered, and subsequently used, one must be sure to wrap it in a context that engages the emotions. Conversely, experiences devoid of emotional impact are likely to be weakly engaging and soon forgotten, leaving nary a mental representation behind. (1999b, p. 77)

What he seems to acknowledge and argue is that emotions are a means to an intellectual end, but he does not recognize that emotional, feelingful "reactions" also form mental representations and form permanent associative links (become knowledge) with all the "disciplined" bits of knowledge Gardner is so concerned about. In my opinion, he misunderstands the nature of foundational knowledge structures in the mind.

Bennett Reimer

Reimer's philosophy of music (1989) is clearly not premised on principles of current cognitive psychology and as such does not offer much for my current considerations. He believes "concepts" require linguistic labels to exist. He believes art is "intuitive" and "non-conceptual" and involves a process he calls "perceptual structuring." This difference is incomprehensible in current cognitive science. His view of the major function of art would be much more convincing to me if he would phrase it within cognitive science. He says:

> The major function of art is to make objective and therefore accessible the subjective realm of human responsiveness. Art does this by capturing and presenting in its intrinsic qualities the patterns and forms of human feeling. The major function of education in the arts is to help people gain access to the experiences of feeling contained in the artistic qualities of things. (p. 53)

I may find Reimer's explanations inadequate, but at least he talks about the experience of music. At least he attempts to account for emotional dimensions of the phenomenon. He expands "understanding" by arguing it involves experiencing the "human feeling" captured by the art work.

Harold Fiske

Rather than discussing Fiske's (1996) dense arguments, I will simply present my favourite quotations (from a hard constructionist):

> [M]usic cognition is a very complex and intellectually exciting mental activity... But complexity does not necessarily mean chaos. (p. 145)

> [C]oncepts—not words—are in charge of thinking. Language does not direct thought, and ideas expressed by words are not equal the words themselves. That is, words are not ideas and ideas do not require words. (p. 148)

> [M]usic-cognitive hypothesis testing consists of comparing incoming tonal-rhythmic percepts with context-derived, expectancy-generated, tonal-rhythmic pattern constructs. (p. 143)

> [L]isteners respond emotionally to music, but their responses, even to the same piece, are personal ones and may vary both in quality and degree. (p. 128)

> [W]hatever musical meaning is, it is in some way about realized inter-pattern relationships expressed as aesthetic attitude belief states. (p. 150)

> [A] listener's emotional, feelingful, passionate, joyous, sad, ecstatic, melancholic, elated, euphoric, or down right turned-on arousal to music validates the human survival-value of aesthetic attitude states. (p. 152)

> Musical comprehension is proportional to the extent of successful negotiation of the hierarchy of tonal-rhythmic pattern-comparison decision-making. (p. 154)

> I would argue that touching an emotional or feelingful button is part of the understanding.

I only differ with the last point because Fiske argues that the outcome of the process of musical comprehension is an aesthetic attitude. Maybe I just do not understand it. The statement sounds like a Leonard Meyer argument to me. Understanding to me includes making the emotional link—this link is an essential aspect of music meaning and understanding. It is not that you understand the music (finished) and then you respond. I would argue that touching an emotional or feelingful button is part of the understanding.

Knowledge as Complex Constructs

Nine-month old Melanie plays with a Persian kitten. She nuzzles its neck, watches it frisk, pulls its tail, holds and shakes it, listens to it meow. Suddenly the kitten is frightened and scratches Melanie. Melanie cries for a little while but soon returns to affectionate play. A few months later, much to the parents' delight Melanie says "cat." One day she sees a little short-haired dog and says "cat" but is quickly told "dog." She sees a short-haired cat and says "dog" but then hears the cat meow and immediately says "cat." Melanie has developed knowledge related to a specific cat and about "catness." She accumulated that knowledge in her mind as a series of registrations of sensory perceptions and bodily responses. *She "constructed" the sum of the sensory perceptions—the sum became a "construct."* An initial visual image distinct from its field established the perceptual "construct," which quickly assimilated touch sensations of fuzziness and warmth, sound sensations, smell, and probably even taste. Melanie's reactions of interest and pleasure also adhered to her cat construct. Quickly the construct had to accommodate the possibility of pain. Melanie's construct received an abstract representation—a name—that she probably remembered as a label long before she spoke it as a word. Her construct was further enriched with other representations (e.g., pictures of cats in books and stories about cats).

The mind of graduate student Pierre plays with questions of creativity for a research study. He wonders whether creativity is an inherent potential or learned ability and then realizes he needs to clarify what he means by "creativity." Pierre reflects on instances when he was told he was especially creative. He remembers the feelings of anguish when he had to improvise in music class and the sense of euphoria when he crafted an exceptional poem. He describes the characteristics of some people he considers creative. He realizes the meaning "creativity" has in his mind is an accumulation of at least (1) personal experiences that were designated "creative," (2) demonstrations of others engaging in "creativity," (3) stories involving "creativity," and (4) the meanings of other words like spontaneous, artistic, novel, unique, and special, associated with creativity. Pierre has constructed this set of meaning connections with creativity over many years. *A complex construct relates to and depends on a multitude of other constructs; it constantly and continuously develops.*

Complex Constructs

There is no neat division between basic, simple constructs and full-blown schema (the explanatory "theories" that are used to predict or guide action). The reason there is no neat division is the nature of complex constructs. As we encounter something new we establish a "place holder" construct (analogy—create a web page) and then begin to make it more complex by adding things to it (put more on the web page) and forming links to other existing constructs (hot button links to other web pages). This IS the process of meaning-making. The complexity of an individual construct is expandable and can in itself take on elements of explanation. When we create a "theory" (or at first a hypothesis) of how constructs are sequenced, linked, and related, we may be creating a new explanatory construct (a construct relation pattern that is stored as an accessible whole) or an awareness of links between simpler constructs (e.g., Melanie will soon predict that if she pulls the cat's tail, the cat will scratch). It may be useful to differentiate between basic denotation and signification level (level one) and explanatory level (level two) meaning constructs.

Level One Constructs. One type of construct at the basic level is the denotative "noun" type. A child's "cat" construct could consist of only perceptions from a picture in a book associated with parents making meow noises. Many constructs begin in that way (almost as dictionary linguistic descriptions) but as such are essentially "empty" constructs (like web pages that have only one thing on them and with no further links, like words remembered as vocables but with no meaning). Connotations can be added to these basic constructs through further verbal and visual connections, but active experience is what essentially develops the richness of the construct, as in Melanie's case. Clearly, a parent or teacher cannot simply "transfer" a fully-formed construct to the child. The person must engage perceptual data and build (construct) or organize it into a mental structure. One type of level one constructs is the noun and verb level—these constructs relate mostly to objects and actions (but always have links to all modes of perception and sensation).

A second type at the basic level of constructs is one that is essentially abstract—involving adjectives and adverbs. These emerge as a locus of meaning from attributions or characterizations of other constructs (objects and actions) and tend to take on values on a dichotomous continuum (e.g., hot/cold, excellent/mediocre, loud/soft). For example, "creative" is a construct that derives from generalized attributions of observations of production and product. There are other types, but I am not trying here to make a complete catalogue and taxonomy of constructs.

Level Two Constructs. A second level of construct is that to which Kelly (1995) refers in his *Psychology of Personal Constructs* and is more recently described by Schema Theory. In schema theory, a person develops a mental structure that encompasses the links and relationships between basic constructs. This connection can be seen as a hypothesis or, with development, a theory. Schemas act as means of making predictions about the world. As a person experiences a stream of sensory data from any or all the bodily senses, these hypothesis-constructs offer "explanations" of the data by allocating them to existing constructs and relationships among constructs previously experienced or introduce "modifications" to existing constructs.

Every level is Complex. Complexity, a property of an object, idea, phenomenon, organism, or system, stems from "compoundness" —multiple parts, layers, or dimensions. In addition, complexity lies not only in an entity as multiple components but also in the interconnectedness or interwoveness of the parts, each of which may depend on or influence the other, neither of which is in a fixed relationship or quantity nor is related to a fixed behavior. Knowledge constructs are complex in their interconnectedness. One construct influences another, and neither is fixed—their meanings continue to change. Complexity, as a quality of being differentiated yet integrated, is commonly regarded as "the direction in which evolution proceeds" (Csikszentmihalyi, 1993, p. 157). Understanding related to particular constructs develops in this "direction"—meaning becomes more differentiated yet integrated into a larger framework of knowledge.

Back to constructs and the website analogy. A construct can be seen as a website. For example, Melanie's cat construct is a mental "website." This site might be structured with a page that has representations of the cat's appearance, a page of words associated with the cat, a page of emotions, a page of sounds, a page of smells, a page of touch, pain, and pleasure, a page of stories and poems of cats, and a page of other cats. Each of these pages has links to other sites. The story page links to many other places, animals, words, pictures, videos, and so on. The page of emotions may have links to parent emotions, sibling emotions, emotion labels, emotion valuing sites and so on. As the person develops the amount of material on each page, the number of pages and the linking to other sites increases. The cat site may be accessed on any page and through other linked sites. To resemble human processing, the web and computer would have to function at a speed making links and pages accessible at fractions of seconds and in multiple channels simultaneously.

Sources of Construct Content

Figure 1 illustrates the possible sources of content for our construct structure. This illustration was adapted from one created by Pandora Bryce, a Ph.D. student at the University of Toronto, to capture a variety of mental representations.

Figure 1. Sources of Construct Content

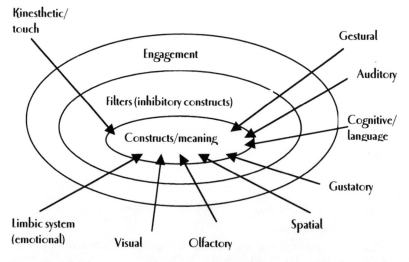

Important to note is that constructs hold important knowledge from many sources other than the evident linguistic form.

Emotional/Feeling Content of Constructs

Emotion is a problem for each of the theorists mentioned. We are afraid of emotion—it does not appear to be rational; it pops up at the oddest times. I would argue that emotion adheres to contructs (it is right there on the web page—as the colour or photo or dancing commercial). It can also be a link to a separate emotional site—sort of an abstraction and objectified emotion—the form of emotion remembered ("cognitive emotions," as Elliott calls them). The biggest lack in the theories of musical understanding, however, is the absence of a thorough integration of emotional tone into every construct. The "playing the violin" construct has emotion on the site. Many "song constructs" have emotion on site. Many specific musical patterns have emotion on their site. Specific sounds have such links—for example a strained, near screaming "sonic event" carries a connection to an emotional site even when the connection does not become specifically conscious. I, of course, focus on this dimension as specifically as possible in designing relaxation music. Specific sonic effects as well as "musical gestures" have links.

A person does not always consciously access each component or button or link. Often it seems that brains do matching iterations. They encounter a stimulus (say a set of oral vocables spoken rather quietly), and the brain does a search for a possible match. Some brains settle for the first match. Others make more iterations and test these possible matches against other context clues.

Inhibitory Constructs

One of the features of brain function is the firing of pyramidal cortical cells; the electrical charge build up starts around the center of the brain, builds up and fires upward, builds up, fires, etc. There are, however, not only excitatory forces. There are also inhibitory forces that resist firing (see Figure 1). Similarly, (not saying this is a function of these forces) there are barrier constructs or filters—inhibitors to the reaching of the web site. So certain meanings or associations may not become conscious, or it may be difficult to reshape an explanatory construct.[1] One of the primary creators of these inhibitory constructs is the emotional reaction. "Belief" or judgments from previous experience can be inhibiting. These inhibitory functions are the opposite of the engagement I will explain shortly in conditions of learning (see Figure 2).

Understanding

Having explained the complex construct and its role in knowledge and understanding, I now finally return to look at what is entailed in the development of understanding. The development of understanding is concerned with: (1) increasing the complexity of constructs (adding pages with more on them to the web site), (2) increasing the associations among constructs (creating more links between sites), (3) increasing the complexity of explanatory constructs, (4) increasing the extent of construct consciousness or clarity, (5) making associations more readily accessible, and (6) increasing facility at accessing and using the links, thereby (7) increasing the accuracy of explanatory constructs to anticipate and predict the future.

Developing Understanding

Jackie Wiggins has already captured many aspects of the pedagogical implication of the constructivist approach I have developed here in her presentation and past writing (Wiggins, 2001; see also chapter 9 in this book). I do not have the space and time to expand on these implications, but a full consideration might start with John Dewey's explanation of "an experience." It would include Vygotsky's activity theory, mediation, and the zone of proximal development. It would include Howard Gardner's thoughts on apprenticeship and the "museum" model of learning, and so on. What I will do instead is to focus mainly on one of the principal concerns of pedagogy and one that is very directly related to the feeling tone that is inherent in every construct—the phenomenon of engagement.

---

[1] Gardner refers to obstacles to understanding. Kelly refers to the permeability of constructs—the capacity of a construct to allow new elements of experience to be admitted.

But first, one short consideration. From the perspective of complex constructs I must emphasize that knowledge exists in multiple forms of representation—each contributing a different form of understanding. One must always assume that knowledge or a meaning construct is linked, for example, to linguistic labels, visual images, musical ideas, feeling tone, and so on. As quoted earlier, Gardner (1999a) says:

> one may believe that this "mental representation" offers the optimal way to convey that particular topic. In contrast, I argue that the best representations are multiple. And so our search should be for the family of representations that can convey the core ideas in a multiplicity of ways at once accurate and complementary. (p. 202)

Facilitating Engagement

Given that understanding will develop in complex relationship constructs, a critical pedagogical element is the facilitation of emotional engagement and the elimination of inhibitory forces. As Gardner (1999b) observes (quoted fully above),

> if one wants some things to be attended to, mastered, and subsequently used, one must be sure to wrap it in a context that engages the emotions. Conversely, experiences devoid of emotional impact are likely to be weakly engaging and soon forgotten, leaving nary a mental representation behind. (p. 77)

The factors that contribute positively to engagement (and their absence to the inhibition of positive learning) are captured in Figure 2 (Cameron & Bartel, 2000).

Foundational to learning is _immersion_ in what is to be learned with many _demonstrations_ of what is to be learned by trusted and esteemed individuals. The context of this immersion and demonstration is positively or negatively coloured by the _emotional tone_ and the presence or absence of a _sense of community_. The central factor is engagement with the _content_ of what is to be learned. To enhance engagement, the content must be _real, meaningful, and relevant_ to the student.

Figure 2. Conditions of Learning

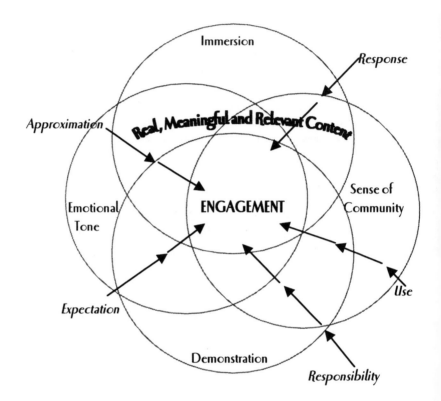

Engagement is facilitated by:

(1) **Expectation.** If students expect to achieve, they achieve; if they expect to fail, they fail. But, the teacher's expectation of the student is particularly influential.

(2) **Responsibility.** To engage effectively in learning, students need to be allowed responsibility "to make their own decisions about when, how, and what 'bits' to learn in any learning task" (Cambourne, 1988, p. 33).

(3) **Use.** Engagement increases when learners have time and opportunity to employ their developing control in functional, realistic, non-artificial ways.

(4) **Approximation.** Especially important in music learning is the need for the learner to be free to approximate the desired model—"mistakes" are essential for learning to occur.

(5) **Response.** For engagement to be sustained, the learner "must receive 'feedback' that is relevant, appropriate, timely, readily available, non-threatening, and with no strings attached" (Cambourne, 1988, p. 33).

Conclusion

Musical meaning and understanding lie in construct complexity—the construct content and construct connections to which they relate. Musical construct complexity includes emotional content and feeling links. To develop musical understanding, music education must foster engagement, involve students in a constructivist manner with musical materials and problems, and encourage links with multiple intelligences and multiple representations through metaphor, cross-modality, and interdisciplinary and integrated art experiences.

References

Bartel, L., & Radocy, R. (2002). Trends in data acquisition and knowledge development. In R. Colwell & C. Richardson (Eds.). *The New Handbook of Research on Music Teaching and Learning* (pp. 1108–1127). New York: Oxford University Press.

Bartel, L. (1988). *A study of the cognitive-affective response to music.* Unpublished doctoral dissertation, University of Illinois at Urbana Champaign.

Bartel, L. (2000). A foundation for research in the effects of sound on brain and body functions. In H. Jorgensen (Ed.). *Challenges in Music Education Research and Practice for a New Millennium* (pp. 58–64.). Proceedings of the Fifth International Symposium of the Research Alliance of Institutions for Music Education. Oslo, Norway: Norges Musikkhogskole.

Briggs, J., & Peat, D. (1999). *Seven life lessons of chaos: Timeless wisdom from the science of change.* New York: Harper Collins Publishers.

Cambourne, B. (1988). *The whole story: Natural learning and the acquisition of literacy in the classroom.* Aukland, NZ: Ashton Scholastic.

Cameron, L., & Bartel, L. (2000). Engage or disengage: An inquiry into lasting response to music teaching. *Orbit, 31* (1), 22–25.

Csikszentmihalyi, M. (1993). *The evolving self: A psychology for the third millennium.* New York: Harper Collins Publishers.

Dawkins, R. (1980). *The selfish gene.* New York: Oxford University Press.

Elliott, D. J. (1995). *Music matters.* New York: Oxford University Press.

Fiske, H. (1996). *Selected theories of music perception.* Queenston, ON: The Edwin Mellen Press.

Gabrielsson, A. (1989). Intense emotional experiences of music. [Not provided] *Proceedings of the First International Conference on Music Perception and Cognition* (pp. 371–376). Kyoto, Japan, 17-19 October.

Gabrielsson, A. (1991). Experiencing Music. *Canadian Music Educator. Special ISME Research Edition, 31,* 21–26.

Gardner, H. (1999a). The *disciplined mind: What all students should understand.* New York: Basic Books.

Gardner, H. (1999b). *Intelligence reframed: Multiple intelligences for the 21st century.* New York: Basic Books.

Kelly, G. (1955). *The psychology of personal constructs* (Vols. 1–2). New York: W. W. Norton.

Reimer, B. (1989). *A philosophy of music education* (2nd ed.). Englewood Cliffs, NJ: Prentice Hall.

Swanwick, K. (1998, October). *Music as culture.* Paper presented at Mayday meeting, Toronto, ON.

Wiggins, J. (2001). *Teaching for musical understanding.* New York: McGraw-Hill Higher Education.

4

Musical Understanding
Cognition and Enculturation

Harold Fiske & Matthew Royal

Introduction

Music educators espouse a range of benefits that result from a musical experience: emotional sensitivity (Langer, 1942), aesthetic values (Reimer, 1989), corporeal effects (Bowman, 1998), spiritual enlightenment (Yobb, 2000), cultural edification (Walker, 2000), and others. In effect, what was once simply viewed as a "covert response" to a performer-determined auditory stimulus (Heller & Campbell, 1988) has more recently been subjected to psychoanalytic-like scrutiny. The impetus for this expansion is largely owed to what some see as undue emphasis on music-theoretic and historical analyses rather than on the benefits of actual on-going musical activity. But while the importance of involved covert responding is undeniable, arguments for these specific effects generally miss an important fact: understanding of a musically intended sound stimulus cannot be found musically meaningful unless it is the outcome of first identifying, discriminating, and relating musical tonal-rhythmic patterns.

A recent theory proposes two levels of consciousness: a subliminal or phenomenal consciousness level and an access consciousness level. Access consciousness is a state in which an experience is available "as a premise in reasoning...poised for rational control of action, and poised for rational control of speech" (Block, 1995, p. 214). Phenomenal consciousness responds experientially or sensuously, but not rationally. An event experienced phenomenally can be felt but not understood rationally or specifically depicted and represented. The taste of a good bottle of wine can be described only metaphorically ("it has the fragrance of aged saddle leather with a hint of broccoli stems," or whatever). It is, therefore, experienced as phenomenal consciousness. An experience available to access consciousness, on the other hand, can be described specifically ("I rode the winning horse across the finish line one length ahead of the second-place winner").

If the above philosophic-structure is true, then the purported benefits of the musical experience, at least as described by some authors, take place on the phenomenal consciousness level rather than the access level. Essentially, this interpretation means that music is experienced sensuously, that is, timbrely, dynamically, and rhythmically, but not structurally. Stretching this claim just a bit, to restrict claims for the value of the musical experience and, therefore, the point of music education, to the phenomenal level of consciousness, is to limit performers and listeners to a sonic "shower bath."

It is clear from animal studies that cats and dogs and other beasts also respond to music. Their behavior has been observed to change in response to timbre, pitch, and dynamic effects in fairly predictable ways. Musical sounds seem to soothe or startle animals' mental states, resulting in their falling asleep or running away. It can be hypothesized, we think, that animals respond to music solely on the phenomenal level of consciousness. If it were the case that animals also identify formal musical structures, then they would respond on the access consciousness level as well (in which case universities would offer music degrees to cats and dogs). But there is no evidence that animals respond to music beyond simple signal-like recognition patterns; an animal's response to music probably takes place primarily on the phenomenal consciousness level.

Humans, of course, respond to music phenomenally. Bundles of research evidence, however, show that musical responding does not stop here, that it occurs on the access level as well (Hodges, 1996). Most importantly, it appears that we do not have a choice: the brain is genetically designed to construct patterns from incoming sensory information. This design reflects a general principle: for survival purposes, brains are driven to build patterns from incoming sensory information. Pattern construction is a fast and efficient means for determining the current state of one's immediate environment. Musical patterns are a secondary outcome of this same principle, secondary because it is very difficult to demonstrate that music experiences hold actual survival value. But musical pattern determination is a primary requirement for understanding and responding to music.

We respond to music on the phenomenal level of consciousness, probably to a richer degree than other animals. But we are also compelled by brain design to respond to music on the access level. To respond musically on the access level means to think in sound (Serafine, 1988), where a musical thought is about identifying tonal-rhythmic patterns and determining their successive and non-successive interrelationships. Limiting music education activities to phenomenal consciousness stimulation while discounting musical thinking impedes the development of musical understanding. The following discussion shows how musical access-level processing occurs.

> Limiting music education activities to phenomenal consciousness stimulation while discounting musical thinking impedes the development of musical understanding.

"Understanding" Is a Construct

Understanding music means understanding something about sound, where "something" means knowing how to produce and/or receive acoustically generated energy of a sort recognized and valued by a particular cultural community. But acoustical analysis of musical events alone tells us very little (or perhaps nothing at all) about how humans come to comprehend those events. So-called modernist writings (e.g., those of Robert Walker—see below) suggest that musical understanding is a sociological phenomenon that can be explained by anthropological investigations exclusively. This extreme view is countered by another no less extreme opinion suggesting that musical understanding should be considered a psychoacoustic and cognitive process only, one that yields an explanation that generalizes across all cultures. This latter position is based on the assumption of uniform brain mechanisms between all humans. Musical understanding, however, is a balance between these two extremes; it involves both sociological phenomenon and cognitive process.

The word "understanding" is a construct. "Musical understanding," therefore, is a special kind of the "understanding" construct. More technically still, a construct (for epistemological matters anyway) is always hypothetical. Therefore, the term "musical understanding" is a hypothetical construct.

The creation and application of hypothetical constructs *par excellence* occurs in physics. "Black holes," for example, have never been directly observed. But scientists are convinced that they exist based upon measurements of gravitational fields surrounding dying stars. Because they are observable only on the basis of secondary events (or indicants) black holes are imaginary. But because these events can be described and predicted with some precision, the scientific community accepts black holes, albeit as a construct narrowly defined.

Another example: flight depends upon a number of hypothetical constructs summarized as aerodynamic theory. Two of these are "gravity" and "wing lift." Both are constructs described mathematically on the basis of various forces imposed upon the otherwise unobservable interactions of air molecules. The pilot's job is to maintain a balance between these two forces in order to keep the plane aloft.

Constructs are not the sole domain of physics. Philosophy, medicine, biology, engineering, geology, and computer science (to name a few) all rely on constructs. For the most part a construct is merely a convenient means for communicating between colleagues. For instance, Fiske (1990) proposed that music is a metalanguage. In doing so, he was able to distinguish music from language. It is important to be able to show this separation since both music and language involve selective use and interpretation of sound and both involve, to a large extent, the same auditory processing brain mechanisms. As Fiske shows in his book, *Music and Mind* (1990), music is the outcome of our ability to generate an indefinitely large number of tonal-rhythmic patterns; but unlike language, musical patterns hold no propositional content. As such, musical content is limited to the found significance of interpattern relationships, a process, in short, captured by the universal construct, "metalanguage."

Explaining a phenomenon on the basis of constructs is a risky business: a construct is not a thing; it is a word, a vehicle for depicting a complex and potentially theoretically messy process. But now we have a problem. Some constructs that we take for granted turn out to be empty of any meaningful content. Recall that a construct is merely a word. What is the difference then between "meaning-full" hypothetical constructs and empty ones? A meaning-full construct normally is narrowly defined and subject to explicit description. A useable construct mostly is confined to specific and very carefully articulated, albeit secondary, evidence shown to predict reliably across a range of tested conditions. Researchers and philosophers invent constructs knowing that they are fictional. As such, however, they take on powerful special technical functions.

A construct is deemed to be empty under a number of conditions: when it is used prior to having supporting evidence in favor of it; when it is used in place of a term already worn down from overuse; when it is used for political expediency; when it is used in the absence of carefully tested theorizing; or when an originally valid construct has eroded through overgeneralization, conflicting or mushy definitions, or misuse by those who have misunderstood its original intent. Here is an example. While the construct *metalanguage* has been shown to be defensible, the term "metacognition"—a word frequently found in the literature—is not. Philosophical analysis of the term metacognition results in the homunculus fallacy, an infinitely regressive chain of mechanisms purportedly explaining concept construction. In effect, "metacognition" is an empty construct.

So, when building or applying constructs we all must be very cautious. As the philosopher Edwin McCann (1995) explains, the fallacy of holding strong beliefs in the reality of constructs, either "full" or "empty," is "that of taking a merely [theoretic] formal unity for a property of empirical things" (p. 345).

Examples of constructs used in music education include: "intelligence," "memory," "talent," motivation," "musicality," "creativity," "achievement," and "aptitude." Again, these are merely words used as a convenient means to talk about unobservable processes. At first glance these appear to be good, solid, well-conceived constructs. A review of relevant literature, however, raises doubt. For example, what is "intelligence"? Is it one general factor? A list of multiple factors? If multiple, how many? Three, eight, twenty-nine? Is music one of these factors? If so, what do we mean by musical "intelligence"? Is it perceptual ability, improvisational ability, knowledge of music history, emotional sensitivity? Or what? There is little agreement within the field because the musical intelligence construct has eroded from its original formulation to one that means just about whatever a writer or speaker wants it to mean. What was once a useful construct has become an empty one. (Incidentally, the music intelligence construct was conceived in 1919 by Carl Seashore, a point missed by more recent theorists who assume it is a contemporary brainstorm.) Thus music intelligence means nothing, or perhaps it means everything.

And what about creativity? Is creativity a construct separate from others such as intelligence? Or is creativity a manifestation of intelligence? For example, is it possible to discern between the creative output of paintings done by 10 year olds from those of abstract expressionists or from those of elephants? From confusing comparisons such as these, the construct "creativity" or "creative intelligence" appears to be devoid of any theoretical meaning and, thus, practical use.

> We want to offer a way of analyzing the construct, "musical understanding," one that is clearly defensible for theory development and practical application.

In this light we want to offer a way of analyzing the construct, "musical understanding," one that is clearly defensible for theory development and practical application. Further, we want to do so while avoiding the bias of musical kinds. For example, we do not want the construct to depend upon and be limited to held assumptions about Western music, ones that would block generalizing a theory of musical understanding to world music.

The Musical Understanding Construct

Let us begin by considering how a musical work is created and how a listener receives it. If we can solve the construct problem for the listener we also should be able to solve it for the performer or composer/improviser/creator. Music is a sonic event occurring through time; no matter one's role in this event, each depends upon involved, attentive listening.

For any of the world's societies, the local musical style is defined by a set of permissible pitch, duration, and timbrel materials agreed upon by members of the particular culture. For Western societies music is produced by mostly vocal, orchestral, and electronic instruments working primarily through well-tempered scales and a hierarchy of bifurcated rhythmic elements. For India, China, Bali and other places, the materials are noticeably different from ours. Let us designate these sound materials—no matter their source or form—by the letter "e" such that the pool of e-resources for any musical culture is designated by: {e1, e2, e3, e4, e5, e6, e7, e8, . . . ej, ek, el}. It is assumed that this pool is, for any culture, constantly expanding. So, the set of sounds available to Western composers is probably larger than it was ten years ago. The same condition presumably applies to the music of other cultures as well.

Now let's assume that a composer (a strictly Western term for a music inventor, but we will use it anyway) selects a few of these materials, piecing them together as a sequence of sounds: {e1, e2, e3, e4, . . . ej}. Although we cannot take the time here, it can be shown that the listener's brain is genetically designed to group like items together into a pattern. It can be shown as well that pattern construction is a universal principle of brain design. Therefore, we will say that the above sequence of e-items will be taken by the brain as a pattern. Call this pattern "pattern P."

Next assume that for the same piece the composer selects more materials resulting in the sequence: {e1, e2, e3, e4, . . . ek}. This group of sonic items consists mostly of the same material as the first group, but it is also a bit different. We will call this group, "pattern P-prime" (P'), the prime indicating that this second pattern is a derivation or variation of the first.

Now assume that the composer dips into the resource pool again and selects the following stream of events: {e5, e6, e7, e8, . . . el}. This group is clearly distinctly different from the other two patterns. Call this pattern, "pattern Pn."

We will take these three pattern types as the first three premises for a theory of musical comprehension, that is, the musical understanding construct.

Now, listeners (or performers or composers) do not merely store patterns as an arbitrary collection of pitch-durational events. Instead, it can be shown that the human brain is designed ("programmed") to compare patterns of sensory information with other patterns of the same kind previously stored in either short- or long-term memory. For music listening this leads to the following three additional premises: P<>P; P<>P´; P<>Pn. These are translated, as "the second pattern is the same as the first," "the second pattern is a derivation of the first," and "the second pattern is distinctly different from the first."

Now here is what is interesting about this last set of premises. First, the set exhausts the kinds of between-pattern comparisons that are possible perceptually. There is no other possible pattern comparison combination. Second, this set of comparison types is universal; the set applies to any of the world's musics or musical cultures. The set is universal because it is the outcome not of theoretic descriptors of particular musical cultures but rather of some known principles of brain design. These principles are genetically, not culturally determined (Fiske, 1990).

While the music of one culture may be quite different from another, it is clear that the members of a culture understand their music according to the same set of *cognitive* principles that determine the understanding of our own music. Cultures take full advantage of these in the evolutionary development of their own, often unique, musical systems. But even in the case of seemingly patternless or improvisatory or aleatoric sonic events, the human brain attempts, usually successfully, to construct patterns. The brain does this not because it was designed to listen to music but because these principles are based upon a basic need: the brain's first priority is the safety and survival of its owner; survival depends upon making sense of incoming sensory information, and such sense or comprehension is governed by identifying patterns and comparing them.

Finally, these principles cannot be overcome through the will of the composer, performer, or listener. (Neither, by the way, can the principles be overcome by the wishful thinking of philosophers or, for that matter, by music teachers who innocently try to impose contrary concepts of musical meaning and understanding upon their students.)

Instead, just as with any other human activity in any part of the world, the musical process works because these brain-design operating principles determine human understanding.

We now have the beginning of a theory of the musical understanding construct. We can claim so far that musical understanding is about the construction and intercomparison of pitch-durational patterns. From this comparison activity, on-going decision-making about successive and nonsuccessive pattern interrelationships is carried out. These decisions are labelled in turn by the technical musical vocabulary germane to the local culture that is relevant to the particular kind of sonic structures that are characteristic of that culture (e.g., fugue or reggae).

We can push this construct design further yet so as to characterize musical thinking. Assume that a listener hears a new pattern P. Prior to anything else occurring, pattern P generates an expectancy profile, an imagined list of pitch-durational possibilities that could reasonably happen next in the piece, each with an associated level of probability. Then, given a second pattern, the listener will conclude—by means of the pattern-comparison procedure described by the premises—either that it is the same as the first, a derivation of the first, or distinctly different from the first. But now furthermore, on the basis of the expectancy profile, the particular pattern outcome will also either confirm one of the items in the expectancy profile or introduce

> Musical understanding entails musical thinking, an *active* time-dependent cognitive process.

another, unexpected, event. The expectancy profile therefore introduces another feature to our theory of musical understanding: musical understanding entails musical thinking, an *active* time-dependent cognitive process. Finally, the listener may self-generate, create, or improvise original continuance of a pattern P on her own without the presence of an actual sound stimulus. That is, she can sing the tune to herself and invent new musical outcomes to her heart's content.

To this point our description of the musical understanding construct takes the following shape: musical understanding means receiving or generating pitch-durational patterns and realizing the relationships that obtain between these patterns. Pattern interrelationships may be either successive or nonsuccessive, and may in some cases result in a complex matrix of realized sonic structures.

Sonic Cues and Tonal-Rhythmic Pattern Construction

So far we have made two principal claims regarding pattern construction and pattern comparison: (1) both are universal and (2) both are necessary (though perhaps not sufficient) for a meaningful rather than empty definition of the "musical understanding" construct. Moreover, claim (2) is dependent upon claim (1): if the construct of musical understanding is to avoid becoming empty through a plethora of different, individual uses, then one must identify what is both intersubjectively and interculturally valid in the construct. In other words, by identifying universal (cross-cultural) constants in cognition, we reach the solid bedrock of the musical-understanding construct. Now, given the importance of our claim (1), it is time to examine the arguments for the universality of pattern construction and comparison a little more closely.

Our view that pattern construction and pattern comparison are universal can be supported both empirically and rationally. The empirical support for universality is, of course, problematic, for, as is well known, it is impossible to show that a behavior or phenomenon exists in all places and has existed at all times. Nevertheless, a large body of experimental work in auditory perception strongly suggests the universality of certain pattern-construction processes. Much of this work up to 1990 is summarized and synthesized as a theory of auditory pattern-construction in Albert Bregman's (1990) *Auditory Scene Analysis.*

Paraphrasing briefly, Bregman identifies two types of processes: (1) primitive, automatic processes and (2) schema-driven or learned processes. Four factors argue for the innate, and presumably cross-cultural nature of primitive processes: they (a) are not affected by long-term learning, (b) are not subject to voluntary attention, (c) are found in neonates, and (d) seem to be performed by anatomically peripheral mechanisms. By contrast, none of these conditions apply to schema-driven processes, implying that the latter are learned, culture- or individual-specific constructs that guide attention and cognition. Auditory and therefore musical pattern construction is a mixture of primitive and schema-driven processes.

There is also a compelling rationalistic argument for the universality of certain elements of auditory pattern construction: it is vital for survival. The purpose of the perceptual system is to tell us something about what exists out there in the environment. Sounds are understood not as a collection of transient frequencies but as objects or sound-sources that have some sort of bearing on our immediate or long-term needs (e.g., a dinner bell, the roar of a tiger, the cry of a child). As Bregman has argued, ascription of certain acoustic events to a particular source is highly complex and must often be carried out in a few milliseconds. In most situations, we simply do not have time to think about such a task, and, thankfully, many of these primitive pattern-construction processes are carried out automatically for us by our auditory system. In short, these primitive processes are hardwired and innate and reflect acoustical universals which humans at all times and in all places have encountered. In respect to innateness, the philosopher Jay Garfield (1995) reminds us that "obviously *something* [about human experience] is innate. Brains are innate. [At the same time] the structure of the brain must constrain the nature of cognitive...development [and the effects of the environment on development] to *some* degree" (p. 367).

> These primitive processes are hardwired, innate and reflect acoustical universals which humans at all times and in all places have encountered.

That being said, each environment also produces sounds that are specific to it: particular animal calls, geographical features (rivers, volcanoes) or weather conditions (thunder, crunch of snow), not to mention the large sonic differences that exist among man-made environments (city streets, mosque, concert halls). Not surprisingly, in response to these differences, we have learned to construct and identify many environment-specific sound patterns.

It is possible to view culture as the historical accretion of learned responses to environment-specific conditions followed by the subsequent altering of that environment. By extension, then, the music or musics of a particular culture are a response to a particular sonic/musical environment, which then, in turn, shape and alter that environment. To point out the wide and obvious differences that might exist between cultures (whether musical or otherwise) does nothing to gainsay the existence of universals. Both culture-specific and universal processes can be active in the brain of a listener; it is simply that these two types of processes co-exist on different levels. Thus one might "understand" a particular musical pattern as, say, a cadenza, a twelve-bar blues, or *kobushi* (the complex ornamentation of a melodic line in some styles of Japanese folk singing). For these culturally specific structures to be isolated, however, they must first be differentiated from what precedes them, from what follows them, and from what sounds concurrently with them. This perceptual act of isolation will rest as much on primitive processes as it does on schema-driven processes.

> Both culture-specific and universal processes can be active in the brain of a listener.

The primitive processes described by Bregman work in the way that they do because of the physiology of the ear and the auditory cortex. One may, however, summarize these processes metaphorically by appealing to the laws of Gestalt psychology. This exercise is instructive so long as one realizes that the Gestalt laws cannot be taken as explanations for auditory behavior but rather are a description of it. The Gestalt laws state that individual elements are more likely to be grouped together as a pattern (1) the closer they are to each other along a dimension (*proximity*), (2) the more alike they are (*similarity*), (3) the more they follow a predictable trajectory across time or space (*good continuation*), and (4) the more two or more co-present elements move in parallel with each other (*common fate*). Correspondingly, boundaries between patterns are likely to be apparent when these laws are broken. Naturally, the dimensions of musical sound along which these laws might apply are several, but limiting ourselves simply to the elemental dimensions, we might identify pitch, time, timbre, loudness, and space. Table 1 shows pattern boundaries that might occur when gestalt laws are broken along certain dimensions of sound.

In general, these boundary cues may be described as changes or discontinuities along each dimension of sound. Now, it is quite possible that the relative perceptual salience of these cues may be culturally determined: while pitch and time (rhythm) are pre-eminent structural dimensions in Western music, timbre or space plays a central role in musics of other cultures (Walker, 1990). We propose, however, that at least some of these boundary cues will be operative in the music of all cultures. Here, an analogy might be drawn between the items listed in Table 1 and the sounds represented in the International Phonetic Alphabet: no language makes use of all the sounds represented therein, but every language makes use of some of them.

Table 1. Pattern Boundaries—When Gestalt Laws Are Broken

	Proximity	Similarity	Good Continuation	Common Fate
Pitch	change in register		change in melodic direction	contrary or oblique motion
Time/ Duration	rests and long notes	change in articulation	change in pulse	asynchronous onsets or offsets
Timbre		change in timbre	unpredictable evolution of timbre over time	asynchronously evolving components of timbre
Loudness		change in loudness, stress	unpredictable change in loudness	differing rates/directions of loudness change
Space	spatially separate sources		unpredictable movement in space	moving in different directions/ along different trajectories in space

Going further, it is even possible that some of these cues are salient in all music. For example, a lack of temporal proximity caused by silence between two events would seem a likely candidate for a universal boundary marker between patterns. (Inadvertent silences are blatant reminders of this perceptual principle.) The same claim might be made for a sudden change in timbre or a sound suddenly emanating from a new region of space. We would suggest (rationalistically) that the brain would have no choice but to ascribe sets of events clearly demarcated by such cues to separate sources. Ironclad empirical evidence for our assertion would require careful collection of both verbal and behavioural data from listeners in non Western cultures.

Effects of Social and Cultural Environment

As we have seen, cognition involves brain mechanisms designed to process certain kinds of stimulus information. But this processing would not make sense if the perceiver could not place the identified incoming sensory information into a workable context. "Brain-in-a-vat" models of cognition do not offer useful explanations of human understanding and meaning. The brain needs to relate incoming information to previous experiences and their former consequences or outcomes, as well as to current beliefs about the immediate social and physical environment. Social and physical-environmental culture provides a context for musical comprehension and meaning, a frame of discourse within which cognitive processes occur.

There are four kinds of context effects. The first we will call *social-cultural theatre*. The social-cultural theatre variable concerns the interaction between music and people and the function of particular musical events within a society. The meaning of these events is obviously defined by that society. This defined meaning is functional; it is about the appropriate or inappropriate use of music with respect to cultural settings. Note that this meaning does not concern the perception of tonal-rhythmic patterns and thus the comprehension of those patterns that constitute the sonic event taking place within a particular cultural function.

> There are four kinds of context effects:
> - social-cultural theatre effects,
> - history,
> - experiences and beliefs, and
> - theoretical and analytical knowledge.

Considerable confusion about this last point is found in recent music education literature. Attempts are being made to replace psychological explanations of musical understanding with sociological ones. To succeed on this score, convincing evidence is needed demonstrating the plasticity of brain design. While descriptions of cultural variance abound, such variance neither provides evidence for brain plasticity nor requires such evidence. While it is the case that brains are designed to readily adapt to their surrounding environmental conditions, coming to terms with those conditions requires hardwired sensory information detectors and pattern construction and identification protocols. The *content* of sensory information can vary considerably; but the manner in which that content is detected, sorted, and identified must be constant across all brains. The evidence for strongly hardwired brain design is overwhelming, and we are very concerned that the field of music education has embarrassed itself lately by ignoring this information and creating stories of musical understanding that are, for the most part, fiction.

> The field of music education has embarrassed itself lately by ignoring this [brain-based] information and creating stories of musical understanding that are, for the most part, fiction.

Sociological descriptors are, of course, needed to complement hardwired brain processing protocols. Otherwise we would be hard put to explain diverse musical kinds and the broad range of cultural affairs in which music is a factor. An explanation of the musical understanding construct requires a cognitive description as well as an explanation of the social-cultural theatre. Music and music-theoretic systems are culture-determined products, comprehension of which partly entails implicit understanding of the music's original cultural and stylistic intent.

The second kind of context effect is *history*. History embraces knowledge of political, social, and economic theory as explanations of music compositional intent, significance, and cultural meaning. Music history entails its own set of constructs, each subject to different interpretations. Note again that considerable variance in a listener's historical knowledge and skill in interpreting heard patterns results in broad differences in musical understanding. Note also the considerable responsibility this breadth places on music teachers and the decisions we must make about curriculum design and day-to-day decision making about musical experiences and information offered to students.

The third type of context variable is the listener's or performer's or composer's *experiences and beliefs*. Experiences and beliefs are the mix of knowledge and personal experiences, musical or otherwise, that affect implicit and explicit understanding of the musical event. These too presumably interact with the outcomes of hardwired musical cognitive processing.

The last type of context variable is *theoretical and analytical knowledge* about music. This type concerns music theory accounts of tonal-rhythmic organization of musical systems and works that are proposed as factual explanations of perceived events. The motivations of music theorists vary. Normally their goal is to formulate and elucidate musical structures. Traditionally these analyses are based on music notation rather than perception, although in the past few years music theory has become increasingly interested in the work of music psychology. There are several different music analysis systems. Sometimes their products seem to bear little resemblance to what we actually hear in a work, although theorists claim that we "might" or "could" hear the work in such ways. Furthermore, the music psychology literature is rife with seemingly inappropriate music theory analyses of "foreign" music based upon premises derived from Western tonal music. (See, for example, Krumhansl, Chapter 10, 1990.) Depending upon one's level of analytical ability, musical acuity, and the theoretic system assumed, the hypotheses that come out of cognitive processing might be interpreted in multifaceted ways.

The interaction between the four context variables and perceptual universals constitutes a cognitive hypothesis-testing process: perceptual outcomes are compared with expectations triggered by the listener's experiences. The results confirm, modify, or refute the listener's assumptions, thereby completing the loop between context and perceptual calculations. Context "holds" model-representations of previously experienced musical works. Because context is flexible and easily modified by new information and experiences, repeated encounters with a work that result in revised perceptual realizations will in turn cause context to change. At the least, cognitive hypothesis testing includes a revised structural concept of the musical work, one that generates modified expectations for subsequent hearings of the same piece. Likewise, new historical or theoretical knowledge, new experiences and beliefs, or immersion in a new social-cultural theatre will each affect context, which in turn affects outgoing perceptual hypotheses.

Hypothesis testing entails both perceptual universals and listener-assumed context. In short, newly realized interpattern relationships may cause changes to any of the four context components, and any one of the context effects may alter the listener's realization and comprehension of a piece, structurally and meaningfully. A theory of the musical understanding construct is incomplete without descriptions of both perceptual-cognitive activity and context effects. Indeed, modifications to the listener's assumptions and beliefs caused by the interaction between cognitive processing and context effects define musical learning itself.

Initial pattern construction, that is, during the first few months of a child's life, is derived from acoustic cues rather than culturally derived knowledge. But both enculturation and training are required before appropriate interpattern schemata are sufficiently built to allow sophisticated cognitive processing. When encountering new musical experiences or for "foreign" music, there are two possible modes of active listening: (1) use of schemata that one already possesses or (2) use of primitive processes until appropriate schemata are eventually formed.

There are inherent problems with both approaches. The first mode will likely be "wrong" for the musical culture in question and may inhibit building a more appropriate schema. For instance, hearing a non-western tuning system as an "out-of-tune diatonic scale" may preclude a growing sensitivity to the nuances of the "local" tuning system. Unfortunately, the second listening mode is difficult to invoke since one's own schemata are deeply ingrained and not readily switched off. The inappropriateness of the first mode and the difficulty of invoking the second mode together cause what we see as a central question in cross-cultural music education: whether or not examples of "foreign" music systems can be taught while preserving the integrity of that foreign culture.

"Foreign" music offers counterexamples to Western music. Therefore, a satisfactory explanation of the musical understanding construct demands that it applies cross-culturally. The following paragraph shows how our theory accomplishes this task.

Musics of different cultures share what the philosopher Wittgenstein called "family resemblances." Musical culture X will possess a number of features, recognizable by a devotee of that music, including particular intended sonic relationships and structures, social-cultural practices, historical perspectives, experience and belief systems, and analytical/theoretical knowledge. Moreover, these features will be represented in the encultured mind as a network of interlocking schemata. Musical culture Y might possess some of the features of culture X but never all of them. The extent to which cultures hold features in common is a measure of the family resemblance between those cultures. A devotee of culture X first approaching the music of culture Y might note the family resemblance between the two cultures. She will, however, (a) possess schemata that are inappropriate for culture Y, (b) lack schemata that are required for culture Y, or (c) both of these. This process, we feel, leads to some crucial questions that must be addressed empirically if cross-cultural music education is to be put on a firmer footing:

- To what extent is it possible to learn to switch off one's own cultural schemata?
- Can one hear music using purely primitive, Gestalt-like grouping cues?
- Can one internalize the schemata of another culture? (Many assume so, but there is no evidence that it is the case.)
- Are there age-related cognitive windows beyond which such additional schema-forming is not possible?
- Are there specific pedagogical methods that facilitate the development of musical multilingualism?

It remains to be seen how research answers these questions.

Conclusion

We have suggested that musical understanding is, like other terms used to describe mental behavior, a hypothetical construct. We have cautioned that without extremely careful philosophical and empirical analysis, methodology, and observation, we risk creating a meaningless and useless (or empty) concept. We have tried to show that musical understanding may be explained both by the contributions of genetically determined brain processes and the less constrained decisions brought about by cultural contextual effects. Based, however, upon the evidence of cognitive science, we strongly suspect that cultural variables remain bound or restricted by the kinds of information human brains are prepared to process. The auditory system is limited to a certain range of pitch, rhythmic, and timbrel complexity. Furthermore, the brain's pattern construction principle appears to have priority over the best or worst intentions of performers, composers, and educators. Nonetheless, musical styles and kinds are culture determined in the first instance, albeit within the perceptual and cognitive constraints we have noted.

So, can listeners voluntarily switch off access consciousness and merely bask in a sonic shower bath, thereby passing cognitive effort entirely? Probably. Should we train our students not to think musically, emphasizing instead the sensuality of sound while ignoring pattern interrelationships? We will leave that choice up to the music teacher. But if access consciousness is discouraged, then we claim that musical understanding is sacrificed as well.

References

Bowman, W. (1998). *Philosophical perspectives in music.* New York: Oxford University Press.

Block, N. (1995) Consciousness. In S. Guttenplan (Ed.), *A companion to the philosophy of mind* (p. 214). Oxford, UK: Blackwell Publishers.

Bregman, A. S. (1990). *Auditory scene analysis.* Cambridge, MA: MIT Press.

Fiske, H. E. (1990). *Music and mind: PhilosophicaL essays on the cognition and meaning of music.* Lewiston, NY: Edwin Mellon Press.

Garfield, J. (1995). Innateness. In S. Guttenplan (Ed.), *A companion to the philosophy of mind* (p. 367). Oxford, UK: Blackwell Publishers.

Heller, J., & Campbell, W. (1988). Studying the communication process in music. In A. Kemp (Ed.), *Research in music education* (pp. 33–44). Reading, UK: International Society for Music Education.

Hodges, D. (1996). *Handbook of music psychology.* San Antonio, TX: IMR Press.

Krumhansl, C. L. (1990) *Cognitive foundations of musical pitch.* New York: Oxford University Press.

Langer, S. (1942) *Philosophy in a new key.* Cambridge, MA: Harvard University Press.

McCann, E. (1995). Philosophy of mind in the seventeenth and eighteenth centuries. In S. Guttenplan (Ed.), *A companion to the philosophy of mind* (p. 345). Oxford. UK: Blackwell Publishers.

Reimer, B. (1989). *A philosophy of music education* (2nd ed.). Englewood Cliffs, NJ: Prentice Hall.

Serafine, M. L. (1988). *Music as cognition: The development of thought in sound.* New York: Columbia University Press.

Walker, R. (1990). *Musical beliefs: Psychoacoustic, mythical, and educational perspectives.* New York: Teachers College Press.

Walker, R. (1987). The effects of culture, environment, age and musical training on choices of visual metaphors for sound. *Perception and Psychophysics, 45* (5), 491–502.

Walker, R. (2000). Multiculturalism and music re-attached to music education. *Philosophy of Music Education Review, 8* (1), 31–39.

Yobb, I. (2000). A feeling for others: Music education and service learning. *Philosophy of Music Education Review, 8* (1), 67–78.

5

Musical Understanding in Critical Music Education

Darryl A. Coan

You must be the change you wish to see in the world. (Mahatma Gandhi)

While "musical understanding" is an idea mentioned more frequently in the last few years, its nature and scope are only now being explored more fully. This interest is warranted and timely since musical understanding has the potential for meaningful curriculum impact. The Victoria *Symposium on Musical Understanding* provided a forum for lively dialogue. As part of my paper at the symposium I attempted to explain a continuum of experiential processes that students pass through as their understanding of musical problems forms. The transmission of those ideas and observations was, in my opinion, only partially successful due to my failure to explain the context in which they were formed—that of critical theory and how it relates to musical understanding. Outside that context, the proposed continuum cannot be adequately understood or explained. This humbling realization was prompted by a comment from symposium attendee and Professor of Education, Robert Wiggins.[1]

As a result, in this chapter I decided to forego the explanation of my continuum, which can be read in its proper context in an earlier paper (Coan, 2000), in order to expand on the way in which I see musical understanding and its definition from a critical perspective. Critical theory seeks to examine self-defeating contradictions between philosophy and

---

[1] Dr. Wiggins did not present, but his character, critical intelligence, objectivity, and depth of thoughtfulness in commentary greatly enriched the experience for all present and served as an inspiration for me.

practice and, from there, build consensus through dialogue. Given the current misunderstanding of critical theory within some music education circles, I address in this chapter some of the confusion and resulting controversy.

As a proponent and practitioner of critical theory in music education, I accept the need for a music education in which

> individual students have been enabled as a result of their musical schooling to want to and to be able to engage themselves in musical praxis in ways and to a degree they find rewarding and empowering in life outside of and after graduation from school. (Regelski, 1998, Part 4, p. 1).

Achieving such a goal begins with a critical consciousness on the part of music teachers of the need to address topics of life-changing potential for the students in our classrooms. Developing musical understanding has the potential to help students take control of their own musical destinies for their own reasons and to the level they want to achieve. It includes helping them unlock doors leading to new musical experience.

In the past few years, I've been renovating an old house and have removed multiple layers left by previous remodels. Looking at those layers and grappling with the obstacles they posed to my progress, it is easy to forget that each layer was considered an improvement by its creator. The time arrived when no more layers could be added and all had to be stripped away to the original skeleton so that the renovating—making new—could be accomplished. It is my contention that the field of music education needs a similar kind of attention that will lead to foundational change in music curricula and classroom teaching in music. Music teachers need to act as agents for that change.

In her paper "...on Music Teacher Agency," Marie McCarthy wrote: "As a curriculum subject, music is poised at a particularly significant juncture between school and society" (McCarthy, 1999, p. 2). She provided an overview of interrelationships between music in our schools and society:

> first, the realities of school music are born out of and channel back into the realities of music in society; second, music teachers are products of musical and educational sub-cultures that are not necessarily cognizant or respectful of the variety of ways in music is present in society; third, the status of music in education is directly related to the public perceptions of the value of music, and fourth, the arts are

transforming agents and the music teacher can be part of the transformative process. (pp. 4-5)

Music teachers can be agents for change where school music (a)
relates to society's perception of the value of music, *and* (b) has
potential for enhancing that value. If one accepts these criteria, it is
worth asking whether school music in the United States is meeting
them.

Leonhard (1991) and Coan (1992) showed a trend of decreasing
time for music in public schools. Boswell (1991), whose attitudinal
study involving 394 middle and junior high school students, revealed
that the two statements about which participants felt most negative
were, "I look forward to coming to school when I have music class," and
"What we do in music class is a challenge" (p. 54). Boswell compared
her work with studies by Pogonowski (1982) and Haladyna and Thomas
(1979) located in different geographical regions. The results showed
similar negative attitudes on the part of music students (pp. 50-51).
When these data are seen in the context of all the energy that has gone
into music education reform in the last several decades, it seems that the
layers of our walls are crumbling. Perhaps this crumbling is due to the
confusion generated by too many individuals attempting to create new
window dressings instead of evaluating and sharpening existing practices.
Or perhaps it is a result of individuals trying to save the field through
constant change instead of carefully examining and updating existing
ideas so we don't throw out the good ones.

If decreasing student numbers and interest do exist and are continuing to develop in music programs, they prompt questions for the
critical theorist. There is an advocacy movement for music education
but is it effective? Is music education, in fact, less valued in our culture
than it has been? What do these trends mean when music stores in the
region where I teach (St. Louis metropolitan area) have waiting lists of
students wanting to study guitar and drums? Why do I have on average
10 to 20 non-music majors coming to me every fall semester to enroll in
our music fundamentals course because they want to learn to read music? Perhaps these people are looking for a certain kind of music education that they did not receive in elementary and high school, an education that fits their *personal* goals for a fulfilling life that includes music as

an important part. Is "music for every student" a motto that we live up to?

Critical theorists don't look at situations through a variety of separate lenses because every problem is situated as part of a totality at a given time, coming from something before, going somewhere else. We attempt to approach a situation critically in all its richness and diversity by exposing places where the paths of philosophy and practice don't intersect, even when the majority fails to notice the weaknesses. For critical theorists, that means examining claims made by groups or individuals regarding benefits that are said to accrue as a result of their particular method or philosophy and using these claims as criteria for evaluating the success or failure at achieving those benefits. [2]

If, for example, a music teacher says, "I teach for musical understanding," what does that mean exactly? If she can't tell us what it means, how does she know she is successful in teaching for understanding? If we do not perform this type of critique, how can members of our profession be accountable for validity claims for school music let alone for particular pedagogical approaches? Whether students actually learned something they can remember and use in their musical lives in the public schools might never be measured or identified unless they become college music majors, and that's too late for elementary teacher accountability.

I cannot agree with the view expressed by some at the Victoria *Symposium* that we can avoid defining what we mean by musical understanding. Agreeing to disagree on a central point avoids meaningful debate and provides an effective smokescreen against criticism. It also implies that what musical understanding means is somehow inconsequential or irrelevant to the practice of music education.

Calling oneself a professional in any field means a willingness to be held accountable for the results of one's actions. For the critical theorist, accountability isn't a matter of public relations or political expediency, like proof of having successfully conditioned students to meet a national music literacy requirement. If music education is a profession, accountability is a matter of *ethics* because our actions involve the minds

---

[2] The word "critical" also connotes a need for immediate or urgent attention.

and lives of fellow human beings and their potential musical communion with society.

If musical understanding is primarily unintentional, then we needn't hold symposia about it as there is no centrality of purpose. If, on the other hand, we consider musical understanding to be something we teach toward, then it is by definition a goal to which we aspire, and toward which we direct our actions. If it is an intended goal—or *the* intended goal of our teaching—then it must be a central issue. If it is a central issue in our profession, then we must approach its attainment in the best possible way we can, professionally and ethically—with *phronesis*, "the ethical discernment by which agents gauge what course of action is right and just in a given situation" (Bowman, 2000, p. 100).

> If musical understanding is a central issue of our profession, then we must approach its attainment in the best possible way we can, professionally and ethically.

Those who purposely avoid defining what they believe is a crucial issue are, at best, creating an internal contradiction or legitimation[3] crisisand, at worst, appearing to promote an ideology that purports that there can be no definition because none would be sufficient.[4] That no one definition might be good enough is an invalid reason to avoid trying.

Finding a right definition for musical understanding is not an easy matter as it exhibits many intangible qualities, as do music and people (therein lies the temptation not to define it); how one person exhibits musical understanding will be different from another in another situation. Therefore, a technicist or scientific definition is not appropriate; no static model would capture all the relevant variables and

---

[3] "These internal contradictions and conflicts make the benefits that are only abstractly claimed in theory progressively more difficult to justify, rationalize or legitimize as being 'good.' ...such 'built-in' crises bring about the need to legitimate the rationality and values of the system" (Regelski, 1998, Part 4, p. 3).

[4] "An ideology, as seen by Critical Theory, is a system of seemingly rational ideas, practices and paradigms that serve to justify or legitimate the values, vested interests, and beliefs of a particular group of people" (Regelski, 1998, Part 4, p. 3). If a group dismisses the arguments of others in order to maintain

conditions. It will not suffice, though, to say, "We'll know it when we see it." If that's true, then there must be some evidence of musical understanding that is tangible. If there is tangible,

> It will not suffice, though, to say, "We'll know it when we see it."

observable evidence of musical understanding, it is observable because it exists within a particular social framework, and we can identify its encouragement and observation as praxis, "a mode of action through which participants constitute themselves, both as a community and as individual members of that community" (Bowman, 2000, p. 100).

Identifying musical understanding in a praxial sense means, then, identifying tangible musical practices that serve important social roles and that have certain clear conditions of accomplishment that can be taught and learned. Thus, we are making ample room for all the tangible and intangible human and social variables because:

> praxis necessarily involves human needs and functions that are not susceptible to formulaic recipe methods or techniques because of the many situated variables that can influence results.... The right action of praxis means an action the results of which benefit the specific but varying needs of the different individuals served by the praxis. (Regelski, 1998, Part 4, p. 9)

Because music itself is a fluid and changing entity, the right action will always take into account the group one is teaching, the individual differences of the group members, the specific teacher, the kind of music, etc.—the whole, or holistic situation: "Phronesis, the ethical discernment that guides right action in such highly variable conditions, is a practice's life blood" (Bowman, 2000, p. 103).

In order to approach musical understanding in a praxial-phronetic mode we understand that the evidence will manifest itself in non-coerced ways during situations of class musical activity and in similar situations outside class. As part of our praxis we are constantly attuned to what students are doing and saying. It is nothing new in our field to interpret observational data; methods of qualitative research have been helpful in these endeavors. In other fields teachers are using student portfolios to build evidence of student learning with the teacher as

---

the dominance of its own position and discourage further debate, it is promoting an ideology.

learning partner, as well as to gain insight into how and why students involve themselves in their own learning (e.g., Galley, 2000). Max Kaplan (1966) suggested the use of case studies for understanding creative people and their activities (p. 81). These techniques have precedents, fit well within the praxis I have outlined, and can be used as cumulative observations to form a basis for communicative action with colleagues to expand our collective understanding of musical understanding. Such activity can be likened to Dewey's (1938) "formation of purposes," which involves:

> (1) observation of surrounding conditions; (2) knowledge of what has happened in similar situations in the past, a knowledge obtained partly by recollection and partly from the information, advice, and warnings of those who have had a wider experience; and (3) judgment which puts together what is observed and what is recalled to see what they signify. (p. 69)

Any definition of musical understanding that would follow from our phronesis must be broad enough to encompass a great number of variables. I favor the one offered by Leonhard and House (1972): "Musical understanding is defined as the ability to bring accumulated musical learning to bear on the solution of musical problems" (p. 133). I would argue to delete the word "accumulated" since musical learning, as I see it, is ongoing rather than accumulated. With that caveat, I would alter the definition to, *the process of bringing musical learning to bear on the solution of musical problems.* This

> Musical understanding is the process of bringing musical learning to bear on the solution of musical problems.

definition allows for a great variety of approaches and can be used with any type of music. It is a definition with which music educators of various philosophical orientations should be comfortable, and leaves open for debate and interpretation three critical points: 1) *how* one teaches for musical understanding, 2) *what* constitutes musical learning, and, 3) *what* constitutes a musical problem. While Leonhard and House outlined their ideas for addressing these three points, one need not conform to their ideas in order to accept the central statement.

The definition has import for those of us interested in the application of critical theory to music teaching. The operative concept of the statement and the goal of teaching for understanding is that understanding is a *process*. In this regard, the definition is situational and multi-contextual; as such, ability is dependent on the musical experience of an individual. In addition, praxis requires the inclusion of the teacher in the formula, to the extent that the teacher (as *agent)* allows and encourages students to communicate that experience both in the present and the future. The use of the verb "bring" also implies *intentionality* or willingness, a necessary ingredient of praxis.

Phronesis requires that in addition to teaching *for* musical under-

> Phronesis requires that in addition to teaching *for* musical understanding, we also teach *with* musical understanding.

standing, we also teach *with* musical understanding. First, by engaging in teaching, we are working to solve musical problems and making use of all of *our* musical learning (in addition to other realms of understanding). Second, each meaningful musical experience adds to previous understanding as an essential ingredient to more understanding for everyone in the situation: "Becoming educated about music is to create the conditions of music educating us in return" (Howard, 1988, p. 34).

Because praxis is not coerced, the teacher as agent uses previous understanding and knowledge of the group to guide the experiences by which the musical problems become apparent and in need of resolution. The agent should view

> teaching and learning as a continuous process of reconstruction of experience. This condition in turn can be satisfied only as the educator has a long look ahead, and views every present experience as a moving force in influencing what future experiences will be. (Dewey, 1938, p. 87)

Musical understanding happens not as a sudden or culminating event but as something that simultaneously accrues, develops, and matures in a number of ways, constantly leading the *experiencer* to reconstruct understanding to bring it to bear on the new experience. In other words, music *is* experience, and musical understanding is the means by which we grasp that *experiencing*. In this construct, musical learning is any (musical and non-musical) knowledge, skill, or insight that provides an active-receptive frame of reference for subsequent musical experience.[5]

---

[5] Active-receptive means that a human is a participatory receptor.

A praxial approach to musical understanding through musical problems (any aspect of music that raises the curiosity of the beholder) requires the teacher's awareness of the entire situation of the class including chronologically (then, now, and in the future all wrapped into one), and including a strong store of musical knowledge, insight gained from research, and understanding (you cannot help someone else understand that which you yourself cannot fathom). It does not call for a recipe book lesson plan or reliance on nice, neat, little activities learned at a workshop:

> Phronetic power of discernment is experiential knowledge that is *essential* to the right action in the here-and-now, real-time, social world, where the ends to which our actions are directed always have significant consequences yet can never be pre-scribed or pre-determined. (Bowman, 2000, p. 102)

For this type of *agenting*, reliance on artificial teaching sequences leaves little room for flexibility and may weaken the teacher's ability to understand what is happening with the group or with individuals right now. Phronesis that leads to the next right action is then thwarted when the inexperienced (or unaware) teacher pushes the boat forward without students on board. As I teach my advanced music theory class I am always aware that each person in the room is at a different level of understanding, and individuals are at different levels of sophistication in their own understanding, with different aspects of music. It is my responsibility to comprehend as best I can where individuals are in their understanding and where the group as a whole is.

Both in practice and on a personal level, teaching for the empowerment of students' current and future praxis involves far more than teaching a certain way; it means *being* a certain way and providing a concrete model for students to see (so they won't see you as a hypocrite, and because they'll likely teach the way they are taught). In helping students attain their goals for a musical life, I see my responsibilities as agent to include illuminating otherwise unknown musical avenues for

> In helping students attain their goals for a musical life, I see my responsibilities as agent (based on my phronesis) to include illuminating unknown musical avenues for my students to explore and allowing students to illuminate for me as well.

my students to explore. Challenging them to listen for and examine musical problems, I initiate classroom discussion about and investigation of problems relevant to potential lifelong musical praxis. As an agent, I also want my students to see me as a practicing musician not just as a music theory or music education teacher who operates outside a personal musical praxis. This holistic type of modeling not only continually deepens my musical and pedagogical understanding but also urges the students to far more than the uninspiring goal of passing a required class.

I contend that a failure to define musical understanding in terms of its qualities and praxial potentials for our students and ourselves will discourage debate and result in its fading from our view as a potent concept of experience; ultimately, musical understanding could be relegated to the well-intentioned but ill-fated fads of music education history. In order to behave like professionals and agents for right action for our students, we must be willing to constantly reconsider what musical understanding consists of for a particular student at a particular time and for particular purposes.

Critical theory is one means through which we can examine not only how we treat musical understanding but other seminal issues in music and music education. Conscientiously practiced, critical theory is a form of action that compels us to be honest in our intentions and open to meaningful discourse; it empowers us to insist on the same behaviour by others. If we are to be truly professional, we cannot abdicate our responsibility to continuously question our practice and practitioners, regardless of the popularity of a person, method, or group. To constantly engage in critical discourse is to make theory active and practice relevant to the real life world of individual students.

In conclusion, the chapters in this book testify to the curiosity that musical understanding incites in the minds of teachers. It is my hope that we continue to capitalize on that curiosity and engage in vigorous scholarly research and discussion on this topic as a piece of the music education puzzle and as a pathway to serious discussion about contradictions between philosophy and practice in music education. We engage in this dialogue for the sake of our students and their musical lives.

References

Boswell, J. (1991). Comparisons of attitudinal assessments in middle and junior high school general music. *Bulletin of the Council for Research in Music Education, 108,* 49-57.

Bowman, W. (2000). Discernment, responsability, and the goods of philosophical praxis. *Musiiki-Kasvatus: Finnish Journal of Music Education, 5* (7–2), 96–119.

Coan, D. (1992). *Computer-mediated communication for survey research in music education.* Unpublished doctoral dissertation, University of Illinois at Urbana-Champaign.

Coan, D. (2000). Charity begins at home: Discourse among teachers of music. *Musiikki-Kasvatus: Finnish Journal of Music Education, 5* (7–2), 59–72.

Dewey, J. (1938). *Experience and education.* New York: The Macmillan Company.

Galley, S. M. (2000). Portfolio as mirror: Student and teacher learning reflected through the standards. *Language Arts, 78* (2), 121–127.

Haladyna, T., & Thomas, G. (1979). The attitudes of elementary school children toward school and subject matters. *Journal of Experimental Education, 48,* 18-23.

Howard, V. A. (1988). Music as educating imagination. In C. Fowler (Ed.), *The Crane symposium: Toward an understanding of the teaching and learning of music performance* (pp. 25-36). New York: Potsdam College of the State University of New York.

Kaplan, M. (1966). *Foundations and frontiers of music education.* New York: Holt, Rinehart, & Winston.

Leonhard, C., & House, R. (1972). *Foundations and principles of music education* (2nd ed.). New York: McGraw-Hill.

Leonhard, C. (1991). *The status of arts education in American public schools.* (National Arts Education Research Center Report). Urbana, Illinois: Council for Research in Music Education.

McCarthy, M. (1999). ...*on music teacher agency.* Retrieved April 2, 2000 from Mayday Group Web site
http://members.aol.com/jtgates/maydaygroup/mccarthy3b.html

Pogonowski, L. (1982). *Attitudinal assessment of upper elementary students in a process-oriented music curriculum.* Unpublished doctoral dissertation, Temple University.

Regelski, T. (1998). *Critical theory and music education.* Retrieved April 2, 2000 from Mayday Group Web site
http://members.aol.com/jtgates/maydaygroup/crittheory.html

The Historical Roots & Development of Audiation

A Process for Musical Understanding

Ronald C. Gerhardstein

When considering the phenomenon of musical understanding, the functioning of the mind upon a given selection of music must be considered. In the musical listening process, the musical mind engages in the following tasks: listening, recognizing, analyzing, and comprehending. Historically, these musical mental tasks, in relation to the aural processing of music, have been labeled aural imagery, although a host of other related terms have been used as well. Since 1975, however, the term audiation has come into vogue. Audiation was coined by Edwin Gordon to lend specificity to the more traditional terms then in use (aural imagery, aural perception, inner hearing, musical perception, etc.). Since that time, Gordon has developed hierarchical stages of audiation and a theory of music learning based on audiation development. Given the certain connection between musical mental processes in regard to musical understanding, music educators and music education researchers should consider the historical development and meanings of these terms. Of particular importance, given its wide usage, is the understanding of Gordon's theory of audiation from a historical and conceptual standpoint, especially in light of its role in regard to musical understanding.

Definition of the Term

The definition of audiation has gone through a number of revisions during the past 25 years as Gordon has broadened his understanding of the term and the process based on his own study and commentary from his students and colleagues. Gordon (1975) originally described audiation as follows:

> Audiation suggests hearing music as compared to aural perception, which suggests just pure sensory reaction to sound. Moreover, there are two types of audiation: basic audiation (through either memory or creation) and notational audiation. Basic audiation takes place when one simply hears music without it being performed whereas notational audiation takes place when one hears music seen in notation without it being performed. (p. ii)

In the 1976–77 edition of *Learning Sequence and Patterns in Music,* Gordon changed the definition to read:

> Audiation takes place when one hears music through recall or creation (the sound not being physically present except, of course, when one is engaging in performance) and derives musical meaning, as compared to aural perception when one listens to music actually being performed by others. (p. 2)

In 1984, Gordon theorized different types and stages of audiation and defined the term as follows: "Audiation takes place when one hears music silently, that is, when the sound is not physically present. One may audiate in recalling music or in composing music" (p. 11). In 1988, Gordon included an entire chapter on audiation in *Learning Sequences in Music: Skill, Content and Patterns* and added the word "comprehension" to his definition stating that "audiation takes place when one hears and comprehends music silently, that is, when the sound is not physically present" (p. 7). In 1993, the definition of audiation was changed only slightly, although Gordon further explained that "sound is not comprehended as music until it is audiated after it is heard" (p. 13).

> Audiation involves both hearing music and the comprehension or understanding of music in the mind. The comprehension and understanding of music, according to Gordon, must include the audiation of musical syntax: tonality, meter, form, style, and musical expression.

In the 1997 edition of *Learning Sequences in Music: Skill, Content and Patterns,* the definition of audiation is as follows:

Audiation takes place when we assimilate and comprehend in our minds music that we have just heard performed or have heard performed sometime in the past.... Sound itself is not music. Sound becomes music only through audiation, when, as with language, you translate the sounds in your mind to give them meaning. (pp. 4–5)

Clearly, audiation involves both hearing music and the comprehension or understanding of music in the mind. The comprehension and understanding of music, according to Gordon, must include the audiation of musical syntax: tonality, meter, form, style, and musical expression.

Gordon's Musical Background

One of the basic tenets of audiation is the hearing or recall of music within the mind. Gordon's interest in this phenomenon began early in his musical career due to the teaching of influential music instructors. This teaching formed the motivation behind the concept of audiation.

While in high school in Stamford, Connecticut (1941–1945), Gordon played double bass in small local jazz bands for a variety of social functions organized by friends from school. His first jazz lessons in the early 1940s were from Sid Weiss, the former bassist with the Benny Goodman Quartet. Instruction from Weiss was accomplished without the aid of musical notation, most likely because Weiss himself did not read music. Without the aid of musical notation, Weiss taught Gordon to "think" what he was to play before he actually played it (Gordon, 1991, p. 7).

Eighteen months of military service with the 302nd U.S. Army Band in Denver, Colorado (1945–1947) brought Gordon more exposure to professional jazz musicians. In the Army Band, Gordon played tuba in the marching and concert bands and double bass in the jazz band. Additionally, many hours were spent jamming with a small group of musicians from the jazz band, including former members of the Ray McKinley Orchestra and the Glenn Miller band. Gordon was especially impressed with the members' knowledge of standard jazz tunes, improvisational skill, and their "hearing" abilities (Gordon, 1991, p. 7; personal communication, May 30, 1998).

Gordon matriculated at the Eastman School of Music in 1947, studying bass with Oscar Zimmerman. Zimmerman was a traditional teacher who taught Gordon the standard classical bass literature. The two did not have a good relationship, in part because of Zimmerman's authoritarian manner and his penchant to "tell" Gordon how music should sound rather than allowing his own musicianship to "hear" and interpret how it should sound. This method was in stark contrast to Gordon's informal and aural musical education in jazz.

In 1950, Gordon performed with Gene Krupa's big band. Like Weiss, Krupa did not read music notation, and Gordon was impressed with Krupa's knowledge of music, especially his vast knowledge of rhythm. Krupa explained that rhythm is comprised of big beats, small beats, and what comes in between (melodic rhythm) (personal communication, February 27, 1997).

In 1953, upon completion of a Master's degree in music performance at Eastman, Gordon studied classical bass with Philip Sklar in New York City. Sklar's teaching, together with instruction from Weiss and Krupa, reinforced Gordon's thoughts on the importance of "hearing" music in the mind before it is performed, even while reading. Sklar insisted that Gordon sing and demonstrate in movement all that he could read in notation. In this non-traditional approach, lessons with Sklar were often spent away from the bass, singing and/or moving to music (personal communication, February 27, 1997). This approach challenged Gordon to reconsider many of his thoughts about musical learning and musical understanding processes.

> Gordon came to believe that musical understanding is associated with one's ability to internalize music, to think and to process music within the mind.

Through his years of study with Weiss, Krupa, and Sklar, Gordon came to believe that musical understanding is associated with one's ability to internalize music, to think and to process music within the mind. Musical understanding is not solely dependent upon one's skill in reading musical notation.

Historical Foundations

Gordon is not unique, of course, regarding the notion of hearing and understanding music within the mind. The latter phenomenon has a long and colorful history that has been shaped by music educators, music psychologists, and cognitive psychologists. The following section lists part of that history, primarily that with which Gordon and his music education contemporaries would have likely been familiar.

The capacity of the mind to see (visualize) internally, or to use the "mind's eye," has historically been labeled "mental imagery" (Galton, 1880, pp. 301–318). Later, the term "auditory imagery" was used to describe the capacity of the mind to hear internally without actual physical sound being present. Robert Solso (1995) defined mental imagery as "a mental representation of a nonpresent object or event" and he explained that mental imagery has progressed through three time periods: the philosophic or pre-scientific period, the measurement period, and the cognitive and neuro-cognitive period (p. 280). Thus, the study of mental images in the philosophic period can be traced to the classic Greek philosophers, Aristotle and Plato, and to the British empiricists, John Locke (1632–1704), George Berkeley (1685–1753), David Hume (1711–1776), and David Hartley (1705–1757). Quantitative assessment of mental imagery in the measurement period began with Sir Francis Galton in 1880 (p. 280).

Carl Seashore (1919b) believed that auditory imagery is an essential component of musicianship (see Chapter 1). Although he was certain that auditory imagery was a primary component of musicianship, he did not test it directly in his *Seashore's Measures of Musical Talents* (1919a). Seashore (1938/1967) did believe, nevertheless, that auditory imagery should have a "central place" in the testing of musical talent (p. 161).

Seashore (1919b) described auditory imagery as follows:

> When we have heard a tune, some of us have the power to hear it over again; it comes back to us; it follows us; it may even be so persistent as to haunt us. It is heard in imagination—more than imagination, in fact, for it is actual hearing in the absence of the outward sound. We can play the tune, hear the counterpoint, follow the resolution of the chord, admire the attack, respond emotionally to the exquisite nuances which are rolled off in our mind's ear. This is call auditory imagery. (p. 211)

Seashore (1938/1967) distinguished between those who had the capacity for auditory imagery and those who did not. As Galton reasoned with mental imagery, so did Seashore believe some individuals would likely have very strong auditory images, some none at all, and others moderately so (pp. 162–163). Seashore (1919b) placed great importance on auditory imagery, for it was the only means to enter what he called the "tonal world." A person capable of auditory imagery "lives for the moment in a tonal world and hears music" while one who is not "does not enter this tonal world but satisfies himself with ideas about music or names for it" (p. 215).

Motor imagery, or kinesthetic sense, is also connected with auditory imagery in music as one hears, recalls, or creates music (Seashore, 1938/1967, pp. 168–169). Seashore believed that one's ability to hear music through auditory imagery affected the ability to appreciate music. What the music listener is able to hear in music "depends upon what he is, or is capable of putting into it, that is, hearing into it" (p. 169). Seashore believed that aural imagery was certainly an inherited trait; it could, however, be developed by use and training, as in the development of thinking (p. 170).

Emile Jacques-Dalcroze (1921) used the term "inner hearing" to describe the musical mental process. He sought to train the musical ear in a meaningful way, different from traditional methods that he believed had failed. Jacques-Dalcroze was exceptionally critical of musical training that taught musical skills apart from training the ear. Concerning the ability to hear harmonic progressions in music, Jacques-Dalcroze believed that it was "impossible to conceive a true sequence of chords without an inner ear to realise the sound in anticipation" (p. 3).

Jacob Kwalwasser (1932) noted that the mark of an experienced musician was the ability to miss a page turn and continue playing in the same style, approximating what the composer had written (p. 81). Children who are taught to read music in such a manner are capable of "reconstructing tones in their imaginations just as the originator of the melody did in conceiving the melody; in a sense, they are re-living the experiences of the composer" (p. 82).

James Mursell (1937/1971) wrote that what comes to the ear of the music listener and what a person hears are two very different things. It appears that Mursell believed that the mind is capable of filtering unneeded sounds and reducing music into patterns (see also Chapter 1). He wrote the following statement about the music listener.

> His ears are subjected to a continuous inflow of vibrations of tremendous complexity. But out of this he selects certain elements which are significant because they stand in intelligible tonal or rhythmic rela-

tions to one another; and he hears, not a bewildering chaos of impressions, but a sequence of coherent patterns. (p. 13)

Mursell (1937/1971) had difficulty believing that the phenomenon of music is best explained simply as the ear responding as the physical receptor of sound. Musicianship, in other words, was not simply a matter of one's physical hearing ability, although surely one needed to be physically able to hear to be a competent musician. According to Mursell, music does not depend on the stimuli that reach the external and internal ear but rather "upon the organizing and transforming operation of the mind upon them" (pp. 50–51). Further, he described a three-step approach to the role of the mind in regard to music:

1. Musical effects depend upon an intricate selective activity carried on by the mind;
2. Musical effects depend upon a whole array of organizing and synthesizing activities carried on by the mind;
3. Musical effects depend upon an array of organizing activities, by which the mind determines the patterns and relationships in which we shall hear what comes to our ears. (pp. 52–53)

G. Revesz (1954) described a sense of pitch, or what he believed was the prerequisite to developing one's musical ear. This sense of pitch included the ability to hear whether two notes are the same or different. Revesz reasoned that the ability to hear same and different in music is far easier and more important than the ability to determine which of two notes is higher (p. 95).

Donald Pond (1978) wrote that music is much more than figures used in musical notation; it is sound. Therefore, a connection must exist between music itself and the notation used to express that particular music. Music notation should not be associated with only the keys of the piano but as a representation of the tonal and rhythmical relationships between sounds. Those who have achieved at a high level in music have the ability to "anticipate mentally the sounds that their fingers are about to produce" (p. 67).

Neal Glenn and Edgar Turrentine (1968) noted that imagery, as it relates to music, is typically associated with one's ability to match a visual symbol with an aural one (pp. 68–69). Glenn (1951) stated that musical perception, or the "understanding of the music that is being experienced," was an important component of the musical process (p. 53). Music perception seems to imply more that just the physical sensation of sound, for it is through perception that musical learning, understanding, and appreciation take place.

Charles Leonhard and Robert House (1959) defined the role of perception in the musical learning process as the "act by which meaning is gained from the sensory processes while a stimulus is present" (p. 110). According to Leonhard and House, perception involves gaining meaning and forming musical concepts together with an awareness of the intensity and relaxation of tonal and rhythmic movements (pp. 110–111). Perception is a critical skill as the authors insisted that aural awareness is the "key to all musical learning" (p. 134).

Claude Palisca (1963) and all of those present at the 1963 Yale Seminar on Music Education regretfully reported that participation in instrumental music had not produced the "capacity to hear internally a musical line," a benchmark for the musician and the perceptive listener (p. 6). They also reported that in many instrumental programs musical drill was emphasized to the exclusion of creativity and musical thought.

Lev Vygotsky (1962) wrote of the relationship between thought and meaning in language. According to Vygotsky, words (or what Gordon refers to as tonal and rhythmic patterns in music) and their meanings (what Gordon refers to as the audiation of musical syntax) are inseparable. Words without meaning, Vygotsky explains, are "empty sounds" (p. 5). Moreover the movement between words and their meaning is a continual process. Two forms of speech, internal and external, are also involved. External speech is a result of moving from thought to words. Internal speech, on the other hand, is a result of the transformation of speech into inward thought (pp. 125–131).

Robert Solso (1995), a cognitive psychologist, did not seem to make a distinction between the differing senses in terms of mental imagery. Mental imagery, therefore, includes not only the visual sense, but also the sensations for hearing, tasting, feeling, and smell (p. 282). The manner in which the brain perceives, codes, stores, and retrieves sensory images is of great importance. With regard to visual images, Solso wrote:

> Visual information is filtered, summarized, and stored as abstract "statements" about the image. Reactivation of the memory then

would consist of recalling the abstract code, which in turn would conjure up the subjective image associated with it. Finally, we could argue that some information is stored visually and some in abstract form, indication that multiple codes exist in the mind. (pp. 281–82)

Ulrich Neisser (1967), another cognitive psychologist, wrote that auditory synthesis, like visual synthesis, requires two stages. The first is a passive, pre-attentive stage during which some units are tentatively identified; the second is an active stage (p. 173). Neisser adhered to a model of auditory cognition that he calls "analysis-by-synthesis." This model involves a set of rules (phonetic, phonemic, syntactic, and semantic) that allows one to generate and properly store spectral patterns rather than entire catalogs of patterns themselves (pp. 194–95). Therefore, a multitude of patterns based on this one set of rules can be generated.

Neisser was also interested in the manner in which sounds are heard, analyzed, and stored. Hearing and sound are temporal events; therefore, an "echoic memory" is necessary so that the listener can hold onto the sound event for a brief moment and then select portions of the sound content for special attention. Echoic memory is a necessary phenomenon because, if the brain discarded all sound information as soon as it arrived, hearing would be impossible. Echoic memory serves as a buffer for temporary storage in the auditory cognitive system. Neisser also explained that echoic memory is necessary for the perception of rhythm (p. 205).

Gordon was well aware of the historical foundations presented in this section (Gordon, 1971; Gordon, 1987; Gerhardstein, 2001). His concept of audiation, although unique in many respects to his predecessors' ideas, is clearly rooted in work of other psychologists.

Gordon Creates Audiation

By the early 1970s, Gordon became dissatisfied with the use of the word imagery in connection with aural events in music. His own use of the terms tonal imagery and rhythm imagery prior to 1975, as well as the concepts of aural imagery and musical imagery were, in his opinion, inaccurate and incomplete. To Gordon, imagery implied only the visual sense; hence, tonal imagery and rhythm imagery were inadequate because they applied only to seeing music notation in the mind rather than comprehension of what one is hearing or has heard. Using a strict inter-pretation, inner hearing was also inadequate to Gordon because it im-plied only hearing musical sound in the mind and not necessarily deriv-ing meaning or understanding from that sound. The term musical per-ception was also not specific enough; Gordon understood it to imply only the ability to physically hear or perceive sounds.

Gordon concluded that a new term was needed. "Audiation" was suggested by Gordon's friend and editor, Claire Ives, in 1975 (personal communication, April 10, 1997). The etymology of the word is a cross between "audition," the action or faculty of hearing, and the verb "ide-ate," to form an idea or to think. The formation of ideas of things not present to the senses, or "ideation," is obviously closely related to audia-tion.

Types and Stages of Audiation

In 1984, Gordon defined seven types and five stages of audiation (pp. 11–19). Later, he expanded the concept of audiation to include eight types and six stages (1997, pp. 13–23). The eight types of audiation are common instances during which one could audiate, including listening, reading, writing, recall, performance, creating, and improvising. The eight types of audiation are listed in Table 1.

Table 1. Gordon's Eight Types of Audiation (1997, p. 14)

Type	Context
1	Listening to familiar or unfamiliar music
2	Reading familiar or unfamiliar music
3	Writing familiar or unfamiliar music from dictation
4	Recalling and performing familiar music from memory
5	Recalling and writing familiar music from memory
6	Creating and improvising unfamiliar music while performing or in silence
7	Creating and improvising unfamiliar music while reading
8	Creating and improvising unfamiliar music while writing

Gordon's six theoretical stages of audiation are hierarchical, cyclical, and cumulative; each successive stage in the process becomes more complex than the previous stage. Gordon's stages of audiation should be considered in the same light as other cognitive models, for it is essentially a musical information-processing model. The six stages of audiation are listed below in Table 2.

Table 2. Gordon's Six Stages of Audiation (1997, p. 18)

Stage	Phenomenon
1	Momentary retention
2	Imitating and audiating tonal patterns and rhythm patterns and recognizing and identifying a tonal center and macrobeats
3	Establishing objective or subjective tonality and meter
4	Retaining in audiation tonal patterns and rhythm patterns that have been organized
5	Recalling tonal patterns and rhythm patterns organized and audiated in other pieces of music
6	Anticipating and predicting tonal patterns and rhythm patterns

Stage one, momentary retention, is similar to Neisser's echoic memory, which allows for sound to be retained in the mind for a brief period. Gordon (1997) describes an "aftersound" that remains for only a few seconds, allowing the listener to give conscious meaning to the sound in stage two (p. 18). In stage two, what has just heard is played back silently in the mind through imitation. Through audiation, meaning is then given as one quickly organizes series of tonal and rhythm patterns containing essential pitches and durations, respectively. Organization of tonal and rhythm patterns occurs due to the conscious recognition and identification of a tonal center and macrobeats (1993, pp. 22–23). In stage three, as a result of stages one and two, one establishes, through audiation, objective or subjective tonality and meter (1997, p. 19). In

stage four of audiation, one consciously retains that which one has organized in the first three stages. One may clarify, assess, and restructure
that which was previously audiated. In stage four one recognizes and
identifies sequence, repetition, form, style, timbre, and dynamics, as well
as other important musical information (1993, p. 21). In stage five, one
compares that which one has just heard to that which has been previously audiated. The more music we have listened to, and the larger the
vocabulary of tonal and rhythm patterns that we possess, the better we
will be able to engage in stage five of audiation (1997, pp. 21–22). In
the final stage of audiation, stage six, one anticipates and predicts music
that will be heard next. Again, the more music one has listened to and
the larger one's vocabulary of tonal and rhythm patterns, the better able
one will be able to engage in stage six of audiation.

Role and Importance of Audiation

When thinking of the term audiation (or related terms) one should not
divorce that concept from the practical musical considerations that encompass musical understanding. Ac-
cording to Gordon and the authors who
described related terms, the mental
processing of music is musical under-

> Music is comprehended and understood as music through audiation.

standing. Music is comprehended and understood as music through
audiation. Musical communication, some would argue, is communication through audiation at some level. Taking the argument to an extreme position, some would argue that understanding music without
audiation (auditory imagery, aural perception, inner hearing, etc.) is an
impossibility except for the understanding of musical text and the mere
feelings that one may associate with a
musical composition.

> Audiation is the vehicle in which this sharing of musical knowl-
edge takes place; between com-
poser and listener, between a
performer and her audience,
between teacher and student,
and between parent and child.

Every musician has two instruments of great importance. One is a
physical instrument (piano, violin,
saxophone, or the voice) while the
other is invisible. The invisible instrument is the instrument of the
mind, or one's audiation instrument. For understanding to occur between two or more individuals, knowledge must be shared. Audiation is

the vehicle in which this sharing of musical knowledge takes place—between composer and listener, between a performer and her audience, between teacher and student, and between parent and child.

The mind is a pattern-making machine. Upon hearing music, the mind creates order out of multiple stimuli (tonal aspects, rhythmic aspects, harmony, timbre, etc.). Meaning (musical understanding) is given to music through the audiation of musical syntax as the mind assimilates tonality, meter, harmony, timbre, form, style, musical modulations, and dynamics. The more ways we understand syntax in music, the better we understand music. Audiation allows us to understand unfamiliar music and to develop musical predictions; thus, we are able to move beyond mere listening to music and to participate in the listening process.

Audiation is also of great practical significance in relation to Gordon's seven published tests of music aptitude. Audiation (or tonal imagery and rhythm imagery as used in his 1965 *Musical Aptitude Profile*) is a central component in Gordon's psychological constructs of music aptitude. Gordon claims that "audiation is the basis of music aptitude"; hence, audiation is given precedence above other possible constructs in his tests. The basic skill used throughout each of Gordon's tests of musical aptitude is the ability to distinguish whether two patterns (or melodies) are the same or different. Using the concept of same and different as a foundation for musical understanding yields a multitude of possibilities in relation to the complex phenomenon of music making (e.g., in-tune singing, matching articulation, performing in an appropriate musical style, improvising to a given harmonic progression, performing a melodic variation, etc.).

Gordon's music learning theory was designed with the notion of audiation at its core. His learning theory is, at its most basic level, a model for instruction (or guidance) in audiation. The skill learning sequence of music learning theory begins with aural/oral (hearing and performing music), and moves through various stages ending with theoretical knowledge about music. Teaching students how to audiate is a matter of teaching what to audiate. As such, Gordon's music learning theory is highly associated with his musical pattern sequences. The combining of audiation with

> Teaching students how to audiate is a matter of teaching what to audiate.

pattern instruction (one of the more controversial components of Gordon's theory) is probably why audiation has been criticized by some. Yet, it is clear that not only Gordon but others throughout music education history have placed the mental processing of musical sound in high esteem in relation to musical learning and to musical understanding. Training in audiation is consistent with long held traditions in music education of teaching sound before sign or "ear training before eye training."

The motivation and foundation behind the theory of audiation is clearly found in Gordon's own musical experiences and in the historical traditions of related terminology. In fact, audiation appears to be more closely related to traditional terms such as mental imagery, auditory imagery, and sense of pitch to a much greater extent than Gordon admits in his writings. Through the musical mental process (audiation), music becomes meaningful and purposeful sound. In terms of musical understanding, audiation should be of concern to all music educators.

> Through the musical mental process (audiation), music becomes meaningful and purposeful sound. In terms of musical understanding, audiation should be of concern to all music educators.

Afterthoughts

Participants at the *Symposium for Musical Understanding* (SMU) seemed to view Gordon's concept or theory of audiation from either a neutral or negative perspective. It appears that audiation itself—if it can in fact be thought of apart from Gordon's tests of music aptitude and his music learning theory—was not a point of contention; there was interest in the historical predecessors of audiation and Gordon's role in that history. Nevertheless, audiation is, in fact, a central component, if not the primary basis, for both Gordon's tests of music aptitude and his music learning theory. It is not surprising that views expressed regarding Gordon's theories at the *Symposium* were strong.

The arguments against Gordon's theory of audiation and his related work stem from the view that Gordon's work is positivist in nature. His theories and tests are described as reductionist and atomistic. Also, of concern were the methods that Gordon and his associates use to teach children to audiate, namely the pattern learning sequences (or learning sequence activities) associated with his music learning theory.

Although there appeared to be a general distrust of both Gordon and his theories at the *Symposium* (perhaps due to supreme confidence with which Gordon presents his own ideas), there was a general appreciation for the presentation of Gordon's ideas in a historical context. I believe this was a valuable outcome and a contribution to the dialogue surrounding musical understanding. The historical underpinnings and the relative merits of Gordon's views certainly stirred lively and meaningful dialogue. I was especially grateful for the opportunity to share ideas with colleagues and to think and learn in such an environment.

References

Galton, F. (1880). Statistics of mental imagery. *Mind, 19,* 301–318.

Gerhardstein, R. C. (2001). *Edwin E. Gordon: A biographical and historical account of an American music educator and researcher.* Unpublished doctoral dissertation, Temple University.

Glenn, N. E., & Turrentine, E. M. (1968). *Introduction to advanced study in music education.* Dubuque, IA: Wm. C. Brown.

Glenn, N. E. (1951). *Teaching music in our schools.* Dubuque, IA: Wm. C. Brown.

Gordon, E. E. (1965). *Musical aptitude profile.* Boston, MA: Houghton Mifflin.

Gordon, E. E. (1971). *The psychology of music teaching.* Englewood Cliffs, NJ: Prentice Hall.

Gordon, E. E. (1975). *Learning theory, patterns, and music.* Buffalo, NY: Tometic Associates.

Gordon, E. E. (1976/1977). *Learning sequence and patterns in music* (Rev. ed.). Chicago: GIA Publications.

Gordon, E. E. (1980). *Learning sequences in music: Skill, content, and patterns.* Chicago: GIA Publications.

Gordon, E. E. (1984). *Learning sequences in music: Skill, content, and patterns* (Rev. ed.). Chicago: GIA Publications.

Gordon, E. E. (1987). *The nature, description, measurement, and evaluation of music aptitudes.* Chicago: GIA Publications.

Gordon, E. E. (1988). *Learning sequences in music: Skill, content, and patterns* (Rev. ed.). Chicago: GIA Publications.

Gordon, E. E. (1991). Gordon on Gordon. *The Quarterly Journal of Music Teaching and Learning, 2* (1/2), 6–9.

Gordon, E. E. (1993). *Learning sequences in music: Skill, content, and patterns* (Rev. ed.). Chicago: GIA Publications.

Gordon, E. E. (1997). *Learning sequences in music: Skill, content, and patterns* (Rev. ed.). Chicago: GIA Publications.

Jacques-Dalcroze, E. J. (1921). *Rhythm, music, and education* (H. F. Rubinstein, Trans.). New York: G. P. Putnam.

Kwalwasser, J. (1932). *Problems in public school music.* New York: M. Witmark and Sons.

Leonhard, C., & House, R. W. (1959). *Foundations and principles of music education.* New York: McGraw Hill.

Mursell, J. L. (1971). *The psychology of music* (Reprinted ed.). Westport, CT: Greenwood Press. (Original work published 1937)

Neisser, U. (1967). *Cognitive psychology.* New York: Appleton-Century-Crofts.

Palisca, C. V. (1963). *Seminar of music education,* Cooperative Research Project No. G-013. New Haven, CT: Yale University.

Pond, D. (1978). *Music of young children.* Santa Barbara, CA: Pillsbury Foundation for Advancement of Music Education.

Revesz, G. (1954). *Introduction of the psychology of music* (G.I.C. De Courcy, Trans.). Norman, OK: University of Oklahoma Press.

Seashore, C. E. (1919a). *The psychology of musical talent.* Boston: Silver Burdett.

Seashore, C. E. (1919b). *Seashore's measures of musical talents.* New York: Columbia Phonograph Co.

Seashore, C. E. (1967). *The psychology of music* (Reprint ed.). New York: Dover Publications. (Original work published 1938)

Solso, R. L. (1995). *Cognitive psychology* (4th ed.). Boston: Allyn and Bacon.

Vygotsky, L. S. (1962). *Thought and language.* Cambridge: M.I.T. Press.

7

Movement and Music

The Kinesthetic Dimension of the Music Listening Experience

Marian T. Dura

Listening is among the most basic experiences we have of music, and movement has been described widely as the "essence" of both music and the musical experience. Music listening has long been a favorite topic of philosophical essays and, in recent years, of empirical research, but few writers have devoted extensive thought and effort to characterizing the involvement of the body in music listening and in musical understanding.

A complete picture of the music listening experience and musical understanding, however, must include this foundational kinesthetic aspect. An experience that can be so profoundly "moving" must at the very least leave its trace or effect upon the body and, at most, involve and implicate the body in its essential workings.

This study examines one portion of this aspect—that of the internal feeling of movement experienced when listening to music, even when one is not overtly moving—and attempts to provide an explanation of the functioning of the body as one essential component of the cognitive/emotional processes employed in musical understanding. It serves as a bridge between the description offered by Harold Fiske and Matthew Royal of the interaction of cultural variables and the brain's auditory networks in musical understanding (see Chapter 4), and the practical application of movement metaphors as gesture and imagery in the choral classroom presented by Marta McCarthy (see Chapter 13).

The interaction between the physical and the cultural in musical experience is described by John Blacking (1974), writing from the point of view of a cultural anthropologist. Blacking, consistent with Fiske, calls music "a synthesis of cognitive processes which are present in culture

119

and in the human body: the forms it takes, and the effects it has on people, are generated by the social experiences of human bodies in different cultural environments" (p. 89). He suggests we might learn more about music and "human musicality"

> if we look for basic rules of musical behavior which are biologically, as well as culturally, conditioned and species-specific. It seems to me that what is ultimately of most importance in music cannot be learned like other cultural skills: it is there in the body, waiting to be brought out and developed, like the basic principles of language formation. (p. 100)

Considering music a communication of feelings between the composer and the listener, Blacking, like McCarthy, says that a performer might be able to reproduce the "rhythmical stirring of the body" that originated the experience by "finding the right movement." He suggests, for example, that a pianist might get a better feeling for the music of Debussy if he or she could discover "how Debussy might have held his hands and body when he played the piano." Blacking claims that such an experience would be "profoundly deep, because you would be sharing the most important thing about music," namely the universal feeling within the body, and that is "probably as close as anyone can ever get to resonating with another person" (pp. 110-111).

The primary research question of the study that was the source of this chapter was "How, precisely, does music produce a sense of movement in the listener experiencing that music?" An attempt has been made to answer that question by reviewing, summarizing, and synthesizing the literature in many of the areas pertinent to the study—philosophy, neurology, psychology, and music theory—guided by the following sub-questions:

> How, precisely, does music produce a sense of movement in the listener experiencing that music?

> **Sub-question 1.** Given what seems to be a simultaneous and inseparable relationship between cognition and emotion, is there some kind of physical involvement, particularly a *movement*-based physicality, among the other identified elements of the musical experience, different from, say, a *tactile* experience, such as the comparison of tone quality to the softness of velvet, or a *visual* comparison to shimmering water?

Sub-question 2. What is the relationship between body, mind, and brain in the processes of audition, cognition, and emotion, particularly during the music-listening experience? Is there something in the way the brain works that might link hearing and movement? Is there organic, visceral, or muscular involvement in audition, cognition, and emotion?

Sub-question 3. What is it about musical structure itself, from the point of view of philosophers, educators, composers, conductors, and music theorists, that might be implicated in the creation of kinesthetic responses?

Sub-question 1: Physical Involvement
as a Component of the Music Listening Experience

According to the philosophers and theoretical writers reviewed, the music listening experience is a complex and many-faceted phenomenon that depends upon the mind's ability to organize sounds into meaningful, understandable patterns. It is a very different kind of experience from that of vision, even artistic vision, since sound is invasive and penetrating, and vision tends to be a distancing sense (Burrows, 1990). Music listening is an active experience, but it is a special kind of activity that confers a kind of subjectivity upon the object, giving it an animated quality and making it appear to have a life and will of its own (Ihde, 1976; Dufrenne, 1973).

It is widely agreed that the music-listening experience does involve the entire body, not only in the physical act of hearing (as, for example, in vibrations felt from approaching jet planes, loud rock music being heard in the stomach, and deaf persons hearing through bone conduction), but also in the physical reaction to heard music (Ihde, 1976). This response appears to be an inseparable, simultaneous integration of cognition and emotion, sometimes characterized as musical perception and reaction, and it does have an identified physical component. The body has an essential, integral role to play in cognition, including musical cognition, since, as Howard Gardner (1985) puts it, our "muscle memories" of past experiences, symbolized kinesthetically, enable us to experience aesthetically (p. 228).

This physicality has been described variously, but these definitions usually include the concept of motion or movement. This motion is expressed as a result of the passing of time, tension and its resolution, cognitive grouping processes, and other characteristics that make listening to music a qualitatively different experience from listening to everyday sounds (Gardner, 1985). The elements of space and time are represented together in movement; indeed, sound cannot occur without the friction and collision resulting from movement (Bartholomew, 1985). The function of motion is thus so basic and foundational to the music-listening experience that this pervasiveness may itself explain its manifestation as a feeling in the listener.

Sub-question 2
The Body, the Mind, the Brain, and the Musical Experience

Early philosophies, such as that of Descartes, considered the mind to be not only separate from but superior to the body (Wis, 1993). Modern scientific theories of the relationship between mind and body are based upon studies of the physical workings of the brain. These emphasize the connection between thought and physical action in the brain, which is the "sending and receiving agent of the nervous system" (Campbell, 1983, p. 20). Parallel and distributed processing—a contemporary explanation of sensory processing—provides one description of the processes by which multisensory integration may take place. In the theory of parallel and distributed processing, it is hypothesized that features of perception are analyzed separately in independent processing modules and then re-united as a single representation. The use of various areas in the brain suggests the possibility of processing sensory input (such as musical sounds) through different modalities (implying visual and kinesthetic associations with the auditory input). The time lag before the reassembly of the representation is suggestive of the role of time in the perception of movement (Dissanayake, 1992; Elliott, 1995).

Gerald Edelman's (1992) account of synthetic properties and higher functions of the brain, called Neural Darwinism, posited a selectionist system, based on perceived need, feeling, and value. There is much support for this theory, which states that the patterns, number, and strength of synaptic connections in the brain are actually formed by the neural connections *created* by experiences undergone by the organism. This is why each brain, even those of identical twins, is unique, and why the brains of musicians may develop differently than do those of non-musicians (Edelman, 1996). Maps, in the sense of patterns of neuron firing activity, are not fixed, and there is evidence that neurons may function in groups (Edelman, 1992). As well, it has been hypothesized that the physical make-up of the cortex is basically the same in all areas, although areas of some specialization have developed through neural selection. These areas of specialization might help to explain the phenomena of kinesthesis, empathy, and synesthesia in terms of mapping, since similar patterns in different areas of the brain may yield equivalent experiences that are manifested, however, in different sensory modalities. At the same time, this distribution of various aspects of the music listening experience (hearing, emotion, labeling through language, motor skills, memory, imagery, etc.) among various areas of brain specialization implies that there is no music "center" within the brain (1992; 1996).

A contrasting suggestion, that some cortical neurons may actually be polysensory, is used to support certain theories of the unity of the senses or sensory correspondences. Such theories date back as far as Democritus and Aristotle and they survive in modern theories of synesthesia, or the "transference of sensory images or attributes from one modality to another" (Marks, 1978, p. 8). This transference has been described as the residue of a primitive general sensory response, which existed in early evolutionary stages but which became more differentiated with evolutionary development, and which may be caused neurologically by nerve patterns deviating from their normal paths (Marks, 1978; Marks & Bornstein, 1987).

Arnheim (1966; 1984), Churchland (1986), Clynes (1977), Dissanayake (1992), and others have speculated on the existence and nature of a relationship between perception, emotional response, and patterns of electrochemical forces in the brain, referred to as isomorphism. This relationship may be implicated in aesthetic experience, as might a hypothesized relationship between posture or gesture and feeling and emotional states. It is suggested that hemispheric specialization might also play a role in aesthetic experience, since the percepts such as images, patterns, music, and emotional intonation that register and are stored in the right hemisphere are not verbalized and thus may not be recognized as part of conscious cognition (Dissanayake, 1992).

Examination of the auditory system suggests that a close relationship may exist between hearing and the inner ear's other functions such as balance and movement. Such a relationship might be seen as contributing to the linkage between music listening and the perception of the feeling of movement.[1]

Many theories of emotion, beginning with that of William James (1887/1961), demonstrate its intimate relationships with both cognition and bodily states. More recent evidence suggests that there may be a quantitative correlation between the intensity of a stimulus and the resulting pattern in the brain (Damasio, 1994; De Sousa, 1990; Mandler, 1984). When this close relationship between an emotion-provoking stimulus and subsequent brain activity is considered in combination with what has been stated above about the equivalence of patterns in various parts of the brain through mapping, this relationship could imply cross-modal representations such as that linking music and movement, particularly in an experience as potentially intense and profound as the music listening experience.

To summarize sub-question 2 thus far, the examination of the kinesthetic dimension of the music listening experience led to an investigation of the respective roles of body, mind, and brain in the processes of audition, cognition, and emotion. Earlier philosophies, which suggested

---

[1]Harold Fiske, "Structure of Cognition and Music Decision-Making," in *The Handbook of Research on Music Teaching and Learning* (New York: Schirmer Books, 1992). See also Donald Paul Barra, "Listening and the Aesthetic Experience" (Ed.D. dissertation, Columbia University Teachers College, 1975); chapter three, "Psychoacoustical Foundations," in *Psychological Foundations of Musical Behavior,* by Rudolf E. Radocy & J. David Boyle, 2nd ed. (Springfield, IL: Cahrles C. Thomas, 1979); chapter two, "The Perception of Sound," in *Music Cognition* by W. Jay Dowling and Diane L. Harwood (San Diego, CA: Academic Press, 1986); and J. D. Hood's chapter, "Psychological and Physiological Aspects of Hearing," in *Music and the Brain: Studies in the Neurology of Music,* (Springfield, IL: Charles C. Thomas, 1977). A readable and entertaining discussion of the auditory system is also offered by Frank Wilson in *Tone Deaf and All Thumbs?* (New York: Viking Penguin, 1986), and a classic description of the mechanics of hearing is offered by Hermann L. F. Helmholtz in *On the Sensations of Tone* (New York: Dover Publications, 1954). See also Donald A. Hodges' *Handbook of Music Psychology,* 2nd ed. (San Antonio, TX: IMR Press, 1996).

a separation of mind and body have been replaced by empirical observations—psychological, physiological, and neurological—of the synergy of mind and body in cognition and emotion. There does not appear to be a great deal of evidence yet for "centers" within the brain, such as for music or for movement, although certain areas of the brain are, to some extent, implicated in such functions. Since, however, sensory input is dispatched to various parts of the brain for processing and subsequently recombined, and since the strength and number of connections between various parts of the brain develop differently in individuals based upon early life experience, it seems entirely likely that there are neural connections between areas associated with music listening and with movement, and that, in certain individuals who have learned to make these associations at an early age, these may be particularly strong. The association between hearing and movement is strengthened when the dual functions of the inner ear—those of hearing and those of balance and movement—are also considered.

There are similarities between physical reaction to music and physical reaction in emotion, and each is closely associated with cognition. This relationship could have implications for many different cross-modal representations. Of particular interest is the possibility that an association of music and movement might leave a lasting trace upon the brain that would be strengthened when repeated in subsequent music listening experiences.

> Of particular interest is the possibility that an association of music and movement might leave a lasting trace upon the brain that would be strengthened when repeated in subsequent music listening experiences.

To continue, the study of metaphor as an integral part of the human conceptual system is also of importance in answering sub-question 2. This approach starts from the premise that humans strive, not only to survive in the world, but also to make sense of it. As Peter Kivy notes, we tend to anthropomorphize or animate objects we see, and we tend to hear music as human utterance, giving it a sense of meaning or significance, based on its quasi-syntactical character (Lakoff & Johnson, 1980). We possess the ability to see and hear movement where none actually exists, as in the phi-phenomenon (observed, for example, when lights which are spread through space and alternately turned on and off appear to be a single entity moving its location between the positions of the lights) and, as well, in music. Our thinking is structured by comparisons with our world, and our experience of listening to music is structured in the same way.

Lakoff and Johnson (1980), for example, consider metaphor to be an inherent characteristic of the human conceptual system, where "understanding takes place in terms of entire domains of experience and not in terms of isolated concepts" (p. 117). Metaphor allows us to understand these domains of experience in terms of each other, and imagination is involved in creating a meaningful and connected experience. This imagination goes beyond visual and aural imagery, organizing mental representations and structuring them into meaningful unities. It has been hypothesized that the image schemata which contribute to this process may be basically kinesthetic, rather than visual in nature, lending a kinesthetic coloring to our thinking (Lakoff, 1987).

Metaphor has been described as an inherent property of the nervous system which can be described in neurological terms and which developed as humans learned to abstract similar characteristics from changing events in order to provide stability for survival. Some of these abstraction skills seem to be innate, while others are learned (Honeck, Kibler, & Firment, 1987). Metaphor may in fact even *create* similarities when the interaction of two referents creates a new understanding or meaning that is greater than the sum of its parts (Wis, 1993).

Music can be seen as a form of metaphor, as symbolic of feelingful life. It has been hypothesized by writers such as Peter Kivy (1989) that the human propensity to anthropomorphize objects, which began as a survival skill, developed into a recognition of the quasi-syntactical aspect of music, related to tone of voice or emotional cast. This more sophisticated recognition allowed music to become symbolic and, to an extent, representational in terms of expressive behavior (p. 83). Kivy's characterization of musical movement emphasizes the relationship between pitch, energy, and motion.

To summarize, then, in answer to sub-question 2, it seems clear that body and brain work together seamlessly in the processes of parallel and distributed processing and mapping, and that the mind constantly attempts to make sense of the world through selective filtering of sensory data, grouping and associating of data, and the use of metaphor to abstract similar characteristics from changing events in order to provide stability for survival.

There may indeed be a function of the brain that links hearing and movement, through the selective neural networks characterized in the theory of Neural Darwinism. The mechanism of the inner ear itself also holds implications for such a linkage between hearing and movement.

There is much evidence from a wide range of psychological, physiological, and neurological sources indicating that organic, visceral, and/or muscular involvement is clearly an element in audition, cognition, and emotion. It has been suggested that musical sounds may even work directly upon the muscles, in a form of bodily cognition or knowledge.

Sub-question 3
Effects of Musical Elements on Listeners

Attention must also be focused upon the elements and structure of Western tonal music,[2] to investigate their role in creating a feeling of movement in the listener. Many authors agree that music possesses the power to affect listeners physically as well as emotionally. They suggest that these effects may vary with the musical background of the listener or the significance and personal meaning the particular music holds for the listener.

Kinetic energy profiles based upon loudness, speed, pitch, and timbre contribute to music's expressiveness and underlie the similarity between sensory modes through their imitation of purposeful, physical actions. Kinetic images conveyed by works of music can even characterize an entire historical period or style (Arias, 1989).

Motion or movement in music is most often associated with the motion of pitch or melody, and this association requires a definition of the space within which the tone "moves." There has been much discussion but little agreement on the question of whether musical space is equivalent to physical space or whether it is merely metaphorical (Dalhaus, 1967/1982). The absence of a vehicle, or carrier, leads some

---

[2] An examination of musics based upon other tonal systems, while relevant and of interest, is beyond the scope of this paper.

authors to deny the reality of musical space. Both musical space and musical movement, they say, should be considered metaphorical, due to their lack of orientation and their failure to observe other physical laws. For example, two tones, unlike other "objects," can exist in the same place. No tone, however, can "move" without becoming another tone (Scruton, 1983, pp. 34, 81). In music there is no *thing* that moves between positions, no positions *between which* movement takes place (Budd, 1983). Other writers acknowledge that pitches are not objects that can occupy spatial positions but that they maintain the *perceived* reality of highness and lowness based on prior associations. Without a system of metaphor, it is suggested, we lose the very essence of the musical experience (Scruton, 1983).

> Without a system of metaphor, it is suggested, we lose the very essence of the musical experience.

Some music theorists have devised multi-dimensional representations of pitch relationships in order to account for the structural identity of melodies that have undergone transformations such as inversion, retrograde, retrograde-inversion, and transpositions to other keys (Deutsch, 1982). In these theories, musical space strongly resembles physical space, and the idea of an actual musical motion is supported at the low level of Gestalt-like neural grouping processes, if not at high-level cognition (Gjerdingen, 1994).

Tonality is also implicated in musical motion due to its ability to imply stability or instability, tension or resolution, and continuation or closure. Victor Zuckerkandl (1956) explains musical motion in terms of the dynamic quality of tones or, more correctly, between tones. The background of tonal motion in his theory is not musical space but a "dynamic field" (pp. 128–129). Tonal motion, in his theory, is ideal motion because it exemplifies the inmost core, the "between" or passing over that takes place between discrete tones (pp. 138–139).

Several authors note the fundamental role played by rhythm and tempo in musical motion. The impression of movement has been attributed to "the perception of tones succeeding each other in time," and it is suggested that a continuous refocusing of perception on groups of tones keeps the listener moving ahead with the music while previous events fade away (Pike, 1970, pp. 16–17). Dynamics and volume (in the sense of voluminousness or intensity) may also have a role to play in musical motion. Volume, in particular, because of its relationship to mass and distance, implies a musical space, with tones varying in size, weight, and location (Lippmann, 1952). Changes in dynamics imply changes in tension and, in turn, a form of motion. Other factors have been implicated in musical motion, such as musical form and structure (particularly cyclical or wave structure) (Brower, 1993), grouping processes during listening (Lerdahl & Jackendorff, 1983, pp. 8–9, 179), the interaction of musical elements, and the interplay of dissonance and consonance. These factors are typically expressed as creating some form of tension and subsequent resolution, which accounts for the perception of motion in musical sounds (Ferguson, 1960).

To summarize, in answer to sub-question 3, virtually every element of music has been implicated in some way in the creation of kinesthetic responses. Cited as factors in this response have been pitch (both in its implications for a musical space and in its role in creating the tensions and goal-directedness of tonality), rhythm and tempo, dynamics and volume, musical form and structure, grouping processes during listening, the interplay of dissonance and consonance, and the interaction of these musical elements.

> Virtually every element of music has been implicated in some way in the creation of kinesthetic responses.

Summary: The Primary Research Question

The primary research question of this study was "How, precisely, does music produce a sense of movement in the listener experiencing that music?" The kinesthetic dimension of the music listening experience can be described as a product of various factors, including physical and neurological characteristics of the human nervous system, cognitive processes such as metaphor, and characteristics of tonality-based musical systems, in this case, specifically music of the European common practice period.

1. Certain identified characteristics of the music listening experience such as the integration of bodily, cognitive, and emotional experience; immersion in sound; the integration of space and time; and the perception of flow, flux, and

ephemerality, are significant contributors to the feeling of movement during music listening.

2. There appears to be a biological basis for a connection between music listening and kinesthesia through parallel and distributed neural processing, where incoming stimuli are directed to various specialized areas of the brain before impulses are reunited into a single representation. As well, the dual functions of the auditory system in hearing and in balance and movement may also hold implications for an association between heard music and felt movement. And it has been suggested that musical sounds may work directly upon the muscles and organs, in a form of bodily cognition or knowledge, where "thinking" is pre-conceptual and what is commonly thought of as "mind" is dependent upon bodily experience.

3. Whether its origins are biological or psychological, the human tendency to attribute life to inanimate objects as a means of anticipating danger in the interests of survival has been mentioned again and again in the studies reviewed here as a significant factor in the kinesthetic dimension of the music listening experience. If this "giving life" to inanimate things, including aural events, is a natural and spontaneous function of human cognition, then the perception of syntax and motion in music would seem to be an almost inevitable consequence of actively listening to it. The "quasi-subjectivity" of music, where it appears to take on a life and personality of its own, is also implicated in the attribution to music of the characteristics of movement. Metaphor plays an essential role in associating the patterns of music with the patterns of life and movement.

Through convention and custom, certain combinations of sounds are culturally interpreted as being goal-oriented and directional, thus implying movement.

4. Finally, elements of various musical systems have traditionally been arranged with the intent to create impressions of tensions, expectations, inhibitions, and resolutions. Through convention

and custom, certain combinations of sounds are culturally interpreted as being goal-oriented and directional, thus implying movement. Musical movement and the musical space within which it takes place have been described variously, but there appears to be support for the assertion that they are metaphors analogous to movement and space in the real world.

So much of our informal enjoyment of music seems to involve overt movement—whether dancing, beating time with feet or hands, drawing or painting to music, or imitating the movements involved in making music, as in conducting recordings or playing the "air guitar." Even singing along with the radio, particularly by people who claim they "can't sing," may actually be more a matter of the pleasure of feeling one's vocal apparatus moving with the music than of hearing one's own vocal production.

This pleasure which we derive from associating movement with music can perhaps account for the many styles of music, in all cultures, that have as their main purpose the opportunity for kinesthetic response. The close relationship between music, emotion, and the release of physical energy can perhaps begin to explain the appeal of the kinesthetic response for young people. For listeners of all ages, the wholeness or completeness of a musical experience that incorporates both the mind and the body in a primal unity can be a profound and deeply satisfying experience. It is likely

> For listeners of all ages, the wholeness or completeness of a musical experience that incorporates both the mind and the body in a primal unity can be a profound and deeply satisfying experience.

that much of the meaning and significance that we derive from music is not only a result of its syntactical resemblance to human utterance and its power to evoke images of lived experience but also because of its intimate connection with our bodies—how we first come to know the world. This "wholeness" (a word related to "hale," "healthy," and "holy") may even be foundational to the healing and spiritual aspects that are attributed to music in all cultures.

It is fascinating to consider that, despite its central position in musical experience, so much remains to be known and understood about music listening. The continued exploration of this area, both theoretically and empirically, is certain to yield results of interest to all those who interact with music, especially to those whose professional responsibility is to offer an education in music to all people.

Recommendations for Further Research

More work is needed to support these conclusions. It is recommended

1. that research be undertaken into the exact mechanism of neural connections between regions of the brain, as well as into the extent and nature of specialization of areas of the brain traditionally associated with the music listening experience and its components, such as cognition, emotion, motor skills, memory, and imagery;

2. that replications of this study take place in order to examine other aspects or dimensions of the music listening experience, such as tactile or visual metaphors for multi-domain associations;

3. that replications of this study take place with a focus on cultures where overt movement is an expected part of the music listening experience; and

4. that the present study be extended into an empirical investigation of qualitative and quantitative differences in kinesthetic response to music, as exhibited by listeners of various ages and musical backgrounds experiencing different musics. Interview data might be combined with physiological data to explore further such topics as developmental aspects of music listening and differences between the listening processes of musicians and non-musicians.

References

Arias, E. A. (1989, February). Music as projection of the kinetic sense. *The Music Review, 50*, 1-31.

Arnheim, R. (1966). *Toward a psychology of art: Collected essays.* Berkeley, CA: University of California Press.

Arnheim, R. (1984). Perceptual dynamics in musical expression. *Musical Quarterly, 70*, 259–309.

Barra, D. P. (1975). *Listening and the aesthetic experience.* Unpublished doctoral dissertation, Columbia University Teachers College.

Bartholomew, D. R. (1985). *A phenomenology of music: Themes concerning the musical object and implications for teaching and learning.* Unpublished doctoral dissertation, Case Western Reserve University.

Blacking, J. (1974). *How musical is man?* Seattle, WA: University of Washington Press.

Brower, C. R. (1993). *Motion in music: A wave model of rhythm.* Unpublished doctoral dissertation, University of Cincinnati.

Budd, M. (1983). Motion and emotion in music: How music sounds. *British Journal of Aesthetics, 23* (3), 209–221.

Burrows, D. (1990). *Sound, speech, and music.* Amherst, MA: The University of Massachusetts Press.

Campbell, D. G. (1983). *Introduction to the musical brain.* St. Louis, MO: Magnamusic-Baton.

Churchland, P. S. (1986). *Neurophilosophy: Toward a unified science of the mind-brain.* Cambridge, MA: MIT Press.

Clynes, M. (1977). *Sentics: The touch of emotions.* New York: Anchor Press/Doubleday.

Dahlhaus, C. (1982). *Esthetics of music* (W. Austin, Trans.). Cambridge, MA: Cambridge University Press. (Original work published 1967)

Damasio, A. R. (1994). *Descartes' error.* New York: G. P. Putnam's Sons.

De Sousa, R. (1990). *The rationality of emotion.* Cambridge, MA: The MIT Press.

Deutsch, D. (1982). The processing of pitch combinations. In D. Deutsch (Ed.), *The psychology of music* (pp. 271–316). New York: Academic Press.

Dissanayake, E. (1992). *Homo aestheticus.* New York: The Free Press.

Dowling, W. J., & Harwood, D. L. (1986). *Music cognition.* Orlando, FL: Academic Press.

Dufrenne, M. (1973). *The phenomenology of aesthetic experience* (E. S. Casey, Trans.) Evanston, IL: Northwestern University Press.

Edelman, G. M. (1992). *Bright air, brilliant fire: On the matter of mind.* New York: Basic Books.

Edelman, G. M. (1995). The wordless metaphor: Visual art and the brain. In *1995 Biennial exhibition* (pp. 32-47). New York: Whitney Museum of American Art, Distributed by Harry N. Abrams, Inc.

Elliott, D. J. (1995). *Music matters.* New York: Oxford University Press.

Ferguson, D. N. (1960). *Music as metaphor: The elements of expression.* Minneapolis, MN: University of Minnesota Press.

Fiske, H. (1992). Structure of cognition and music decision-making. In R. J. Colwell (Ed.), *Handbook of research on music teaching and learning* (pp. 360–376). New York: Schirmer Books.

Gardner, H. (1985). *Frames of mind: The theory of multiple intelligences.* New York: Basic Books.

Gjerdingen, R. O. (1994). Apparent motion in music? *Music Perception, 11* (4), 336–369.

Helmholtz, H. L. F. (1954). *On the sensation of tones* (A. J. Ellis, Trans.). New York: Dover Publications.

Hodges, D. A. (Ed.). (1996). *Handbook of music psychology* (2nd ed.). San Antonio, TX: IMR Press.

Honeck, R. P., Kibler, C., & Firment, M. J. (1987). Figurative language and psychological views of categorization: Two ships in the night? In R. E. Haskell (Ed.), *Cognition and symbolic structures: The psychology of metaphoric transformation* (pp. 103–120). Norwood, NJ: Ablex Publishing.

Hood, J. D. (1977). Psychological and physiological aspects of hearing. In M. Critchley & R. A. Henson (Eds.), *Music and the brain: Studies in the neurology of music* (pp. 32–47). Springfield, IL: Charles C. Thomas.

Ihde, D. (1976). *Listening and voice: A phenomenology of sound.* Athens, OH: Ohio University Press.

James, W. (1985). *Psychology: The briefer course.* Notre Dame, IN: University of Notre Dame Press.

Kivy, P. (1989). *Sound sentiment: An essay on the musical emotions, including the complete text of the Corded Shell.* Philadelphia, PA: Temple University Press.

Lakoff, G. (1987). *Women, fire, and dangerous things: What categories reveal about the mind.* Chicago, IL: University of Chicago Press.

Lakoff, G., & Johnson, M. (1980). *Metaphors we live by.* Chicago, IL: University of Chicago Press.

Lerdahl, F., & Jackendoff, R. (1983). *A generative theory of tonal music.* Cambridge, MA: The MIT Press.

Lippman, E. A. (1952). *Music and space: A study in the philosophy of music.* Unpublished doctoral dissertation, Columbia University.

Mandler, G. (1984). *Mind and body.* New York: W. W. Norton.

Marks, L. E. (1978). *The unity of the senses: Interrelations among the modalities.* New York: Academic Press.

Marks, L. E., & Bornstein, M. H. (1987). Sensory similarities: Classes, characteristics and cognitive consequences. In R. E. Haskell (Ed.), *Cognition and symbolic structures: The psychology of metaphoric transformation* (pp. 49–65). Norwood, NJ: Ablex Publishing Corporation.

Pike, A. (1970). *A phenomenological analysis of musical experience and other essays.* New York: St. John's University Press.

Radocy, R. E., & Boyle, J. D. (1979). *Psychological foundations of musical behavior* (2nd ed.). Springfield, IL: Charles C. Thomas.

Scruton, R. (1983). *The aesthetic understanding: Essays in the philosophy of art and culture.* London: Methuen.

Wilson, F. R. (1986). *Tone deaf and all thumbs: An invitation to music-making for late bloomers and non-prodigies.* New York: Viking Penguin.

Wis, R. M. (1993). *Gesture and body movement as physical metaphor to facilitate learning and to enhance musical experience in the choral rehearsal.* Unpublished doctoral dissertation, Northwestern University.

Zuckerkandl, V. (1956). *Sound and symbol: Music and the external world.* Princeton, NJ: Princeton University Press.

Part 2
Perspectives in Practice

Learning made cymbal

8

Harvard's Teaching for Understanding
Applications to Music Education

Brenda Bush Poelman

When I left Harvard after an intensive week at the Project Zero Classroom 2000: Views on Understanding Institute, my most vivid memory was of my growth as I began to connect the unfamiliar terminology used in the Teaching for Understanding (TfU) framework to my own teaching and beliefs about learning. The Institute was a journey into the Project Zero perspective during which I slowly assimilated someone else's language and ways of thinking about teaching.

I observed a variety of comfort levels among participants over the course of my week at Harvard. Some sought answers in the form of formulas and prescriptions to take back and share with other teachers in their schools. Some asked many questions, while others sat quietly absorbing the TfU framework. Many participants furiously wrote down each word being spoken, possibly hoping that if they returned to the words of these master teachers, the approach would begin to make sense. Others nodded their heads affirmingly, while another handful of participants appeared to shut down.

Lois Hetland, a researcher at Harvard Project Zero, shared a children's poem with us during the Institute. I believe that it expresses admirably the sentiments of those attending the TfU Institute. Not only were we confused about TfU but, when we began to question our teaching and think differently about the level of understanding our students gained in the classroom, we became very uncomfortable. It is distressing to think that I had been satisfied primarily with atomistic tasks in the classroom and expected little thinking beyond that.

A centipede was happy quite
Until a frog in fun,
Said, "Pray which leg comes after which?"
This raised her mind to such a pitch,
She lay distracted in a ditch
Considering how to run.
    Anonymous

A week of experiences with TfU did not provide easy or clear answers. There were no recipes. Nevertheless, not only did I experience learning for understanding, but the presenters modeled behaviors and techniques that represented teaching for understanding. That was exciting. There was no disconnection between what the presenters said and what they did; their lives as scholars mirrored their lives as learners. As a participant, not only did I gather knowledge but I was asked to do thought provoking tasks such as explaining, making generalizations, and working to apply my understanding on my own and with others. The Institute included large group plenary sessions, small study groups, open question-and-answer periods, mini courses where participants put knowledge from the week into action, and ongoing assessment through journaling in reflection pages. Social receptions allowed participants opportunities to get to know each other and provided a forum for open discussion about the topics of the week.

Do we teach for understanding? "Teaching for understanding? Everybody does that!" may be a first response. But I would challenge each of us to think more deeply and ask ourselves more questions. We must confront our own naïve theories about learning. In addition, we must face our misconceptions about teaching and learning and their impact on our students. While this is not a comfortable process it is one that we cannot afford to ignore. The purpose of my chapter is to share my initiation into the Project Zero TfU framework; it was an experience that transformed me as a teacher. My intent is to assist other educators who wish to make understanding a more achievable goal in their classrooms. I will begin by examining three challenges that we face in implementing TfU in contemporary schools.

Obstacles to Teaching for Understanding

Understanding becomes an unlikely outcome of schooling when you look at the counter-forces present in education as a whole. Students' naïve concepts, counterproductive disciplinary traditions, and mindless practice in schools present three serious obstacles facing educators.

The first obstacle relates to the naïve concepts or theories children form during their early life experiences and bring with them to the classroom. Some of these theories about the world are useful. Some of these ideas, however, are not well grounded and will delay or prevent deeper understanding. They are misconceptions or misunderstandings.

These misconceptions do not disappear with age but unfortunately endure in our attempt to cover too much material in a superficial manner and in our inability to recognize their persistence (Gardner, 1999, p. 73). Identifying students' naïve concepts is not an easy task. The only way to correct this miseducation is by providing stronger theories to confront and change naïve theories. A teacher needs information about students' existing understandings in order to promote conceptual change and a new comprehension of a topic that students can put into action.

Teaching for understanding requires us to "unlearn" deeply held knowledge and many protected misconceptions about the process of teaching and learning. We undoubtedly possess "working theories" of pupils' musical development that are implicitly formulated (Hargreaves, 1996). We typically, however, build these working theories on the basis of our experience and neither seek to articulate nor test their usefulness. We need to uncover our conceptions so we can examine them to expose misconceptions and link our ideas to educational research and sound practice. We must support our practice with research that takes into account the social, cultural, and educational context in which our teaching occurs rather than just good intentions.

A second obstacle involves the counterproductive disciplinary traditions that are frequently employed in our educational systems. Curricula in all subjects abound with topics taught because of their *perceived* importance to the discipline. For example, while children may be able to perform a rhythm ostinato to accompany a song, the objective is cut off from the function and social contexts of music in students' lives. There is little consideration as to whether these topics contribute to students' understanding of the discipline (Perkins, 1988, p. 40). This obstacle is reinforced by the strict adoption of prescribed methods that do not foster musical understanding and by strict adherence to the U.S. Voluntary

National Standards in music education (Consortium of National Arts Education Associations, 1994) as a disconnected series of accomplishments. Music educators frequently fail to develop in children an understanding of how to learn, create, describe, and interpret music well enough to continue music making beyond the music classroom. In too many cases, students can successfully imitate teachers and/or follow specific directives in the classroom, but this method limits their musical development. Too many students leave the classroom unable to function musically after school lessons are over. We can cover all curricular requirements and still have students who are leaving our classrooms without understanding. Raising standards without developing more skillful teaching and more supportive schooling will only result in greater failure.

Music educators often hesitate to work with music outside their own culture or outside their own mental representations. We too often listen to children with a preconceived adult schema of Western art music. This myopia can create destructive disconnections between students, teacher, and music. To omit music initiated by the voices of our students is to hinder the growth of musical understanding. Music must be experienced in a personal way cognitively, emotionally, and physically (Camp, 1981).

Baily and Doubleday (1987) suggest that the study of enculturation is one of the keys to building upon students' musical understanding. Taking into account the interrelationship between culture and music can assist teachers in recognizing how cognitive schemata are built up and reveals the kinds of information necessary for the development of deeper understandings. Cultural understanding and an awareness of self and world help to illuminate the nature of musicality.

A third obstacle is the prevalence of mindlessness in schools today. Classroom structure involves prescribed automatic routines. Much of our school day is spent in overly structured tasks. Assessment tools encompass traditional evaluative practices such as true-and-false, fill-in-the-blank, or multiple-choice paper-and-pencil tests. And unfortunately, teachers still operate in authoritarian information structures that strip students of the respect central to democratic practice and good schooling.

In many ways, mindlessness is systemic. Our views quickly become anchored as a result of our experience and our interaction with like-minded individuals. The substance of our own learning often pigeon-holes us into our perspective, confines our view, and limits how we will respond in the future. In the course of our automatic actions we lose sight of how our positions and mindsets are constructing our thinking (Meier, 1995). Asking critical questions is dismissed. We see our behavior as "normal."

Teaching for Understanding

Typically we believe we can determine if a student knows something. Indeed, we feel affirmed when a student can reproduce knowledge upon request. Students are familiar with the cycle of practicing and remembering, but do they understand? Knowing is not enough. "The mystery boils down to this: Knowing is a state of possession. But understanding goes beyond possession. The person who understands is capable of going beyond the information given" (Perkins, 1992, p. 77). Gardner (1991) clarifies the issues:

> "Understanding involves a mastery of the productive practices in a domain or discipline, coupled with the capacity to adopt different stances toward the work, among them the stances of audience member, critic, performer, and maker."
> (Gardner, 1991)

> Production ought to lie at the center of any artistic experience. Understanding involves a mastery of the productive practices in a domain or discipline, coupled with the capacity to adopt different stances toward the work, among them the stances of audience member, critic, performer, and maker. The "understander" in the arts is one who can comfortably move among the various stances. (p. 239)

Unfortunately, many of our students leave school without understanding, and even the best students in our best schools do not understand much of their curricular content.

> Students at MIT and Johns Hopkins perform credibly in classroom exercises. But consider what happens outside of class, when they are asked to explain relatively simple phenomena, such as the forces operating on a tossed coin, or the trajectory of a pellet after it has been propelled through a curved tube. Not only do more than half fail to give the appropriate explanation; even worse, they tend to give the same kinds of answers as peers and young children who have never

studied mechanics. Despite years of schooling these college students remain fundamentally unschooled. (Gardner, 1991, p. 46)

Some of our teachers have similar problems when it comes to teaching music. Recently, a first grade teacher shared with me that she was helping reinforce the work I was doing on steady beat with her class. When she and the class demonstrated their progress, I was shocked to find that they were clapping the rhythm of the words and calling what they were doing "clapping the beat." This teacher had completed her educational training without ever understanding the difference between beat and rhythm in music. No wonder students don't understand.

Teaching for understanding is not a new idea, but despite all of our educational endeavors, understanding still seems elusive. The TfU framework originated in 1988 with three faculty members at the Harvard Graduate School of Education—Howard Gardner, David Perkins, and Vito Perrone—who wanted to explore with teachers what teaching for understanding would look like. Subsequently, research teams at over a hundred institutions dedicated five years to defining understanding, determining what classroom practices support understanding, and establishing how best to assess understanding. The TfU framework is the result of this commitment.[1]

Teaching for understanding requires that the learner move beyond the conceptual to performance: the TfU framework helps students put knowledge into action to demonstrate their understanding. Teaching for understanding closes the gap between ideas and actions. Understanding something is a matter of being able to think and act flexibly with what you know.[2]

Developing understanding means doing things and using knowledge in new situations to solve problems.[3] Understanding occurs when knowledge takes action. Thus, students demonstrate understanding

[1] For more information on the history of the TfU project go to http://pzweb.harvard.edu/.

[2] I am writing on the basis of my experiences with the TfU framework, which includes access to an extensive bibliography, conversations with educators using the framework, and participation in a number of related conferences, including Project Zero Classroom: Views on Understanding 2000.

[3] For a more extensive exploration of the dimensions of understanding see Chapters 6 and 7 in M. S. Wiske, Ed., *Teaching for Understanding: Linking Research with Practice* (San Francisco: Jossey-Bass Publishers, 1998).

when they generate music (in performing, composing, or writing what they hear), listen perceptively (to performances of their own compositions and the compositions of others), and think critically about what they are hearing (thinking on the spot and reflecting over time, in speech, in writing, or in non-verbal ways). The most effective learning occurs when these modes are combined (Davidson et al., 1992). The language of understanding is possessive: students have an understand-

> Students demonstrate understanding when they generate music, listen perceptively, and think critically about what they are hearing.

ing, possess an understanding, grasp something, apprehend something, get it!

TfU is a thinking frame. It is not a formula. David Perkins' term "thinking frames" suggests how the ideas of the TfU framework can work. Perkins defined thinking frames as "representations intended to guide the process of thought, supporting, organizing, and catalyzing that process" (1986, p. 7). A thinking frame organizes our thinking much as the viewfinder gives focus and direction to our compositions as we take pictures. The thinking frame does not define in advance the answers we will get; it is up to us to fill in the content of a frame.

The TfU Language

What the framework has helped me do is find ways of thinking that guide my process of thinking and understanding about music, children, learning, teaching, and instructional contexts. Understanding can become explicit using the pedagogy of TfU. The TfU framework highlights four key elements: generative topics, under-

> The TfU framework highlights four key elements:
> - generative topics,
> - understanding goals,
> - performances of understanding, and
> - ongoing assessment.

standing goals, performances of understanding, and ongoing assessment.[4] This language fosters curricula that address the questions sur-

---

[4] These four elements are discussed in a number of sources related to the TfU framework including Blythe and Associates (1998), Hetland (1997), Perkins (1992), Unger (1994), and Wiske (1998).

rounding understanding. Teaching for Understanding is neither a prescriptive nor a linear process. The elements do not necessarily have to be approached in any order, but the following sequence provides access to the process.

Generative Topics

No matter what the curriculum, teachers must make choices about what to teach. The nature of these choices is significant. In making a decision to "get through" all the material in a curriculum, teachers assume little responsibility for making selections among given topics. In addition, the use of standardized tests in music is impacting on the curriculum. Standardized testing can alter the content and pacing of instruction and compel teachers to teach to the content of the tests (Darling-Hammond & Wise, 1985). Test-based instruction prompts teachers to equate student learning with test results and promotes the adoption of fast-paced teaching directly to the test. Nevertheless, even under these restrictive conditions teachers remain the ultimate decision-maker concerning what to teach. How will valuable classroom time be used?

Developing understanding takes more time, and as a result, places a greater burden on the teacher to determine what is worth knowing (especially in the limited amount of class time allocated to music instruction). How can teachers decide which topics are worth the investment of time it takes to promote understanding? What material will be the most enticing, interesting, informative, and awakening? The TfU framework's answer to these questions is *generative topics*.

> "Generative topics are issues, themes, concepts, ideas, and so on that provide enough depth, significance, connections, and variety of perspective to support students' development of powerful understandings." (Boix Mansilla, James, & Jaramillo, 1998)

Generative topics are central to the discipline, exciting to students and teachers, accessible to students, and also foster multiple connections, think-points, and entry points (Hetland, 1997). "Generative topics are issues, themes, concepts, ideas, and so on that provide enough depth, significance, connections, and variety of perspective to support students' development of powerful understandings" (Boix Mansilla, James, & Jaramillo, 1998, p. 25). Issues that foster understanding allow students to gain the skills and understandings necessary to advance successfully to more sophisticated work in the domain. These tend to be issues that would be of interest to professionals in the field. Topics that are central to a discipline should also connect with other related disciplines.

A good generative topic is engaging and accessible. These features allow students to engage the topic successfully and enthusiastically. The generativity of a topic varies with the cultural and social contexts, the personal interests of the teacher and students, and the students' past experiences and ages. It is vital that the topic be accessible through varied and appropriate resources so that it can be addressed through a number of different strategies.

A teacher's passion and curiosity about a topic should help drive the motivations of students. The teacher models how to explore, question, and investigate unfamiliar territory. A teacher with a passion for a topic will approach it with more zest and imagination and display a greater readiness to engage students in deep learning. Teachers can be resources while students assume more responsibility for their own learning, much as do professional musicians. Our efforts to understand naturally engage us.

Finally, the generative topics selected should foster multiple connections, think-points, and entry points (ways into the topic). A generative topic can be connected to diverse themes within and beyond the discipline and connect to students' lives and past experiences. The degree of relevance a topic has to the lives of the students will determine the degree of student motivation. A good generative topic contains an element of openness to the development of increasingly deeper understandings. In music, examples of generative goals are: How do the elements of music combine to create music compositions? Why does some music stick around for so long? Why is music important to people?

Understanding Goals

The maze of opportunities created through generative topics can be very overwhelming. Generative topics require careful consideration and, in turn, scrupulous selectivity of understanding goals. In determining understanding goals or throughlines[5] begin with the question, "Just what is it that the learners should strive to understand?" *Understanding goals* are statements or questions that focus

> Understanding goals are statements or questions that focus instruction on learning what is most important.

instruction on learning what is most important in a domain. They can be thought of as a system of bridges between a conceptual world of thought and a world of practical activity and exploration. Understanding goals help teachers see connections as they are planning instruction and help students make those connections as they construct their learning.

Goals can be stated: "Students will understand..." or "Students will appreciate..." or they can be phrased in the form of open-ended questions: "What are the important similarities and differences...?" Understanding goals are identified by the teacher, who may invite suggestions from students. The TfU framework recommends three, but no more than five, understanding goals per topic. Understanding goals help teachers and students stay focused during the learning process. Students need to be informed of what teachers are asking them to pursue so that they can join in defining and pursuing the primary agenda. The important thing to remember is that the purpose of throughlines/understanding goals is to help clarify what it is important to learn and which of the many possible teachable moments is most valuable.

Student understanding is an internal event that can be assessed when mental representations are made public through actions or performances. An ongoing process of informative feedback enhances both performances and mental representations (Boix Mansilla, 1998, p. 50). Through engagement in work that requires thinking and that is directly

---

[5] The word "throughline" is frequently used by Project Zero faculty interchangeably with "understanding goals." The idea of throughlines originates from Stanislavski's method acting school; it signifies a fundamental theme in a play on which an actor can focus the portrayal of his or her character. The term is used in the context of TfU because understanding goals tend to be ones that teachers and students revisit over the course of a year or semester.

linked to understanding goals, students transform ideas on the topic into more comprehensive and systematic understanding.

Understanding Performances/Performances of Understanding

As stated previously, understanding something is a matter of being able to think and act flexibly with what you know. Thoughts and actions that show such flexibility and expand understanding further are called understanding performances or *performances of understanding*. "In performances of understanding students reshape, expand on, extrapolate from, and apply what they already know. Such performances challenge students' misconceptions" (Gould, 1998, p. 62).

> "In performances of understanding students reshape, expand on, extrapolate from, and apply what they already know. Such performances challenge students' misconceptions."
> (Gould, 1998)

Early in the learning process performances should provide opportunities to begin working with and exploring a topic. The next phase may be a more guided inquiry with a more systematic approach on several aspects of the understanding goals. A culminating performance might involve an effective performance of an individually chosen activity. Words such as "doing, thinking, linking, singing, collaborating, acting, interviewing, explaining" are examples of the language of the process. In performances of understanding learners need to: generalize, classify, predict, infer, and make analogies; challenge misconceptions, stereotypes, and rigid parameters of thinking; and try again and think again over and over, refining and reiterating throughout the process.

There are some criteria that will assist teachers in selecting performances of understanding. First, performances should relate directly to the understanding goals for the given unit. Understanding performances should encompass a number of activities that progress from introductory understandings to deeper and broader understandings. These performances should engage multiple learning styles and forms of expression. The performance must demand critical reflection in conjunction with an action. Finally, understanding performances need to be visible in their outcomes, if not in their process. Learners have to be able to self-assess their own performances, and an opportunity for others to offer feedback should be provided. When understanding is the goal, students need to participate in performances of understanding from the beginning to the end of every unit.

Understanding performances vary in the form in which understanding is made visible. For example, a teacher may have students brainstorm all the ways in which we use music in our society. The next performance of understanding may ask students to keep a log of all the places and ways in which they experienced music in 24 hours. In small groups students might discuss the music they encountered and decide when they enjoyed the experience and why. Students may be asked to create a presentation entitled "If there were no music...." In small groups, students might choose a piece of music and share their responses to it. Students might debate the use of music in different forms of media (examining patterns or structures that link certain forms of music to specific forms of media). Finally, students might work in small groups to create a plan for developing awareness about the presence of music in their community. All the activities should help students deepen their understandings. Understanding goals state what students should understand, and performances of understanding are what students do to develop and demonstrate those understandings.

There are challenges to be addressed related to this process. Many students and teachers are not used to making understanding explicit. There may be resistance to thinking and acting with what you know about music. Reflecting about music, writing in music class, recording work, analyzing music, exploring instruments, making presentations in music, debating issues in music, or having homework in music may be new actions in the music classroom. Guidance, instruction, creating a safe environment, and modeling the technique or system of providing constructive feedback will be important parts of the teacher's role. In addition, it is vital that the teacher be the exemplar of good questions and critically framed responses. Teachers and students are not necessarily familiar with explicit documentation of musical learning.

In selecting performances of understanding, teachers encounter the challenge of assessing the cultural relevance of a specific performance (Boix Mansilla, 1998, p. 50). Do the performances we ask our students to carry out represent the conduct we expect from them as members of a society? Performances of understanding are context-dependent. David

Elliot (1995) wrote about the context-dependence of developing musicianship:

> Developing musicianship is essentially a matter of induction: students must enter and become part of the musical practices (or music cultures) they intend to learn. This is so because music is context-dependent. The musicianship underlying any practice of music making and listening has its roots in specific communities of practitioners who share and advance a specific tradition of musical thinking. (p. 67)

Performances of understanding emphasize the root of our educational efforts: to help students understand the social, natural, and cultural world around them and to prepare them to perform in such a world as active contributors of their society (Gardner, 1993). When students engage in performances that resemble the actual performances valued by society it is possible to make a better prediction about how these students are progressing toward their educational goals. Performances of understanding provide us with a more valid assessment of students' abilities to use what they know in innovative contexts.

Ongoing Assessment

Understanding is not just something one has or does not; it is something that grows over time. Therefore, teachers must use effective *ongoing assessment* to check regularly about understanding. Ongoing assessment is the fourth element of the TfU framework. This category recognizes that feedback is an essential tool in learning. Learners benefit from the opportunity to refine performances, repair misunderstandings, and revise products. Teacher's benefit from using assessment as a means of informing instruction. Both benefit from making standards of work explicit.

Identifying principal components of the ongoing assessment process will help in establishing a supportive pattern of ongoing assessment. Having clear criteria that are closely related to the understanding goals helps

> Ongoing assessment needs to evaluate student progress and, in turn, inform future planning.

students. Opportunities for multiple sources of feedback should be provided. Ongoing assessment can be formal and planned or more casual, such as a class discussion. Finally, ongoing assessment needs to evaluate student progress and in turn, inform future planning. Ongoing assessment, both formal and informal, by students and by teachers reveals profiles of development and fosters learning and new levels of achievement.

There are a number of difficulties related to selecting modes of assessment in music. Music consists of sequential aural sensations. Any musical performance is based on sensations produced by the brain of the teacher and the performer. While both may agree on objective assessment of correct notes, many decisions about phrasing, tone quality, tempi, and ornamentation are the subjective decisions of individuals. The assessment of a musical experience is based on subjectivity, but a subjectivity tempered by cultural traditions. This subjectivity can make it difficult to determine exactly what is being measured in a performance of understanding, unless cultural norms are considered.

A further difficulty involves determining students' representations of knowledge. How one initially thinks about a problem can determine how difficult it is to solve (Bruner, 1993, p. 291). Sometimes, a poor initial representation, naïve theory, makes it impossible for students to solve a problem. With ill-structured problems the initial representation can influence not only how we solve a problem but also what we accept as a satisfactory answer. We must be sure to provide opportunities that transform representations into solutions that guide our students' understanding performances. It is important to provide quality examples.

Jeanne Bamberger (1991) has done a great deal of research on the concept of musical representation or schemata. She observed children solving problems in puzzling ways and began to test assumptions concerning the nature of melodic structure and the implications built into our system of description as these refer to pitch and pitch relations. The subjects worked with Montessori bells[6] in order to build a tune—"Hot Cross Buns" or "Twinkle Twinkle." The second part of the experiment asked participants to make instructions so someone else could play on the bells as they had set them up. Bamberger observed:

---

[6] Montessori and Maccheroni designed the Montessori bells. Each individual bell is mushroom shaped; a metal bell attached to a wooden stand. The bells are all the same size, shape, and color, and the only way to distinguish differences in

a crucial part of that process for which change in inner strategies for constructing musical relations is one of *progressive articulation*: a gradual coming apart of the possible features and relations of musical structures that are initially taken as unitary wholes and that are rigid particularly in their sequential ordering. As a result of this rigidity, the constituents of musical structures—for example, pitch, duration, tune-events, the embodiment in the bells, and the sequence of actions on them—can at first only be given meaning in *the fixed order in which they occur*. (p. 264)

Teachers must be able to recognize this developmental factor and work to liberate representations from their dependence on fixed order. Through a multitude of performances of understanding children will begin to construct new understandings. Bamberger commented on the learning process.

In order to understand the conventional names that are given to objects, a child must first differentiate, sometimes even construct, and then pull out from the multiple *possible* features of objects, the particular property that is the relevant one—the one that names names. (p. 282)

There are two important questions teachers should ask: (1) How can we deepen and expand our understanding of children's construction of their knowledge and skills? (2) What are the connections between the mental images recalled from memory, verbal language, and visual language? These questions can be drawn into the discipline of music in a number of ways. Children hear music everyday, but what do they really hear in the music? Do they sense that it has an important presence? What do they know about music? What relationships do they have with music? Understanding how students represent knowledge will not only assist teachers in recognizing the needs of their students but will enable teachers to develop effective modes of assessment that measure change and growth.

---

pitch is through actually playing the bells. This feature allows students to focus solely on pitch.

Implementing TfU

The TfU Graphic Organizer (see Figure 1) facilitates visual connections among the TfU elements: between unit-long understanding goals, unit-long understanding goals and the performances that support them, performances of understanding and ongoing assessment processes, and performances of understanding and the skills students need to carry them out.

Figure 1. A Graphic Organizer for TfU Units

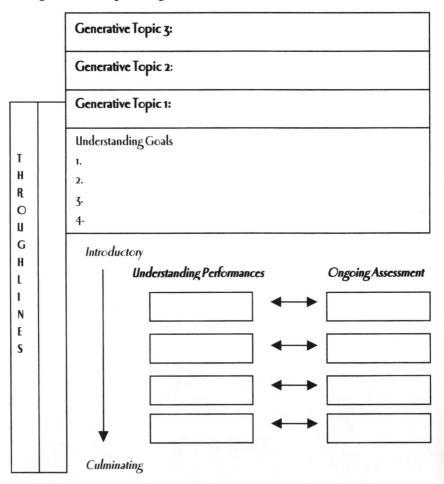

This organizer is just one possibility for representing and documenting a TfU unit. It is helpful in that it is possible to see how all of the elements fit together. The Graphic Organizer is *not* the TfU framework; it is merely one representation of the framework. After becoming more comfortable with the language of TfU, teachers are urged to create their own representation. The one presented in Figure 1 is mine.

Planning curriculum and classroom lessons is a very personalized activity. Each teacher may approach the process differently. There are teachers who have used the framework and shared their strategies. The following are recommendations they have made for implementing the TfU framework.

Start small and with something familiar. Go back to a unit or lesson that you felt was successful and recast it using the TfU language. Write some understanding goals for your lesson. Continue by examining and analyzing the lesson or unit. How could you refine and improve the unit? How are you helping students develop understandings? What can your students demonstrate as a result of this lesson or unit? These questions are vital to the process of teaching for understanding.

An additional recommendation involves finding your support systems. If we are isolated in our thinking it is difficult to get out of our pigeonholes. Get on-line; read books that will serve as good models; and find some insightful and mindful colleagues to use as sounding boards. We are more engaged with our work when we have a community that shares educational goals, when we are given encouragement to improve our teaching, when we share in developing practice, and when we relate to one another as persons outside the school context (Bryk & Driscoll, 1988).

Reflection is vital to success. Keep a journal and record your thoughts, questions, concerns, and attempts. Use your journal as a safe place to challenge your own intellect. Seeing this information in written form may provide you with the new perspective you need.

Demonstrate your understanding of the TfU framework by talking to others about it. Use your new language very deliberately. Disseminate information to parents, colleagues, and your students. Teachers need strong school-wide and community support in the enterprise of education. The more clearly the language is understood, the more people will be empowered to dialogue with you. Their support may help you in achieving your goals.

Lastly, be clear and make choices about when you are going to use the framework. You can, from time to time, put memorization up front. Learn when the interactive constructivist forms of teaching and learning are called for and when more traditional strategies might be appropriate. Biting off more than you can chew will most likely result in failure. Decide how and when you will use your TfU approaches and when you will not.

Difficulties in Implementing TfU

Implementing this framework is not without its difficulties. It seems as though more and more is being asked of us and of our time. We are to the point where understanding is just one of many agendas. When I was teaching in Waukesha, Wisconsin, our teachers were implementing a yearlong program addressing bullying. We were also working to promote a campaign for positive attitudes. Many of the students in our school were in special education and required additional time for lesson modification, behavior tracking programs, and consultation meetings. These were some of the demands in addition to the typical appeals for time. such as after school and recess duty. Musical understanding was but one of many goals.

As teachers, we often feel powerless about making our own decisions about our practice. The public sector embraces substantial diversity in the form and function of schools. Trends toward the increased control of teachers strip us of our capacity to make professional judgments. These outside forces are sometimes strong enough to shape our judgments about our practice and defeat a desire to improve our teaching.

Another very serious issue is testing. There is more and more pressure on teachers to improve the test scores of their students. This direction is unfortunate because these tests typically do little to support understanding. There is a high premium on the quantification of educational results. Unfortunately, it is difficult to quantify understanding in this way.

Making everyday choices about what material, activities, and assessments will best support teaching for understanding is a very time consuming process (Perkins, 1998, p. 11). Teaching for understanding requires content knowledge but also pedagogical knowledge.

A final difficulty is that there are very few music teachers utilizing TfU in their classrooms. Six months after the Project Zero Institute I contacted nine of the participants on the roster who had listed themselves as being involved with music. After questioning them about their success in implementing TfU into their work, I received no positive responses of marked progress. While there is significant research reporting on the use of TfU in science and math studies, research in music is scarce. The issues are complex and call for serious reflection. Even if there are difficulties, shouldn't understanding be a priority?

Through transformative reflection and critical thinking we can make adjustments in our representations of intelligence, learning, and the role of educational research. As we become willing to reflect and as our students increasingly become able to use what they are learning in meaningful and diverse contexts, the cloud over understanding will be lifted. In our willingness to risk and seek better ways, we will begin to find understanding. I have accepted the challenge.

References

Baily, J., & Doubleday, V. (1987). Patterns of musical enculturation in Afghanistan. In F. Roehmann & F. Wilson (Eds.), *Music and child development* (pp. 88–99). St. Louis, MO: MMB Music.

Bamberger, J. (1991). *The mind behind the musical ear: How children develop musical intelligence.* Cambridge, MA: Harvard University Press.

Blythe, T., & Gould, D. (1998). Performances of understanding. In T. Blythe (Ed.), *The Teaching for Understanding Guide* (pp. 55–70). San Francisco: Jossey-Bass Publishers.

Blythe, T., & Associates. (1998). *The teaching for understanding guide.* San Francisco, CA: Jossey-Bass Publishers.

Boix Mansilla, V. (1998). Beyond the lessons from the cognitive revolution. *Canadian Social Studies, 32* (2), 49–51.

Boix Mansilla, V., Phillip J., & Jaramillo, R. (1998). Generative topics. In T. Blythe (Ed.), *The Teaching for Understanding Guide* (pp. 25–34). San Francisco: Jossey-Bass Publishers.

Bruner, J. (1993). *Schools for thought: A science of learning in the classroom.* Cambridge MA: MIT Press.

Bryk, A., & Driscoll, M. E. (1988). *An empirical investigation of the school as community.* Chicago, IL: University of Chicago School of Education.

Camp, M. (1981). *Developing piano performance: A teaching philosophy.* Chapel Hill, NC: Hinshaw Music.

Consortium of National Arts Education Associations. (1994). *National standards for arts education.* Reston, VA: Music Educators National Conference.

Darling-Hammond, L., & Wise, A. E. (1985). Beyond standardization: State standards and school improvement. *The Elementary School Journal, 85* (3), 315–56.

Davidson, L., et al. (1992). *Arts PROPEL: A handbook for music.* Cambridge, MA: Harvard Project Zero and Educational Testing Service.

Elliott, D. (1995). *Music matters: A new philosophy of music education.* New York: Oxford University Press.

Gardner, H. (1999). *The disciplined mind: What all students should understand.* New York: Simon & Schuster.

Gardner, H. (1993). *Multiple intelligences: Theory into practice. A reader.* New York: Basic Books.

Gardner, H. (1991). *The unschooled mind: How children should think and how schools should teach.* New York: Basic Books.

Hargreaves, D. (1996). The development of artistic and musical competence. In I. Deliège & J. Sloboda (Eds.), *Musical Beginnings* (pp. 145–170). Oxford, UK: Oxford University Press.

Hetland, L. (1997). Teaching for understanding. In S. Veenema, L. Hetland, & C. Chalfen (Eds.), *The Project Zero classroom: New approaches to thinking and understanding* (pp. 20–39). Cambridge, MA: Project Zero.

Meier, D. (1995). *The power of their ideas: Lessons for America from a small school in Harlem.* Boston, MA: Beacon.

Perkins, D. (1986). Thinking frames. *Educational Leadership, 43* (8), 4–10.

Perkins, D. N. (1988). Art as an occasion of intelligence. *Educational Leadership, 45* (4), 36–43.

Perkins, D. N. (1992). *Smart schools: From training memories to educating minds.* New York: The Free Press.

Perkins, D. N. (1998). Understanding understanding. In T. Blythe (Ed.), *The teaching for understanding guide* (pp. 9–16). San Francisco, CA: Jossey-Bass Publishers.

Unger, C. (1994). What teaching for understanding looks like. *Educational Leadership, 51* (5), 22–23.

Wiske, M.S. (Ed.). (1998). *Teaching for understanding: Linking research with practice.* San Francisco, CA: Jossey-Bass Publishers.

Teaching Music through Problem Solving

Jackie Wiggins

Learning is a constructivist act. In order to learn, people need to have opportunities to construct their own understanding. Based on this perspective, learning theorists suggest that the optimum learning situation is one in which students engage in interactive problem solving. If learning occurs through problem solving, then teachers need to conceive of the process of lesson planning as problem setting.

Perspectives On Problem Solving

References to the connections between problem solving and learning date back to some of the earliest writings on education, including the work of early theorists like Plato, Locke, and Rousseau. Throughout the early twentieth century, John Dewey wrote prolifically about a progressive vision of education that was based on learning through hands-on, real-life problem solving experiences. In his 1938 publication *Experience and Education*, he talked about the nature of good teaching problems as those which allow the learner to work at his present level of expertise, using what he has already mastered but piquing the curiosity of the learner such that he will be motivated to move beyond his present level of expertise to pursue higher levels of understanding and competence. The solutions of well-constructed problems should lead to interest in new problems such that learning becomes a continuous process:

> [P]roblems are the stimulus to thinking....Growth depends on the presence of difficulty to be overcome by the exercise of intelligence....
> It is part of the educator's responsibility to see equally to two things:
> First, that the problem grows out of the conditions of the experience

157

being had in the present, and that it is within the range of the capacity of students; and, secondly, that it is such that it arouses in the learner an active quest for information and production of new ideas. The new facts and new ideas thus obtained become the ground for further experiences in which new problems are presented. The process is a continuous spiral. (p. 79)

In the 1960 landmark publication *The Process of Education*, Jerome Bruner considered "mastery" or expertise in a field of knowledge to be reflected in an individual's ability to solve problems within that field.

Mastery of the fundamental ideas of a field involves not only grasping of general principles, but also the development of an attitude toward learning and inquiry, toward guessing and hunches, toward the possibility of solving problems on one's own. (p. 20)

Bruner was the first to articulate that mastering a field of knowledge means formulating understanding of the structural elements of that field. It is his work that caused music educators to begin focusing on teaching musical concepts in the late 1960s and early 1970s. In his view, part of the development of competence in a field involves the ability to use structural understanding to solve problems.

In 1983, when Howard Gardner set forth his theory of multiple intelligences, he proposed a definition of an *intelligence* that included the ability to both solve problems and identify new problems within a particular field of knowledge: "An intelligence is the ability to solve problems, or to create problems, that are valued within one or more cultural settings" (Gardner, 1993, p. x).

He went on to describe the role of problem solving with a vision not very different from Bruner's perspective:

To my mind, a human intellectual competence must entail a set of skills of problem solving—enabling the individual *to resolve genuine problems or difficulties* that he or she encounters and, when appropriate, to create an effective product—and must also entail the potential for *finding or creating problems*—thereby laying the groundwork for the acquisition of new knowledge. (pp. 60-61)

Learning Through Problem Solving [1]

Solving problems requires students to use what they know, but also provides opportunities for them to construct new understandings and clarify existing understandings. Some teachers view problem solving as a way of evaluating how much a student understands; therefore, they use it more as a means of assessment than as a teaching tool. It is important to realize that the process is much more complex than that—in the process of using what they know to figure something out, students are also increasing their knowledge base. While students' ability to solve problems certainly provides the teacher with information about the level and depth of their understanding, what is more important is that problem solving is an opportunity to further learning.

Teaching Through Problem Solving

Teaching through problem solving is more of a mindset and approach to classroom experiences than it is a "methodology." If teachers truly understand that students need to figure things out for themselves in order to learn, their way of being in a classroom and ways of interacting with students will reflect that understanding. Sometimes a problem might take only seconds to solve, as in the scenario in Box 1, which draws from an actual case.

Box 1 (Vignette)

> The tenth-grade band was on stage for the final dress rehearsal before their winter concert. As they were playing through one particular work, their teacher stopped the group and asked quickly, "Clarinets, the people who are not with my beat, are they ahead or behind the beat?"
> Students quickly responded, "Behind," to which the teacher replied, "Then can you fix it?" and the rehearsal continued.

---

[1] The remainder of this chapter has been reproduced from *Teaching for Musical Understanding* (Wiggins, 2001), with the kind permission of McGraw-Hill Company.

This momentary exchange lasted less than a minute. What makes it a problem-solving situation is that the teacher put the onus on the students to figure out what the problem was and to solve it rather than telling them what they ought to be doing. Whether teachers plan extended units requiring solutions to complex, long-term problems or simply adjust their ways of interacting with students to put the onus on them to figure things out, the more problem solving they can incorporate into their teaching, the more productive and healthier the learning experiences they design will be for their students.

Collaborative Problem Solving

When students are given opportunities to work with others to solve problems, they learn even more than they might learn working alone because they benefit from the perspectives that others bring to the situation. Interacting with others provides them with a wider range of alternatives and possibilities, helping them see things in ways they may not have thought of on their own. Since knowledge includes not only factual information but also procedural and contextual information, solving problems in collaboration with others provides opportunities for students to expand their palette of choices of procedures and contexts.

Teachers who view problem solving as a "test" of individual progress sometimes see collaboration as "cheating." It is only cheating if there is an expectation of only one right answer and a need to find out who knows that answer and who does not. A well-designed problem has a multitude of solutions, and learners can gain a greater perspective by being a part of more than one of those solutions rather than by seeking the "right" answer.

Further, collaborating with peers provides support for individual learning because it provides individual opportunities for immediate feedback on their ideas. This puts students in the position of having to explain, clarify, or defend their ideas to the group, which causes them to think things through more carefully and often results in a higher level of understanding within the group and on the part of the initiator of the idea. Collaborative problem solving also creates opportunities for modeling. Students can benefit from observing the ways in which both teachers and peers approach problems. From working with others, students can learn new strategies and ways those strategies can be used, providing both procedural and metacognitive models.

The Nature of Good Teaching Problems

The best problems for learning are those that reflect problems that occur in real life within a particular discipline—problems that require students to deal with ideas and understandings intrinsic to that discipline. Solving real-life musical problems means solving problems using the same *thought processes* and *procedures* that real musicians use when they solve musical problems.

Music students need to engage in the same processes as expert musicians do—performing, listening, and creating. Even the youngest students engage in these processes and do not pretend to engage in them in some superficial way. While students will not think and act with the same level of expertise as someone who is highly accomplished in the field, the nature of their thinking and acting should parallel what experts in the field actually do.

The classroom should be a place where students feel that any and all ideas are both welcome and valued by teacher and peers, which makes multiple perspective possible. Not every idea can be expressed through verbal communication. Students need to have available a multitude of ways of expressing their understanding and ideas, including non-verbal means of expression such as gesture and movement, graphic representation, musical expression such as singing, visual expression such as drawing, and so on.

Problems should be designed in a way that allows students to draw upon relevant prior experience to make solving the problem a possibility. This is an important consideration in instructional design. Learning experiences need to be connected in ways that allow students to draw upon previous experiences to solve the problem at hand (see Box 2).

With this understanding, let us consider what teaching music through problem solving might look like.

Box 2. The nature of good teaching problems

In general, good teaching problems:
- reflect real-life problems that occur in the discipline.
- require students to engage in the actual processes of the discipline, thinking and acting in the same way as experts in the discipline.
- require students to deal with the ideas and understandings intrinsic to the discipline
- enable students to formulate and understanding of concepts in a context that is genuinely appropriate to the discipline
- have a multitude of solutions and require students to make choices and decisions based on their understanding of the discipline
- allow for a variety of ways for students to express what they know
- provide opportunities for support from peers and teachers
- require and enable students to use what they know to figure things out for themselves

Teaching Music through Problem Solving

Allowing students opportunities to solve genuine musical problems may prove to be the best way to nurture musical independence in our students. Since students should be engaged in performing, listening, and creating, time spent in a music classroom should entail working to solve performance-based problems, listening-based problems, and creating-based problems. Students should be solving musical problems through engaging in vocal and instrumental performance experiences, analytical listening experiences, and compositional and improvisational experiences. Solving musical problems should enable students to have opportunities to manipulate and make decisions about musical ideas based on what they know and understand about music. Problems should be designed to enable students to develop conceptual understanding of the structural elements of music (pitch, rhythm, form, texture, timbre, etc.) within the context of a genuine musical work (not a work contrived to teach the concept).

Good musical problems involve *musical* thought, which is more than verbal thought *about* music. They should be designed such that students will need to engage in thinking in sound—in hearing musical ideas in their heads, including pitch, duration, timbre, dynamics, tempo, form, texture, and so on. Good musical problems will enable students to act on those musical ideas, either by performing the music they hear in their heads, by analyzing their perceptions of what they hear during listening experiences, or by using their musical ideas to generate original compositions or improvisations—and by evaluating their own musical ideas in all of these contexts.

Teaching music through problem solving can mean designing complex problems that require extended time to solve. Older and more experienced students, in particular, enjoy engaging in long-range, complex projects or units that require a multitude of decisions and actions on the part of the learner. Often, older and more experienced students may work with one particular problem for an entire class period or even longer. They might, for example, participate in a unit that entails a small group composition project based on understandings developed during performance or listening experiences. The performing and/or listening experiences that comprise the introductory stages might occur during one or two class sessions. Students might then tackle the compositional project for two or three class sessions. Followed by a communal sharing of ideas and a culminating lesson extending what was learned during the entire unit. A unit such as this might last as long as six or seven class sessions and might include a series of interconnected problems—an initial performance-based problem, followed by an analytical listening problem, followed by a compositional problem, ending with another analytical listening problem.

Extended units of problem-solving experiences are often necessary to enable students to feel at home in music of an unfamiliar culture. Understandings developed through a long-term series of projects, including opportunity for listening and performing, are essential to the development of understanding of world musics. After extended experience with music of an unfamiliar culture, students might then be asked to improvise or compose in the style of the music they have studied.

However, teaching through problem solving does not always mean designing complex problems that require extended time to solve. It might mean asking students to engage in solving a series of small problems throughout one particular class session. Most often, this will be the case in designing instruction for young and/or inexperienced students. The very youngest students will need to work with more teacher guidance and support, and they will probably not be ready to work independently or to sustain on a project over a long period of time. Older students with little prior work musical experience will not have the knowledge base to work without teacher support although, developmentally, they may be better prepared to maintain attention to a project over a longer period of time. Also, some material is more appropriately organized into a series of smaller problems. This is often the case with introductory experiences where students are experiencing a musical idea for the first time. Such experiences are likely to be organized as whole-group, teacher-guided lessons where the teacher poses a series of problems for the class to work together to solve. In this case, the key often lies in the ways in which the teacher chooses to phrase questions. Teachers can phrase questions in ways that might elicit one "correct" answer or in ways that imply a multitude of possibilities. Teachers can phrase questions in ways that lead students to particular answers or in ways that encourage them to figure things out for themselves (see Box 3).

What does a musical problem look like? Following are some sample musical problems rooted in performing, listening, and creating experiences. It is important to note that in most cases, a problem utilizing one of these musical processes connects to a new problem that utilizes a different process. In other words, listening-based problems often lead quite naturally into creating-based problems that deal with the same musical elements. Performance-based problems often lead quite naturally into listening-based problems, particularly where students listen to and analyze recordings of music they have performed. Creating-based problems are most successful when related to prior performing or listening experiences. Therefore, in the sample problems described below, you will note that they are often linked to additional problems that utilize a different musical process.

Box 3 (Activity)

Which of these questions would you consider to be good, open-ended, problem-solving questions?

* Last week we said that, when a song has two different melodies, we would call the first melody "A" and the second melody...?
* Listen to this song and raise your hand when you think you hear a new section of the melody has begun.
* How can you tell when the music changes its speed? What are some of the things you might be listening for in order to tell?
* Which part of the music in your text looks like it would sound like the music I am singing? Why do you think that?
* How many beats does a quarter note get in 2/4 time?
* If the instruments sound to you like they are not playing together, what might people need to do to fix that problem?

Performance-Based Problems

Performance-based problems can take many different forms, the common thread being that students solve the problem primarily through performing. In some ways, just learning to perform a new song or piece is a musical problem. However, learning to perform the work through imitation of a model is quite different from learning the work through solving problems related to specific aspects of the work. Asking learners to mimic a song line by line does not challenge their ability to reason musically as much as asking them to figure out specific aspects of the song does. Students might be asked to figure out the melodic contour or rhythmic characteristics of a new song or to figure out its form or textural make-up. They might be asked to determine the harmonic structure so they will know what chords to play to accompany their singing. They might be asked to determine appropriate dynamic or tempo changes based on the way they think the work should sound. In each of these cases, they would need to hear the song performed in its entirety many times to make decisions or solve problems. In this way, they become increasingly familiar with the song before ever attempting to sing it themselves. In this process, the teacher is still presenting a model, but the students are learning through their experience with the details of the song and not simply through imitation of the teacher's model.

There are many ways to teach music for performance besides asking students to imitate the teacher—ways that help students to focus on particular elements of the music and to formulate their understanding of the work in terms of those elements. Even in a performance ensemble setting, students can make many of the decisions. They can make decisions about the appropriateness of a particular dynamic level, tempo, choice of chord progression, choice of phrasing, choice of accompanying instrument, or overall balance or intonation of the ensemble. In order to grow as musicians, students need to develop an understanding of *why* musicians make these kinds of decisions and *how* the decisions are made.

Example 1. Sample performance problem. The following is an example of a performance problem based on the round "Hey, Ho! Nobody Home." The problem is designed to help students understand both the contour of the melody and the texture of the round, in addition to learning to perform the melody in a round with peers.

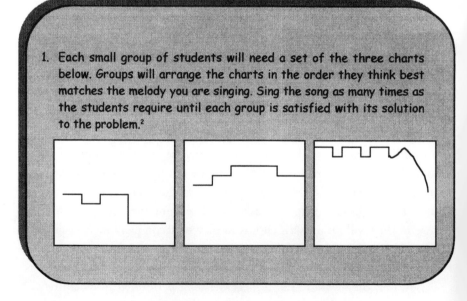

1. Each small group of students will need a set of the three charts below. Groups will arrange the charts in the order they think best matches the melody you are singing. Sing the song as many times as the students require until each group is satisfied with its solution to the problem.[2]

---

[2] Many of the ideas for designing performance problems come from Eunice Boardman, who also advocates teaching music through problem solving.

As they work together to solve the problem, students will most likely sing or hum the melody, or segments of the melody, to themselves. They will also need to talk quietly with peers. This talk will reflect their understanding of the contour of the melody and their ability to describe and communicate their understanding.

2. Once finished arranging the charts, students are generally eager to sing through the melody in its entirety, often tracing their charts as they sing. It would be appropriate at this point for the whole class to try singing the song together, perhaps with teacher accompaniment. The teacher might even suggest that group members trace their contour charts as the class sings to double check their solutions to the problem.

3. This performance-based problem can easily be tied to an analytical listening problem by playing a recording of the song performed as a round and asking the students to describe what they hear. In this case, the problem to be solved is: "What do you hear in the recording that sounds different from our class performance of the song?" Students will probably point out numerous differences, which is appropriate and desirable.

4. Once students have analyzed the recording for its important points, an additional performance-based problem can be introduced. Challenge the students to sing the melody in a round as they heard it on the recording. Ask them to describe what they will have to do in order to carry this out. This is an important step because it can enable those who are uncertain to learn from strategies shared by peers and be more successful as a result.

As suggested in this scenario, these two performance-based problems and one listening-based problem can be combined to create one continuous lesson plan for the students. Upon completion of the lesson, students should have a better understanding of melodic contour and of the texture of a round. They will have had opportunities to improve their personal skills in both graphing and singing melodic contour and in performing one melodic line against an opposing melodic line as a member of an ensemble, an ensemble that shares a common sense of underlying pulse, tonality, and simultaneity. The students are also likely to develop a far greater sense of these musical ideas than they might have in a setting where they were taught solely through imitation of the teacher. A further extension of this lesson could involve students working in pairs using xylophones or keyboards to develop original rounds. Students working from this knowledge base generally produce a melody that they then attempt to play as a round. At this level of experience, one cannot expect that the rounds will define "traditional" harmonies or even operate within a logical rhythmic organization, but the two aspects that have been studied by the students (melodic contour and canonic texture) generally appear in their work in this context.

Learning to perform music through problem-solving experiences fosters a greater understanding of the music performed and of music in general. It is important to approach performance in ways that will enable students to participate meaningfully. This means going beyond asking students to perform through imitation of the teacher—beyond echoing or chanting and then playing a part. It means providing students with the wherewithal to know how to decide what should be played or sung and how and why it should be played or sung in that way.

Listening-Based Problems

Listening-based problems can also take many different forms, the common thread being that students solve the problem primarily through listening—analytical listening, which requires listening for particular features of the work to solve the problem.

One characteristic that is unique to the process of listening is that an observer has no way of knowing what an individual is hearing unless he or she communicates it in some way. A teacher cannot tell whether a student is listening or what he or she is hearing by simply observing what the student is doing. Someone might be gazing out the window but listening intently.

In order to deal with this teaching situation, it is essential that listening-based problems include at least one means of representing and communicating what students hear. Students might be asked to make a gestural or graphic representation of what they hear. They may be asked to organize "puzzle pieces" that graphically represent what the music sounds like. They may be asked to move in a way that shows what they hear. Students sometimes fill in charts with information they glean from the listening experience. They might try to represent what they hear through participating in another art form, such as language arts, visual art, drama, or dance. In each of these cases, it is essential that the focus remain on the music and how the music expresses. One can easily maintain this focus by asking students, "What did you hear in the music that made you decide to move that way (or paint that way, or write that dialogue, etc.)?"[3]

In solving listening-based problems, students might be asked to represent their understanding of formal or textural characteristics of the work or of the organization of dynamic or tempo changes within the work. They might be asked to represent their understanding of pitch, harmonic or rhythmic characteristics, or even stylistic characteristics. Through analytical listening experiences, students broaden their understanding of the ways in which music is put together and the ways in which it operates. One of the perks of asking students to engage in these kinds of activities as they listen is that they find themselves needing to ask to hear the music again and again in order to know how to solve the problem at hand. This aspect is invaluable because repeated listenings afford students opportunities to become more familiar with the music and therefore to experience what the composer and performers are trying to express.

Example 2. Sample listening problems. The following two examples of analytical listening problems are based on a 16th-century Renaissance dance, "Saltarello Giorgio" and represent two different approaches to the same work. The problems are designed to help students use what they know about melodic contour to understand the form of a work.

Version 1

1. Students listen to the piece and in small groups decide how they will move (or walk) to reflect what they hear in the music. As they work, they will need to listen to the music again and again. When ready to share their ideas with the class, the different groups

---

[3] Many of the ideas for designing listening problems are from Lawrence Eisman, Queens College, CUNY, and Magne Espeland, Stord/Haugesund University College, Norway.

probably will have chosen to represent various aspects of the work—perhaps melodic contour or rhythm, quite often the meter, and sometimes various stylistic characteristics as well. However, because the form is so obvious in this work, most students also choose to represent the arrangement of the two thematic ideas in their motions, making it easy to focus their attention on the form of the work during follow-up discussion.

2. Class discussion of the various solutions should focus on which aspects of the music the groups have chosen to portray, answering the question, "What do you think they heard in the music that made them decide to move that way?"

3. A logical follow-up experience would be to ask students to compose an original bithematic work based on what they learned about how professional composers create a work out of two contrasting themes. Students work in small groups using classroom instruments, synthesizers, or composition software to develop a work that has an A theme and a B theme. To carry this out, each group will need to develop thematic material and decide how it will be arranged and repeated within the work.

Version 2

1. A different approach to the same piece is to ask students to work in a whole-class setting with a graphic representation of the rhythmic and pitch aspects of the melody. The piece consists of two distinctive melodies that appear in a typical dance form: AABBAABB. Students first consider graphic representations of the thematic material and predict what they think the music might sound like.

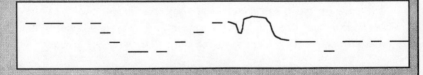

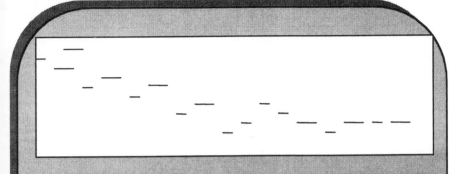

Ask the students, "How do you think the music will sound? What makes you think that?" Students might then listen to the recording and compare their predictions to what they hear.

Focus attention on the rhythmic aspects of the melody. "Can you hear that this music is made up of mostly a pattern of long and short sounds?" [The piece has an underlying rhythmic pattern of ♩♫♩♫♩]

2. Challenge the students to walk in a circle in a way that reflects the long/short pattern that is the predominant rhythmic pattern in the work. As they walk to the rhythm, can they circle to the right on the A theme and to the left on the B theme?
3. This version can be used to launch a composition project where students are asked to make up their own music that uses a combination of long and short sounds, causing them to focus on the rhythmic aspects of their work.

In listening-based problems, it is important to create a situation in which students need to hear the music played many times in order to solve the problem. This enables them to become intimately involved with the music, increasing their capacity to understand the music, and therefore, their capacity for response to the music. *Familiarity and increased understanding foster lifelong valuing.*

Creating-Based Problems

Creating-based problems can take many different forms and include the processes of composing, improvising, and even arranging. The common thread is that the students solve the problem primarily through the generation and organization of original musical ideas. Often, problems are constructed such that students are asked to work within particular parameters as they compose, improvise, or arrange. These parameters generally reflect particular elements of music, often linked to concepts learned through prior performing or listening experiences. By the nature of creative processes, students engaged in creating are solving musical problems. When composing or arranging, they are planning and evaluating solutions ahead of time—before the premiere performance of the work. When improvising, they are solving problems instantaneously as they perform.

Example 3. Sample creating problems. The following is an example of a composition-based problem based on understanding of the role of direction in melody.

> Once students have experienced working with melodic direction through analytical listening and performance-based activities, they may be ready to use their understanding of the concept to create an original composition. In previous lessons, they may have engaged in such activities as listening to "leap Frog" from Bizet's *Jeux d'Enfants* (Children's Games), reflecting their understanding of the melodic direction through gesture or other movement or through graphic representation. They may have analyzed songs for passages that move "up and down," and they may have learned some songs where the melodic direction is a particularly pronounced and important aspect of the song, perhaps used to portray the lyrics.
>
> 1. Students can work in pairs or small groups to develop an original composition that is driven by melodic direction, where extremes in melodic direction are a central characteristic. Depending on the nature of their prior experiences, they might be asked to create an instrumental piece using barred instruments and/or keyboard instruments. Some students might try creating a piece using computer software, if available.[4] They may also be asked to write a song, setting a text where the lyrics are concerned with something related to the concept of "up and down"—or might be asked to create original lyrics as well.

---

[4] *Freestyle* (1994, Cambridge, MA: Mark of the Unicorn) and *Making Music* (M. Subotnick, Voyager CFD-ROMs) work well for assignments such as this one.

2. Once students have established how they will use melodic direction in their work, they may opt to add accompanying figures or nondirectional percussion parts.

3. In the final product, listeners ought to be able to hear how melodic direction has been used, but they should also be able to discuss other decisions made by the composer—decisions not necessarily related to melodic direction.

4. Students working on such an assignment might work during one class session to plan and practice their piece and then share their products with the class during the next session. As students share their work, the teacher should focus attention by asking, "How did this group decide to show up and down in their work?" and "What else did they decide to do? What other decisions did they make?

Box 4

Take some time to consider the sample problems you have just read. In each problem:

- What is the teacher trying to help the students learn?
- What are the students learning?
- What did the students need to know in order to be able to solve this problem?
- What is the problem? Can you articulate it?
- What did the teacher do to prepare the students to be able to solve the problem?
- How would the teacher know whether or not the students have understood what he or she was trying to teach?

Participating in these kinds of experiences fosters the development of conceptual understanding that enables students to function as musicians. Regardless of subject matter, students need to understand the ideas intrinsic to the discipline in order to know how to function within it. If students' personal understanding has not grown to the extent that they can apply what they now know to new situations (without the teacher), then they have not learned. Like students in other subject areas, music students need opportunities to initiate original musical ideas and ideas about music. As music students work together to solve performing, listening, and creating problems, these experiences both draw upon and enhance their understanding of music—and enable musicianship and musicality. Music instruction should enable them to move toward a degree of autonomy in music. Music instruction should empower students with musical understanding so that they can become musically proficient and eventually musically independent of their teachers.

References

Bruner, J. (1960). *The process of education.* Cambridge, MA: Harvard University Press.

Dewey, J. (1938). *Experiences and education.* Chicago, IL: University of Chicago Press.

Gardner, H. (1993). *Frames of mind: The theory of multiple intelligence* (2nd ed.). New York: Basic Books.

Wiggins, J. (2001). *Teaching for musical understanding.* New York: McGraw-Hill.

10

Musical Understanding
in the Elementary School

Amanda Montgomery

Introduction

Musical understanding is *the ability to think and act musically with personal meaning* (Montgomery, 2002). Indeed, children with such understanding have the competence to act flexibly and ultimately bring personal intervention to any of their daily musical encounters.

> Musical understanding is the ability to think and act musically with personal meaning.

According to Howard Gardner (1999),

> [i]f a person understands music…if a person can think musically, that means he or she has certain categories, certain institutions, certain schemas that came out of his or her exposure to previous music…. It means when a person approaches a *new* work of music, or even creates one, that person can draw on that knowledge. (p. 15)

This "knowledge" comes from children's active engagement with the "stuff of music"—that is, the structural components and stylistic syntax of musical patterning. Students need opportunities to learn how to recognize musical patterning and make musical connections regarding these structures whenever they are engaged in musical behaviour: performing, composing, or listening.

For example, as *listeners*, children need to learn how to perceive and determine relationships in musical patterning in order to derive personal meaning; such meaning comes from children's musical cognition of the syntax of a particular musical style in combination with the social and emotional background they bring to the listening experience. As *performers*, children need to learn to perceive and determine these structural relationships; familiarity and recognition of the various components in musical patterning will lead to the flexibility to make artistic and expressive decisions within musical performance. And as *composers*, children need to gain a working knowledge of musical structure in order to abstract particular components for re-construction into their own unique, personalized musical compositions (Montgomery, 2002).

> Musical understanding is not an intellectual expression of musical knowledge, but rather, is evident whenever children are able to make meaningful musical decisions while engaged as performers, composers, or listeners.

Clearly, musical understanding is not an intellectual expression of musical knowledge, but rather, is evident whenever children are able to make meaningful musical decisions while engaged as performers, composers, or listeners. The more sensitive children become to the way music is put together, the greater their chance at exhibiting such musical understanding in any of these three modes of musical behaviour.

Educators such as Newton (2000) believe "understanding moves from the authorized or public understanding to a personal one" (p. 23). Presumably, children should gain experience with the standards of normalcy within whatever musical style and syntax they study in school in order to gain the confidence to bridge towards novel ways of interpretation and creation. Whether engaged as performers, listeners, or composers, children must become familiar with the commonly occurring structural patterning in any musical style in order to increase their abilities at making meaningful and artistic decisions within that style (Montgomery, 2002).

The Elementary School Music Curriculum

Music education in the elementary grades can play an important role in the development of musical understanding by intensifying and enhancing each individual's capacity to think and act musically. This curriculum needs to be designed in such a way as to heighten children's ability to perceive, relate, and act upon the music they encounter in their everyday lives. Classroom experiences should engage children in reflection, analysis, and interpretation of *both* the music (i.e., musical syntax and structure) they encounter *and* the actions (i.e., musical skills) they take regarding that music (Montgomery, 2002). These experiences should place the child at the center of the music learning process but will require a thoughtful teacher to set the stage for a developmentally appropriate journey towards musical understanding.

Elementary music teachers will need to be cognizant of the importance of the diverse social, emotional, and spiritual backgrounds that each child brings to the classroom music experience, as both a working knowledge of musical patterning combined with the child's personal background play a role in developing musical understanding. Multiple meaning-making by students will therefore be expected and valued (Montgomery, 2002).

Classroom experiences in the elementary curriculum should be drawn from a broad spectrum of musical encounters in order to facilitate multiple exploration of the individual components of musical structure. These experiences could include singing, playing classroom instruments, moving with music, composing, improvising, and listening to music. Engagement with the syntax and musical patterning of the music selected for these classroom experiences should form the critical core for the curriculum. This focus in the elementary school on the "stuff of music" will provide children with the working knowledge necessary for supporting their musical decision making whether performing, listening, or composing.

The elementary music curriculum should also include the teaching of musical literacy, as literacy development plays a key role in the growth of children's musical understanding (Montgomery, 2002). Children require competent skills in reading and writing music in order to richly experience performing and composing. Without music literacy skills, students are wholly dependent on others to deliver music to them aurally. Although children may learn how to play music by ear, they can only learn the music that is either performed for them live or has been recorded. This means children without literacy skills have little independent access to a variety of musical styles thereby limiting their chances at deriving personal meaning from any music other than what is presented to them by someone else.

The ability to read notation also opens the door for students to perform music independently or in ensemble with others. Such music literacy also provides access to singing or playing music that is too long or complex to learn by rote. In addition, reading notation provides students with the opportunity to re-experience the history of music from the Western hemisphere through the performance of music that was written down hundreds-of-years ago (Montgomery, 2002). Thus, an elementary music curriculum designed to lead children towards a comprehensive musical understanding includes attention to the process of nurturing student's musical literacy. Figure 1 provides a graphic description of an elementary music curriculum designed to promote the development of musical understanding.

Sample Classroom Activities

The following elementary classroom activities are included as concrete examples of the pedagogical implementation of the elementary music curricula designed to promote the growth and development of children's musical understanding. All activities place the child at the center of the learning process, allowing for opportunities for reflection by the student on the musical decisions made during this process.

Activity 1—*Telling a story with an instrument.* With the guidance of the teacher, children discuss a variety of actions they do on a daily basis, such as riding the bus to school, playing outside at recess, or doing their homework. Individual children select one of these actions and either a body-percussion or a non-pitched percussion instrument with which to "play the story." Given a set time limit (e.g., one minute), children are invited to "play" the actions of the story on their instrument using as many different sounds as needed to convey the meaning. Children should be encouraged to reflect upon and describe verbally or in written form the musical choices (timbre, tempo, rhythm, etc.) they chose for their "story telling" (kindergarten–grade 3).

Activity 2—*Adding instruments to heighten the expressive power of a rhyme, poem, story, or song.* Here children are divided into small groups and invited to explore and subsequently select non-pitched percussion instruments to play at selected moments during the chanting of a rhyme or poem, the telling of a story, or the singing of a song in order to heighten the expressive power of the text.

Figure 1. A Curricula Designed to Teach towards Musical Understanding

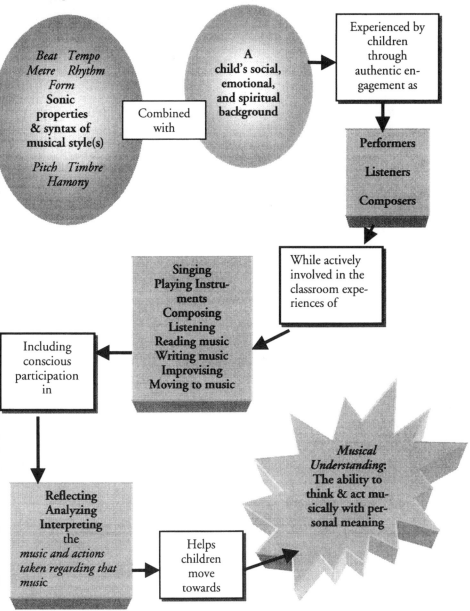

Teaching Towards Musical Understanding, Amanda Montgomery, 2002. Reprinted with permission by Pearson Education Canada.

Groups might be asked to invent their own graphic or iconic notation in order to write down (notate) the instrumental parts that accompany the rhyme, story, or song. By doing so, the children experience the
power of permanently recording their accompaniment such that it may
be brought back and performed at a later date (grades 1–3).

Activity 3—*Writing rhythmic ostinati for accompaniment of rhymes
or songs.* In this activity, children are invited to write a four-beat rhythmic ostinato pattern to be played as an accompaniment to a song on a
non-pitched percussion instrument. Students might be asked to reflect
upon the harmonic parameters of their ostinato, that is, how does the
ostinato support or add variety to the song? Older children may then be
asked to transfer their written ostinato to score form, either on the board
or on paper, such that children can visually see how the various parts,
melody, and ostinati accompaniment, are written together (grades 1–6).

Activity 4—*Writing a short rhythmic motive.* Children are directed
to write a short rhythmic motive (e.g., four measures) with concrete ma-
nipulatives, pencil and paper, or computer software using specified
rhythms (e.g., quarter, eighths and dotted quarter notes) and meter (e.g.,
6/8 time). In order for the activity to have musical context rather than
simply be perceived as an isolated exercise, children could be invited to
perform their rhythms on non-pitched percussion instruments as intro-
ductions or codas to favourite class songs (grades 1–6).

Activity 5—*Writing a rhythm to a given set of pitches.* In this activity, children are presented with a set of pitches and invited to add
rhythm such that the pitches are turned into a melody. This new melody
could be sung or performed on pitched percussion instruments or recorder and recorded for permanent record in a student's individual music portfolio (grades 1-6).

Activity 6—*Improvising a piece in rondo form.* In this activity,
children experience the process of improvising short motives that can be
utilized to build a composition that is constructed using traditional
forms such as rondo (ABACA). Children might sing a familiar song for
the A section. During the B, and C sections, individual children would
be asked to improvise a short melody on the recorder or on pitched per-

cussion. This kind of activity could be repeated any number of times using other known songs as the A section. Improvisations can be video taped for later viewing and written reflection by the student (grades 3–6).

Activity 7—*Sound Walk.* Here, children are divided into small groups of 5–7 children each and invited to take a sound walk together along a pre-determined route in or around the school. Groups are directed to listen for and attempt to remember as many sounds as they can during their walk. Upon returning to the classroom, children are asked to reflect and write down all the sounds they heard in the order that they heard them. Each group then writes a composition on poster size paper using graphic notation to illustrate their individual sound walks. Compositions are performed by each group using either body percussion or various non-pitched and pitched percussion instruments. Children should be asked to reflect on the compositional process involved in the activity (grades 3–6).

Activity 8—*Musique Concrète.* In this activity, children are asked to collect a variety of sounds (e.g., screeching tires, leaky faucet, horn blowing, etc.) they hear in their environment using a small tape or CD recorder. These recorded sounds are then brought to the classroom for re-sampling into a synthesizer or recording directly into a computer. Children are then asked to edit these sounds by putting them into a meaningful compositional order on the synthesizer or computer for playback. Completed compositions can be burned on to a CD for permanent record. This is an excellent individual or small group project for the upper grades and can yield very interesting musical results (grades 5–6).

Activity 9— *Constructing a theme and variations using a pre-composed melody.* Children are presented with a simple known melody and asked to compose a series of variations on this melody. Here children receive practice at employing a variety of compositional techniques including:
1) altering a melody through tempo or dynamic changes,
2) altering a melody by changing its rhythmic structure,

3) altering a melody be adding passing or neighboring tones,
4) altering a melody by changing it from major to minor,
5) altering a melody by adding a variety of instrumental accompaniments,
6) altering a melody through augmentation or diminution, and
7) altering a melody through use of a canon.

Practice with these kinds of sophisticated compositional techniques will help children develop a variety of techniques from which to draw upon when they compose their own pieces (grades 4-6).

Activity 10—*Composing a whole composition including text, music, and movement.* Children are invited to write a poem, set this text to a rhythm and a melody, orchestrate this new song with accompaniment utilizing non-pitched and pitched percussion instruments and/or recorder, add movement and/or costumes, rehearse, and finally record their work as a music video. This activity may take the form of an individual or small group project taking several weeks to complete. The results can be stunning, with children gaining an incredible sense of pride in their growing understanding of how music is put together (grades 5–6).

Summary

The elementary grades can be an important time for the development of children's musical understanding. A carefully guided curriculum based on the recommendations discussed in this chapter will contribute directly to student growth in this direction. Teachers should be urged to take advantage of the eagerness of students at this age by organizing classroom instruction such that the children occupy center stage in the learning process. By doing so, teachers can take great satisfaction in knowing that they have made a significant contribution in helping their students gain the ability to think, act flexibly, and ultimately bring personal intervention to all their future musical encounters.

References

Gardner, H. (1999). Keynote address: Cognitive Processes of Children Engaged in Musical Activity Conference honoring M.P. Zimmerman. *Bulletin for the Council for Research in Music Education, 142,* 9–21.

Montgomery, A. (2002). *Teaching towards musical understanding.* Toronto: Prentice Hall Canada.

Newton, D. (2000). *Teaching for understanding.* New York: Routledge.

11

Eastern Ears in Western Classrooms
Musical Understanding in Cultural Contexts[1]

Carol P. Richardson

Preliminary Remarks

I want to begin by thanking Betty Hanley for inviting all of us to grapple with the notion of musical understanding. Without Betty's invitation to consider the issues surrounding musical understanding, I certainly would not have spent the last few months worrying about it. And worry I have, in an effort not only to understand what the Project Zero folks (Wiske, 1998) intend to convey when they defined "Understanding" (note the capital U; see also chapter 8 for a discussion of TfU) but to clarify my own conception of musical understanding in light of the program of research that I've undertaken over the last few years. I accepted the task of formulating a definition of musical understanding with great trepidation and humility, fully aware that Zora Neale Hurston's quotation from her 1942 book, *Dust Tracks on the Road*, applies here: "Nothing that God ever made is the same thing to more than one person."

In this chapter I will attempt to do two things. I'll begin by walking you through the research studies I conducted to learn about the interaction of Eastern-eared children and the music typically heard in Western music classrooms. I'll then conclude by outlining for you the conception of musical understanding that resulted from my research.

---

[1] I wish to acknowledge the generous support of a National Academy of Education/Spencer Postdoctoral Fellowship for the study reported herein.

Introduction to the Studies

In the United States, music classrooms of the first decade of the 21st century include a much wider demographic base than in any previous decade. According to Zucker and Zucker (1987), the 1980 Refugee Act reversed the established immigration patterns that overwhelmingly favored Europe and Scandanavia by abolishing the country-by-country quotas that since 1924 had made it difficult for anyone from the Third World to immigrate to the United States. Zucker and Zucker pointed to the dramatic effect of this legislation by comparing immigration statistics from the periods both before and after this legislation. During the decade of the 1960s, of the 3.3 million legal immigrants arriving in the United States, 46% came from Europe and Canada, 40% from Latin America, and 13% from Asia. During the decade of the 1980s, overall legal immigration increased to 7.3 million, of which only 13% came from Europe and Canada, while Latin America remained at 42% and Asia increased to 42%. This trend toward immigration from Latin America and Asia was maintained during the decade of the 90s, though with some variation. Of the 6.9 million legal immigrants to the United States during the 90s, 17% came from Europe and Canada, while those from Latin America increased to 48%, and those from Asia decreased somewhat to 31%.[2] Zucker and Zucker (1996) put it succinctly:

> Today's newcomers are primarily people of color. Census projections foretell that by 2040 about 40 percent of the population will consist of people of color: immigrant and native-born Latinos, Asians, and Blacks. (p. 106)

The impact of this major demographic shift can most easily be seen in the elementary classrooms of large urban areas, the destination of the majority of immigrants. Here children from a multitude of cultures and musical traditions are taught the Western European art music canon by specialist music teachers who are themselves the product of a canon that underpins the core curriculum in schools of music and conservatories in

---

[2]U.S. Immigration and Naturalization Service. (1999). *Statistical Yearbook of the Immigration and Naturalization Service.* (Washington, DC: U.S. Government Printing Office), 25-26.

this country. Due to the time constraints of serving as the sole music teacher for hundreds of children, often as an itinerant teacher moving between several schools, these specialist teachers instruct large groups of elementary children in listening, singing, moving, playing, and creating music as if they were homogeneously drawn from the same musical background as the teachers'. This faulty assumption of homogeneity can be attributed, in part, to the historical "melting pot" view of the public schools in the U.S. democracy as places where new arrivals to this country become "American," forsaking their foreign ways and adopting ours. In this setting, a single music curriculum is assumed to fulfill the needs of all learners, though the delivery system may be subject to modification to meet the various identifiable differentiated learning requirements of some students, most notably those with "special needs."

In addition to time constraints, some of the blame for a music teacher's unified approach to students from various musical cultures lies with music teacher preparation programs. Coursework in special education is a standard requirement for American pre-service music teachers; the typical content for such courses focuses on a survey of various learning problems and ways to modify instruction to better serve the special student. What these courses typically fail to include is any discussion of immigrant children and the unique needs they bring to the music classroom. In spite of a 40-year tradition of disciplinary research findings on a wide range of music teaching and learning concepts, the music education profession knows very little about the effects of cultural background on musical perception and understanding, and it is within this context that I studied the cognitive processes involved in music listening with refugee children from Cambodia. I was interested in the ways in which children from musical traditions based on different harmonic and melodic systems, including various forms of Asian music, respond to and make sense of the music usually found in the general music curricula in the United States.

The study was the third in a research program dealing specifically with the cognitive processes by which individuals make sense of the experience of listening to music. In the first study (Richardson, 1988) I developed a model outlining the cognitive processes used by an adult musical expert (music critic) as he listened to an orchestral concert. The four basic components of this model include *expectation* (the process during which the listener uses prior experience to formulate a set of expectations of upcoming musical events), *comparison* (the process of

> The four basic components of this model of cognitive processes in the listening experience include expectation, comparison, prediction, and evaluation.

making comparisons between prior musical experiences and the music currently experienced), *prediction* (the process of using prior musical experiences to formulate predictions about what will happen next in the music), and *evaluation* (the process of formulating musical judgments based on personal criteria formulated through prior experience).[3]

As a follow-up, the think-aloud procedure developed in the 1988 study was used with musically trained children in grades 1 through 8 as they listened to short musical examples drawn from a wide variety of musical styles and genres (Richardson, 1995). The results indicated that the think-aloud procedure could be used with elementary school children and that the model of the adult musical expert's thinking did, in fact, encompass the sophisticated musical thinking of the musically trained child. Though there were differences in the level of detail, vocabulary, and musical understanding, the musically trained children's statements revealed similar cognitive components.

The purpose of the present study was to go beyond the confines of the student and adult upper middle class suburban population to embrace additional types of listeners, particularly those from musical traditions with a different harmonic and melodic system. How do children familiar with other musical traditions process and understand the music used in U.S. classrooms?

The specific research questions addressed in the present study were:

1. What music listening processes are evident in elementary aged Cambodian refugee children?

2. How do their listening processes compare to those of similarly aged children trained in the Western European art music tradition?

---

[3] A more detailed explanation of the theoretical model can be found in Richardson (1996a and 1996b).

3. Do the listening processes exhibited by the Cambodian children when listening to their own traditional musics differ from their processes when listening to Western music?

4. What are the implications of these findings for classroom practice?

Review of Literature

Prior to this study of Cambodian children, no extant has addressed the question of the universality of children's music listening processes or documented the ways in which cultural differences in musical background influence children's music listening processes. Two bodies of literature, however, relate to this study: cross-cultural research in musical perception (Kessler & Hansen, 1984; Walker, 1987) and audiation (Gouzouasis, 1993), and research using verbal protocol analysis to uncover cognitive processes (Bundra, 1993; Richardson, 1988, 1995; Whitaker 1989, 1996; Zerull, 1993).

Two cross-cultural studies illustrate the approach typically taken by researchers interested in the effects of culture on musical perception. Kessler and Hansen (1984) compared the perception of Western and Balinese melodies by 21 listeners from California and 27 listeners in a remote Balinese village. Melodies were played in either Western (diatonic major or minor) or Balinese (five-note pelog or five-note slendro) scales. Subjects were asked to rate how well an unrelated probe tone fit into the scale. Results indicated that both groups made their choices based on the tonal schemata of their own musical culture, leading to the conclusion that cultural learning has "an appreciable effect" on the perception of music (p. 164).

Another cross-cultural study of musical perception was undertaken by Walker (1987). Two-hundred children from five different groups (musically trained urban, musically naive urban, Inuit rural, Indian rural north, and Indian rural west) were asked to choose a visual shape to represent the changes in frequency of four synthesized pitches. The musically trained children were able to represent visually the changes in frequency as upward and downward movement, while children in the four other groups seemed to have no conception of pitch direction. Walker concluded that cultural background was not as important a factor as musical training in the perception of pitch changes.

While the two previously-cited studies looked at the effects of cultural background on musical perception, Gouzouasis (1993) was interested in the effects of cultural background on children's ability to audiate the tonal and rhythmic patterns of Western music. The researcher administered the tonal and rhythm subtests of Gordon's *Primary Measures of Music Audiation* (PMMA) to 281 5-year-old Canadian children from three different cultural backgrounds: Chinese, East Indian (Sikh), and Western European. Gouzouasis found that children from all three groups were able to audiate both the tonal and rhythmic patterns of Western music, although the East Indian children scored significantly lower than the other two groups on the tonal subtest. The researcher attributed this difference more to the Western content of the subtest than to the children's ability to audiate tonal patterns.

The current study differs significantly from the cross-cultural perception and audiation studies for several reasons. The musical stimuli of these studies, experimentally contrived melodies and manipulated pure tones, are atomistic in nature and divorced from a meaningful musical context, while the current study included intact musical examples from both traditional Cambodian (Khmer) and Western European art music. The "testing" context of the previous studies required the participants to come up with the right answer from a set of offered choices, most often in a school environment. The present study allowed participants to respond freely in their own language, with half the participants meeting at their local community center for the procedure and the other half at their Khmer school. The greatest difference between the cited studies and the present study, however, is the global nature of the "think-aloud" task.

Verbal protocol analysis or the think-aloud procedure is described and documented by Ericsson and Simon in their 1993 book, *Protocol Analysis: Verbal Reports as Data*. The specific procedure used in this study is concurrent verbalization, where the participant is asked to verbalize all the thoughts going through her or his mind during a particular task. Ericsson and Simon support this type of verbal report as a close reflection of the cognitive processes involved and make a strong case that verbalization does not change the course or structure of the participant's thought processes (p. 106). Two previous studies by this researcher established that the think-aloud procedure could be used successfully to trace the cognitive listening processes of the adult music critic (Richardson, 1988) as well as elementary children trained in the Western European tradition (Richardson, 1996a). Other music education researchers have used think-alouds to document adult musical decision-making (Whitaker, 1989; 1996), adult musical imagination (Zerull, 1993), and children's responses to musical stimuli (Bundra, 1993).

Procedures

The 60 participants in this study were Cambodian refugee children in grades 1 through 8, drawn from two contrasting populations at sites in both Chicago and Sydney, Australia. The actual age range of both populations was 6 through 16 years, due to the fact that these children had widely diverse educational backgrounds, solely dependent on what was available in the refugee camps in which they lived before immigrating. The Chicago children had been resident in America for a minimum of three months, but no more than two years. They had been born and lived in refugee camps on the Thai border before coming to Chicago. Many were orphans who had been taken into other families while still in the camps. They all spoke fluent English and preferred to speak in English during the think-aloud procedure, rather than relying on my Khmer interpreter. I met with them at their Cambodian-American neighborhood center in an impoverished Chicago neighborhood during their regular Sunday morning Khmer language lessons.

The Sydney participants included only those children who were classified as "new arrivals," having been in Australia for less than a month, and with these children I worked through a female Khmer interpreter to administer the think-aloud procedure. I met with the Sydney participants at their public elementary school on the western outskirts of the city. The school served a large population of "new arrivals" from Cambodia and Viet Nam with self-contained ESL classrooms where children were taught the core curriculum in their native language during the morning and, in the afternoon, had intensive English language instruction with an ESL teacher as well as their native language teacher.

At each site the think-aloud procedure was administered to each child individually in a room separate from all other activities. To warm up the children for the think-aloud task, I asked them questions about their musical background, likes, and dislikes and whether their families sang or played music with them at home. I then read them a standard set of instructions for the think-aloud task that instructed them to tell me everything they were thinking as they listened to each musical example. To maintain the integrity of the think-aloud procedure, the only prompts given them throughout the 30-minute procedure ("Tell me what you're thinking now." and "What are you thinking now?") were aimed at eliciting further responses if the participants were silent for more than five seconds. I was careful to stick to the scripted prompts suggested by Ericsson and Simon to avoid such teacher-like behaviors as giving positive reinforcement for any particular response or posing a leading question, as these would derail the child's thought processes and ruin the data.

The children listened to eight short recorded examples (maximum length = 2.5 minutes) drawn from two contrasting traditions: four from typical general music listening sources (Beethoven, Mozart, Brahms, and 20th century avant garde) and four from traditional Cambodian music (two examples from the traditional Cambodian wedding ceremony, one folk song, one pop ballad). The children listened to the musical examples through headphones, and their statements were recorded via a lavalier microphone.

I then transcribed all the English verbal responses, while the Cambodian translator translated and transcribed those in Khmer. The Khmer transcripts were then submitted to a second Khmer translator who listened to the tapes and noted on the transcript any alternate translations or corrections. I coded each statement using the model developed in the previous studies as the theoretical framework and had my coding checked by two colleagues who are experts in think-aloud procedures.

Results: Step One

The results indicate that Cambodian refugee children exhibited music listening processes similar to those of their musically trained age-mates from the Western art music tradition. They evaluated the music, noted the similarities and differences between pieces, used imaginative language (metaphor and analogy), classified the music by labeling musical timbres and function, elaborated by adding details, and predicted the next musical events or musical outcome. The points of difference evident in the refugee children's musical thinking include vocabulary, imaginative content, and level of affective response.

> *This is music of...In this music, they are dancing, playing flute. They are hitting something. They are playing drums.* (6-year-old girl, Sydney, listening to Phat Chay)

> *They blow horn again.* (8-year-old boy, Sydney, listening to Varèse)

> *This music is slow and fast, and slow and fast.* (12–year-old girl, Sydney, listening to Brahms)

> *I like how they make the sound with the hand, I like that.* (13-year- old girl, Sydney, listening to Coconut Shell)

> *I don't like it; it's too fast but it's normal.* (9-year-old girl, Sydney, listening to Mozart)

> *I think this person playing the piano is very talented.* (12-year-old girl, Chicago, listening to Brahms)

> *Bad song. Why does it always have to a boy singing? They are bad singers, but good background. This is pretty good than other song.* (10-year-old boy, Chicago, listening to MilliVanilli)

> *Like something happening, and a bomb. It's soft and then it's loud again.* (10-year-old girl, Sydney, listening to Varèse)

> *I hear some bird fly.* (6-year-old boy, Chicago, listening to Varèse)

> *It looks dark over there where that snake...snake is coming. They fighting with a...sword.* (9-year- old girl, Sydney, listening to Varèse)

Interestingly, the Cambodian children said less about the Khmer music than they did about the Western musical examples.

Though the Khmer children made fewer statements than the musically-trained Western children, their statements were much more structured than those of their musically educated peers. This may be attributable to the fact that, in spite of the care I took to get them comfortable in speaking with me before the think-aloud procedure, they may have felt the need to give what they thought was the "right" answer in the form of a well-composed, complete sentence. I cannot ignore the reality that my presence (white, middle-aged, female academic) in these two research settings could most probably have affected what they said, as well as how they said it.

The older Cambodian children used much more imaginative language than did their musically trained peers, and both Cambodian and Western music elicited from them higher levels of affective response. What they lacked in musical terminology was compensated for by their depth of response. Their statements contained much more emotion at the middle school level than the statements of their musically-trained counterparts. It may be that they were less sophisticated at masking their feelings than were the musically trained participants.

Results: Step Two

After analyzing the transcripts for evidence of cognitive processes, I took another look at the children's statements, this time looking at the outlier statements, those that had not fit in the coding system based on the cognitive processes model. What I found this second time was a rich source of information about what was going on with these children, transplanted from one musical culture to another and faced with the need to make sense of this new experience. This second look at their statements gave me the sense that I had discovered a small window into the secret, interior lives of these children, which Cristina Igoa described beautifully in her 1995 book titled *The Inner World of the Immigrant Child*. Looking carefully at what the children said about the Cambodian music, I saw a high level of affective engagement with the music. Two recent arrivals in Sydney expressed it this way while listening to a Khmer folk song in which the singer describes how he is a poor but happy farmer, riding along on his ox through the tall grass:

> *It makes me feel homesick...that I miss my family at the countryside.* (12-year-old girl, Sydney)

> *I feel homesick. I remember that I used to ride a buffalo (laughs)...yes. I remember that in Cambodia we used to work hard...remember that I always feel pity for poor people.* (15-year-old girl, Sydney)

From field notes made while sitting with each child during the procedure I recorded affective changes. I noticed these changes only happened while the children listened to the Khmer musical examples. These included changing from a normal speaking voice to whispering, and even ceasing to talk altogether, in spite of my prompts to "tell me what you're thinking now." In some cases I noted a change in breath rate (usually faster), averted eyes, and fidgeting. Clearly, the Khmer music elicited a high level of affective engagement from these children.

In the following excerpts I found evidence of a high level of negative affective engagement with the same Cambodian folk song described earlier. It seems that pre-adolescents from all parts of the world wish to distance themselves from the music of their parents, a desire complicated here by the need to identify with the music of the new country.

I usually hear this song at home. It's terrible loud voice. I don't know what he's talking about, anyway. (10-year-old boy, Chicago)

I hate Cambodian song because it's so boring, and I practically don't know any of the words and they're not like American songs, and they are so boring. Why do those Cambodian songs sound so boring? (11-year-old boy, Chicago)

These children explained to me later that their parents played the Cambodian music on a tape player in the living room at home, while they played "their rap music" in their own rooms.

The children's responses to the Cambodian music reiterate what we already know: that the music of one's home culture is a powerful link to the child's prior experience and serves as the individual's "musical home." In the case of one of the participants in this study, the home music can be a powerful means to unlocking the door for a child who is in the "silent stage."

Igoa (1995) describes the silent stage as a period during which children who experience the school culture as different from their own are unable to communicate with their peers because of a language of cultural difference (p. 38). She explains that the silent stage is a coping mechanism that may last for a year or two. The child whose transcript appears next was known by her Cambodian ESL teacher to be in the silent stage, even in his Khmer-based classroom where she had said nothing since her arrival a few weeks earlier. He thought she would not participate but sent her to me anyway, as her uncle had wanted her to participate in the study. She said notl.ing during the first two Western musical examples, despite my prompts, and then the Cambodian wedding music began:

> *This music is rather pleasant and the music sounds like national anthem.
> And sounds like they are ringing a bell. And it is very nice and I like it.
> This music is like a wedding music. And they parade along and they (?).
> And it is like a Kartin Parade (Cambodian festival parade). And I am
> very happy. Last time I sent to this parade…and it is a very happy occa-
> sion. And my brothers are still in Cambodia; they have not come here yet.
> And I just arrived from Cambodia. And I and my brother. He, he had an
> exam. And he had a few days off. And one of my uncles asked my other
> uncle to let me go to school. My uncle said there are not clothes and said to
> borrow from my brother. This brother has two jumpers (sweaters)—one
> thin and one thick. And so I come to school and I start grade one. I am
> very happy now because I am busy writing something. That's all.* (6-year-
> old girl, Sydney)

At the end of the listening example, she took off the headphones,
said goodbye to the interpreter and me, and went back to her classroom.
Her teacher came to see me at lunchtime to ask me what had happened.
He was puzzled because she would not stop chattering in his class and he
wanted to know what we had done to make her talk. I explained that the
wedding music had done it and that the interpreter and I had just
watched it happen.

The final examples illustrate another major finding that this second
level of data analysis revealed, and this is one that music educators may
find most difficult to face: Children from musical cultures outside the
Western canon seem to have no way to take in, interpret, and understand Western music. In short, music is not the universal language that
we may have held it to be, in spite of the fact that all cultures have some
form of musical expression. Here are just four of many similar statements made by the children while listening to the Western music:

> Music is not the univer-
> sal language that we
> may have held it to be,
> in spite of the fact that
> all cultures have some
> form of musical expres-
> sion.

I don't think anything. (7-year-old boy, listening to Beethoven)

I don't know how to listen to it. (10-year-old
girl, listening to Mozart)

*I don't understand this music. I don't know what
it is.* (10-year-old boy, listening to Brahms)

I'm not thinking, I'm listening. I feel like wanting to listen. (14-year-old
girl, listening to Brahms)

Implications for Practice

Though music is clearly not a universal language, the results of this study reveal that there are cognitive processes for making sense of musical experience that seem to be universal and innate—unimpeded by either the presence or absence of music instruction. Children from these two diverse musical cultures, both musical novices and musically sophisticated, seem "hardwired" to listen to, analyze, and evaluate the music of their home musical culture.

> There are cognitive processes for making sense of musical experience that seem to be universal and innate—unimpeded by either the presence or absence of music instruction.

The results of this study sound a powerful wake-up call for the music education profession and could have a tremendous impact on the way we music teachers address children from musical cultures outside the Western canon. At its very best, current practice includes some instructional modifications for learning- or physically-challenged students, although predicated upon one teacher dealing with large groups of children for 30-minute periods between one and three times each week. Understanding that the musical listening processes of children from two diverse musical cultures are apparently similar and much more sophisticated than we've given them credit for, requires a rethinking of our pedagogy.

We must find better ways to pose questions, phrase explanations, and introduce musical terminology to students from cultures where music has a more specific ritual or social function. We must recognize that music from outside one's home culture is often incomprehensible and rethink ways to include music from children's home cultures in our "post-melting pot" classrooms. We must also recognize that music from the home culture can be a powerful emotional link for the immigrant children in our schools and offer ways to help classroom teachers make use of this musical link too.

A Definition of Musical Understanding in Cultural Context

Musical understanding is the result of the perception of and response to the music we hear. It is the internal, intuitive, ineffable result of growing up in a particular place and time on this planet and it forms and develops within a particular cultural and historical context. It is shaped by both the affective and cognitive elements that come into play as we attempt to make sense of the music that we hear. Most importantly, musical understanding exists untouched by efforts to teach for it because it is part of the human condition that is, fortunately for us as musical beings, beyond the reach of music teachers. Contrary to TfU, musical understanding does not really require our strenuous efforts as educators because students come to us with it already in place, though usually without the words or images with which to express it in our expert musical language. Thus it is not our task to "teach for musical understanding" but to tap into the student's already-formed musical understanding in a way that both acknowledges its presence and honors its origins, in whatever musical tradition it is grounded.

> Musical understanding does not really require our strenuous efforts as educators because students come to us with it already in place, though usually without the words or images with which to express it in our expert musical language.

What we provide, as music educators, is the context in which children can express their musical understanding, whether it is the music classroom or the rehearsal. But we usually require our students to express it in our own terms, not theirs. We specialize in telling them "how" to talk about music "our way," aiming for analysis in the language of musicians. Each individual in our classes and rehearsals, however, brings a personal understanding of music that continues to develop over a lifetime, from daycare center to nursing home. It is imperative that we recognize the unique individual musical understanding that each student brings to our classrooms and rehearsals. Music educators must begin to understand and act on the fact that each student is someone whom we cannot be, whose musical understanding *is not like ours*. We may then begin to use this knowledge as the starting point in asking students to perform *their* musical understanding for us.

References

Bundra, J. I. (1993). *A study of music listening processes through the verbal reports of school-aged children*. Unpublished doctoral dissertation, Northwestern University.

Ericsson, K. A., & Simon, H. A. (1993). *Protocol analysis: Verbal reports as data.* (Rev. ed.). Cambridge, MA: MIT Press.

Gouzouasis, P. (1993). Music audiation: A comparison of the music abilities of kindergarten children of various ethnic backgrounds. *The Quarterly Journal of Music Teaching and Learning, 4* (2), 70–76.

Hurston, Z. N. (1942). *Dust tracks on a road.* Philadelphia: J. B. Lippencott.

Igoa, C. (1995). *The inner world of the immigrant child.* New York: St. Martin's Press.

Kessler, E. J., & Hansen, C. (1984). Tonal schemata in the perception of music in Bali and in the West. *Music Perception, 2* (2), 131–165.

Richardson, C. P. (1988). *Musical thinking as exemplified in music criticism.* Unpublished doctoral dissertation, University of Illinois at Urbana-Champaign.

Richardson, C. P. (1995, April). *Toward a global model of children's music listening processes.* Paper presented at the annual meeting of the American Educational Research Association, San Francisco.

Richardson, C. P. (1996a). A theoretical model of the connoisseur's musical thought. *Bulletin of the Council for Research in Music Education, 128,* 1–10.

Richardson, C. P. (1996b). Understanding the critical process: A paradigm for the music critic's thought. *Journal of Aesthetic Education, 30* (1), 51–61.

Walker, R. (1987). Some differences between pitch perception and basic auditory discrimination in children of different cultural and musical backgrounds. *Bulletin of the Council for Research in Music Education, 91,* 166–170.

Whitaker, N. L. (1989). *Reflective thinking as exemplified in musical decision making.* Unpublished doctoral dissertation, University of Illinois at Urbana-Champaign.

Wiske, M. S. (Ed.). (1998). *Teaching for understanding: Linking research with practice.* San Francisco, CA: Jossey-Bass.

Zucker, N. L., & Zucker, N. F. (1987). *The guarded gate: The reality of American refugee policy.* San Diego, CA: Harcourt Brace Jovanovich.

Zucker, N. L., & Zucker, N. F. (1996). *Desperate crossings: Seeking refuge in America.* Armonk, NY: M. E. Sharpe, Inc.

Zerull, D. S. (1993). *The role of musical imagination in the musical listening experience.* Unpublished doctoral dissertation, Northwestern University.

12

Constructing Musical Understandings

Joseph Shively

On face value, the notion that we should teach for understanding seems rather obvious. One would think, after all, that every teacher strives to guide learners toward understanding. Nevertheless, how we go about teaching for musical understanding is neither obvious nor simple. The challenges come in determining what it means to teach for understanding, how we go about teaching for understanding, and how we know that the learner understands. Teaching for musical understanding requires that we consider both the nature of musical experiences and how learning might best occur within a music classroom. In this chapter, the implications of a constructivist approach to teaching and learning music will frame the discussion.

> The challenges come in determining what it means to teach for understanding, how we go about teaching for understanding, and how we know that the learner understands.

This discussion of musical understanding is grounded in my background as a band director. While this chapter reflects a general overview of constructivism and musical understanding, my original thinking about this topic focused on making performance-based classes more conducive to moving beyond learning to play large ensemble music toward constructing rich, deep knowledge bases about music.

Constructivism

Constructivism is an epistemological view that holds that

- there is a real world we experience but we impose meaning on that world—our world does not exist independently of us;

- there are many ways to structure the world; and
- there are many possible meanings or perspectives brought to any event or concept.

While there are many variations on constructivism, Duffy and Jonassen (1992) provide a helpful overview. Their constructivist view of knowledge has strong implications for the learning process. For constructivists, knowledge is produced through the active process of interpreting the world. In making these interpretations, individuals apply their knowledge base; any interpretation, however, is tentative and requires constant reexamination. While interpretations emerge from the experience of individuals, the experience itself is embedded in an environment that includes other learners. The social interaction that occurs in this environment provides multiple perspectives to both enrich the constructive process and to place constraints on that process. Knowledge construction is both an individual and a social process.

The context of the constructive process serves to index knowledge, to provide meaning within one context that may change when applied in a new context. As the ongoing process of knowledge construction continues, the indexing of knowledge within the base guides construction in a new context. Context is also reflected in knowledge domains, the knowledge used by expert practitioners in a field. Both the constructive process and knowledge base are distributed across learners and their environment, which includes individuals, learners, and teachers, as well as artifacts. The flexibility of knowledge from experience to experience mirrors the reflexive nature of the constructive process and its resultant knowledge base. Reflexivity is dependent upon the variety of experiences that constructivists highly value.

Experiences in the classroom should serve to both broaden and deepen knowledge bases. A reflexive knowledge base is constructed when:

1) engaging learners in experiences reflecting practitioner culture;
2) engaging learners in experiences involving individual and group knowledge construction;
3) engaging learners in experiences reflecting multiple means of representing knowledge; and

4) engaging learners in multiple means of representing knowledge. (Shively, 2002)

This approach provides an authentically complex learning environment where the experiences in which learners are immersed encourage the reflexive use of the knowledge base and the ability to transfer knowledge to a new context. The musical understanding that results allows learners to use knowledge in new ways and within new experiences. It is in the application of the knowledge base that

> It is in the application of the knowledge base that learners demonstrate understanding.

learners demonstrate understanding. It is critical for teachers to recognize the music knowledge base learners bring to their classrooms and to build upon this knowledge, working with more familiar musical experiences toward less familiar ones. It is in the application of the knowledge base developed in the class to musical experiences inside and outside the classroom that understanding is demonstrated. It is in learning a musical idea—such as form—in one context and applying it in another that learners demonstrate further understanding, applying the knowledge in an unfamiliar setting, thereby deepening and broadening their knowledge base.

Knowledge as Tool

If knowledge is constructed, it is critical to consider the relationship between knowledge and understanding. Knowledge is a tool, and it is in the application/use of knowledge that learners demonstrate their understanding. Because it is new knowledge that is being constructed in the learning process, constructivism appears to focus on knowing rather than understanding. This is not, however, the case. Knowing deals with being able to bring forth on demand (Blythe, 1998, p. 12). Knowledge is not an end unto itself but, rather, a tool that is used to foster understanding. This is hardly a new idea. John Dewey championed knowledge as an instrument of the mind in 1958. Contemporary discussions (Brown, Collins, & Duguid, 1989) of knowledge as a tool emphasize knowledge as active. The constructivist idea of knowledge is in opposition to inert knowledge. Knowledge is not stagnant; it is a tool to be used in the active process of coming to understand our experiences:

"Conceiving of knowledge as a tool thus helps break down the dualism between knower and known" (Bredo, 1994, p. 30). The knowledge a learner uses in the constructive process is embedded in that process and indexed by that particular experience. Using knowledge as a fluid tool supports the ongoing process of knowledge construction. Each new constructive experience alters learners' present knowledge base, thereby strengthening the tools they bring to any experience. It is the active use of knowledge that allows learners to construct deeper knowledge bases.

Knowledge construction requires individual interpretations that are placed into social contexts for further interpretation. Knowledge construction is both an individual and a social process. As learners construct knowledge, they must constantly evaluate its placement within their broader knowledge base. Creating a learning environment where learners are comfortable, with constant mediation in learning, is crucial to success. The ability of the learner to "test" knowledge requires both an understanding of and a positive attitude toward the evaluation process.

Knowledge Representation

Representation is the means through which individuals can make their knowledge explicit. It is the "process of transforming consciousness into a public form" (Eisner, 1993, p. 6). The manner in which music knowledge is represented provides a necessary and welcome diversity in the engagement of learners with music experiences. Aural phenomena are not the only way to represent music knowledge but they are the source of all music knowledge; all means of representing music knowledge emerge from some manipulation of aural phenomena, whether direct or indirect. Representation is the means by which someone can make his or her knowledge explicit. It is the "process of transforming consciousness into a public form" (p. 6). Practitioners in music domains typically represent their knowledge through performance, creation, and description, ways of representing our experiences with aural phenomena. When we speak of these ways of representing knowledge, we are also speaking of the activities in which domain practitioners are involved. I do not, however, claim that knowledge only exists after it has been publicly represented or that performance, creation, and description can only occur outside the mind. I claim that through performance, creation, and description individuals can make their music knowledge public. Making tentative constructions public is a crucial component of the constructive process because of the need for social negotiation and feedback.

Performance is a directly aural form of knowledge representation. It is the primary way that instrumental musicians represent their music knowledge. As a point of clarification, performance is an all-encompassing term for performing on an instrument (including the voice) and does not denote solely formal performances with an audience. Creation reflects the aural phenomenon of music but is not always explicitly represented in an aural fashion. To share composition in a public form, descriptive musical tools, such as music notation, are often used. Some exceptions to this practice are electronic compositions and improvisation. Description, such as analysis or criticism, involves responses to aural phenomena. In all these forms of representation, aural phenomena are present, even if only as a mental image.

Each of these general forms of knowledge representation takes on different characteristics that are specific to the domain. For instance, performance very often involves the re-creation of another's composition. Regardless of whether it is a performance of another composer's work or an improvised performance, the results are performers' aural representations of their knowledge of music at a particular instance. Furthermore, overlapping forms of knowledge representation frequently arise. For example, an improvised performance involves both performance and creation.

Creation, as a form of knowledge representation, is manifested in several ways. As discussed previously, improvisation is a type of creation. Composition is another way of representing an individual's music knowledge through creation. In this case, a composer might use music notation to descriptively represent his or her knowledge of manipulating aural phenomena in a creative manner.

Knowledge representation through description also occurs in different ways. The term description commonly denotes the use of language and can be used as a means of representation for music knowledge. This would be the case in much of music criticism, music theory, and music history. These practices, however, are often combined with another descriptive representational form, such as notation.

The Social Nature of Knowledge Construction

Knowledge construction requires support. Learner interaction provides crucial support. Learning environments should be structured to encourage learner interaction. While individual knowledge construction is part of the process, music teachers must consider the collaborative potential of the musical experiences that take place in their classrooms.

If we accept that the construction process takes place on a continuum, the nature of the musical experience and the constructive process almost always leads toward group knowledge construction. Learners will eventually want to perform a composition they have practiced or have someone perform the piece that they have composed. It is during this interaction that learners work together to construct knowledge.

Certain experiences within the music classroom lend themselves to group knowledge construction. Working as a group of composers allows a great deal of vital interaction that can contribute to students' knowledge base. In performance classes, some ensemble experiences are critical, as they allow learners greater control over their work and group interaction. While large ensembles are certainly authentic, even in real settings much of the musical decision making is made by the conductor. Occasions must be provided to allow students greater opportunities to be meaning makers. Of course, the classroom should include opportunities for learners to function in the role of conductor.

The social construction of knowledge, while not fostering absolute truths, does not take refuge in a relativistic state. It reflects the need for balance between the individual learner and the community of learners. Speaking about constructivism, Jerome Bruner (1990) stated: "The best we can hope for is that we be aware of our own perspective and those of others when we make our claims of 'rightness' and 'wrongness'" (p. 25). Throughout the constructive process a learner should interact with other learners. This interaction should reflect the way in which domain practitioners distribute real-world activities in their everyday settings. Additionally, learner interaction provides multiple perspectives and aids in the negotiation of meanings.

Musical Decision Making as Musical Understanding

Problem solving within authentic practitioner domains provides learners with an opportunity to construct musical understanding. If problem solving reflects the constructive process, what are we referring to, for example, in music performance? Simply stated, the constructive process in the knowledge domain of the music performer revolves around the musical decision making process. From the first experience with music, all knowledge that is constructed within the domain of the performer serves as a tool in the musical decision-making process. It is the active use of music knowledge that leads to a depth of understanding that is primarily reflected in representation through performance. Of course the experiences in other domains should continue because they afford learners opportunities to represent their knowledge in other ways, thereby deepening their understanding of music. As are domain practitioners, learners are involved in thinking about music when they apply and reapply their knowledge base to authentic experiences.

> Problem solving within authentic practitioner domains provides learners with an opportunity to construct musical understanding.

Musical decision making does not occur only with interpretive decisions. It happens in every phase of performance, from sight-reading through rehearsal, to performance. In the case of improvisation, the decision-making process of the performer is also a creative one. If learners are reading the notation, making decisions about intonation, phrasing a line, making overall interpretive decisions, or deciding about the use of different playing techniques, they are making musical decisions. Because these are decisions about music using knowledge that emerges from music, it might be said that we are talking about "thinking musically."

Every experience requires learners to make musical decisions or to apply their knowledge base. Application of the knowledge base, the constructive process, leads to a new knowledge base. This view of the constructive process emphasizes the use of knowledge as a tool. These tools allow the leaner to make tentative decisions in response to a musical experience and to test and revise these decisions.

Large ensembles with a teacher/conductor present a different circumstance for the relationship of individual and social knowledge construction. Musical decision making brings us to the crux of the constructivist challenge in instrumental music. Traditionally, decisions have been made by the teacher/conductor. Yet, the purpose of music education should be to immerse the learner in the process of musical decision making, the process of knowledge construction in music. Learners bring relevant domain knowledge, as well as knowledge from other domains, to bear on this process. The constructivist music class should reflect an environment where learners are empowered to understand music through meaningful experiences.

Consider the positive case of the chamber ensemble. In a small ensemble setting, the performers are actively involved in the decision-making process. Consider the potential for knowledge construction in the case of a brass quintet as the students learn a new composition. Sight-reading the composition allows the performers to represent their musical knowledge, with each performer representing his or her own music knowledge, but there is also the potential for almost instantaneous mediation of that knowledge. The learners in the ensemble alter their performance and reconstruct their knowledge based on their responses to the other players in the ensemble; this process reflects the social negotiation of knowledge. As this ensemble moves through continued experiences with the composition, each member of the ensemble constructs new knowledge that reflects individual as well as social processes. The relationship between the learners and the composition, from sight-reading through each of the myriad musical decisions required along the way to performance, typifies the constructive process in music.

The performer as soloist shifts social negotiation to later in the constructive process. Where ensembles allow for the social negotiation of music knowledge every step of the way, the soloist is deeply involved in the self-mediation of knowledge construction. Only when the individual "performs" for someone else does that learner's knowledge construction enter into public consciousness.

Individual constructive processes are not exclusive to solo performance; they are present in all performance experiences. Performers in a small ensemble seek to balance their lines within the musical whole, carrying responsibility for making decisions about an individual musical line as well as the collective musical decision making of the ensemble.

The different forms of knowledge representation in music allow individual learners to present their constructions in public. Learners construct knowledge based on experience but use these means to "test" that knowledge in a public forum.

Different performance settings support different constructive processes. The interactions between a soloist and a composition or the members of a small ensemble and a composition or the members of a large ensemble, its teacher/conductor, and a composition create experiences that support varying constructive processes. Each of these settings can contribute to the perspectives within the knowledge domain of the instrumental musician if this potential is acknowledged. Of critical importance is adhering to constructivist learning principles in the classroom.

Constructivist Music Teachers

Constructivism may not be a theory of teaching but it does hold strong implications for teachers who choose to develop a classroom grounded in this perspective. Certainly, teachers taking a constructive approach must be prepared to rethink their purpose in the educational process. In making the transition from a traditional classroom to a constructivist classroom, the constructivist music teacher must function as the primary agent for change.

The greatest challenge for the constructivist music teacher is the necessity to function as a domain practitioner. While the constructivist classroom represents a shift of the responsibility for learning from the teacher to the learner, it nonetheless requires the teacher to model the processes of music practitioners. Teachers need to make the thought processes of musicians explicit. Further, to help learners look at musical experiences from different perspectives—such as composer versus performer—music teachers must themselves have sufficient experiences in the varied domains. This approach also has significant implications for the preparation of music teachers.

The knowledge domain of teachers is reflected in teachers' knowledge bases developed over time from the first encounter they had as a learner. This idea is reflected in the adage, "We teach how we were taught, not how we were taught to teach." The base continues to grow through field and course work as an undergraduate or graduate student and in the field as a working professional. This consequence, too, reflects the tentative nature of a teacher's knowledge base. Teachers need to model their understanding and how they develop it to help their students gain greater musical understanding. Music teachers must continue to immerse themselves in experiences that will deepen their knowledge bases within the domains of both music and teaching.

Experiences in the Music Classroom

The nature of constructing musical understandings is reflected in philosophy. In *Of Mind and Other Matters* (1984) and *Languages of Art* (1968), Nelson Goodman advanced a constructivist philosophy of art. For Goodman, "much of knowing, acting, and understanding in the arts, sciences, and life in general involves the use—the interpretation, application, invention, revision—of symbol systems" (1984, p. 152). Music is a symbol that is used to make meaning out of the world, to construct a world. Opportunities to interpret, apply, invent, and revise music should be at the core of musical experiences—experiences that lead to musical understanding. When realized in these four ways, musical experiences provide opportunities for learners to manipulate music.

Adding to the complexity of teaching for musical understanding is the nature of representing knowledge of musical experiences. Language is often view as analogous with knowledge representation. As learners represent what they know, however, knowledge can take on many forms, for there are as many worlds as ways to describe them (Goodman, 1978). It may be that "Everything said is said by someone," (Knuth & Cunningham, 1993, p. 168), yet "Not everything can be 'said' with anything" (Eisner, 1993, p. 7). Music is a potentially powerful and sometimes more appropriate way of representing what a person knows. Additionally, learners need multiple means of experiencing music and of representing what they know about music. These experience should include the opportunity for learners to compose, improvise, perform, conduct, coach, and write about and discuss music (Shively, 2002). These opportunities indicate the need for experiences reflecting practitioner culture, individual and group experiences, experiences reflecting multiple perspectives, and multiple means of representing knowledge.

Composing

Compositional activities are critical in music classrooms. It is in these activities, as well as through improvisation, that learners are provided the ultimate opportunity to manipulate sound. Performance-based music teachers who see composition as beyond their purview or as something that will take too much of their class time, should consider that through the manipulation of notation and the organization of sounds, students' music reading skills will also improve. Most importantly, however, learners will develop a much keener understanding of the relationship between sound and notation.

Improvising

Send learners home the first day "making up" songs, Even in performance courses have them start using the pitches they have learned immediately. Improvisation provides an excellent opportunity for them to explore music.

Any time that composition and improvisation are discussed, there is typically some discussion of quality of product and limitations of creative abilities. While these issues should be discussed, the benefits of creative experiences should place them at the forefront of music education. This raises the question—what then of performance?

Performing

There continues to be significant discussion about the role of performance in music education and the degree of emphasis it should receive. In performance-based courses, we often walk a very fine line. The claim may be made that participation in a band, chorus, or orchestra allows the learner the opportunity to think like performing musicians. Every effort, however, must be made to shift the responsibility for musical thinking to the learner away from the teacher, in this case usually also the conductor. Even in authentic settings, practitioners have the least opportunity for personal music making in large ensembles. It is much easier to share the responsibility for musical thinking in smaller ensemble, where traditionally it is the ensemble members who have the responsibility for musical thinking or decision making.

I do not intend to diminish the importance of performance-based courses; rather, I hope to get teachers of these courses to consider what will provide learners the most fertile opportunities to develop musical understanding. Music educators must work to provide learners with the best possible environment within which to foster musical understanding.

Writing About and Discussing Music

Verbal representation is important even in the music classroom. Writing and talking about music provides learners with opportunities to share their experiences with music in another representational mode, one in which many of them will be comfortable.

Conducting and Coaching

Learners need an opportunity to look at scores and to hear what an ensemble sounds like from the front of the room. Even more basic than this need is that learning basic conducting patterns provides greater insight into what they see the conductor doing as they play. Learners need opportunities to conduct their own compositions.

The opportunity to coach an ensemble provides another means for learners to represent their knowledge. Further, the discussion that results not only with the coach but also among members of the ensemble will provide an opportunity for learners to share what they know and for each of them to solidify further their knowledge. In this case, they are discussing music with one another in a rich, authentic context.

ഇരൽ

The context in which the classroom experience occurs serves to index the knowledge that is built. If the learner is given a music vocabulary list, for example, the knowledge that results will be simplistic, temporary, and most disconcerting of all, inert. If musical terms are learned and used in the context of musical experiences, however, the result should be knowledge that will be constantly re-applied and a new knowledge base that will be constructed, reflecting a greater depth of understanding. After all, it won't take long for a learner to realize that *piano* and *forte* are much more than soft and loud but are dependent on the style of music, the instruments in the ensemble, and the nature of the orchestration. In other word, learners must think and listen. Two of the most important aspects of the experiences the teacher should consider are authenticity and multiplicity.

Authenticity is determined by the extent to which the learning environment reflects real-world experiences. The teacher should consider what instrumental musicians, as well as other musicians, do and how they think about what they do.

Multiplicity is reflected in both multiple ways of representing knowledge and multiple sources of knowledge. As discussed earlier, involving learners in activities such as performing, composing, conducting, improvising, coaching, and discussing music, provides not only multiple ways for them to demonstrate music knowledge but also multiple ways of building the knowledge base. This variety of experiences will contribute to much richer knowledge and understanding.

To provide multiple perspectives the music that is used in class should be as varied as possible in almost every way imaginable—for example, use of styles, meters, and modes. Certainly, music that learners know when they come into the classroom from their experiences both in and outside school should be used.

Conclusion

Musical understanding is the ability of a learner to apply his or her knowledge base to make meaning of a new musical experience. This application of the knowledge base reflects the nature of the constructive process and the nature of what it means to develop musical understanding. A constructivist approach to learning provides fertile experiences for fostering musical understanding.

> Musical understanding is the ability of a learner to apply his or her knowledge base to make meaning of a new musical experience.

Teaching for musical understanding is a very challenging idea requiring that we, as a profession, continue this conversation. Furthermore, we as a profession must provide teachers with the ability they need to create classrooms that will provide the necessary experiences to help learners develop musical understanding. Steering the focus of music teachers in this direction will require both a rethinking of current practice in the classroom and the courage to change practice as needed.

References

Blythe, T. (1998). *The teaching for understanding guide.* San Francisco, CA: Jossey-Bass Publishers.

Bredo, E. (1994). Reconstructing educational psychology: Situated cognition and Deweyian pragmatism. *Educational Psychologist, 29* (1), 23–35.

Brown, J. S., Collins, A., & Duguid, P. (1989). Situated cognition and the culture of learning. *Educational Researcher, 18,* 32–42.

Bruner, J. S. (1990). *Acts of meaning.* Cambridge, MA: Harvard University Press.

Dewey, J. (1958). *Experience and nature.* New York: Dover Publications. (Reprint of 1958, 2nd ed., La Salle, IL: Open Court Publishing Co.)

Duffy, T. M., & Jonassen, D. H. (1992). Constructivism: New implications for instructional technology. In T. M. Duffy & D. H. Jonassen (Eds.), *Constructivism and the technology of instruction: A conversation* (pp. 1–16). Hillsdale, NJ: Lawerence Erlbaum.

Eisner, E. (1993). Forms of understanding and the future of educational research. *Educational Researcher, 22* (7), 5–11.

Goodman, N. (1968). *Languages of art: An approach to a theory of symbols.* Indianapolis, IN: Bobbs-Merrill Publishing.

Goodman, N. (1978). *Ways of worldmaking.* Indianapolis, IN: Hackett Publishing.

Goodman, N. (1984). *Of mind and other matters.* Cambridge, MA: Harvard University Press.

Knuth, R., & Cunningham, D. J. (1993). Tools for constructivism. In T. M. Duffy, J. Lowyck, & D. H. Jonassen (Eds.), *Designing environments for constructive learning* (pp. 163–188). Berlin: Springer-Verlag.

Shively, J. L. (2002). Learning and teaching in the beginning instrumental classroom. In E. Boardman (Ed.), *Dimensions of musical learning and teaching: A different kind of classroom* (pp. 169–185). Reston, VA: Music Educators National Conference.

13

Using Gesture and Imagery
Enhancing Musical Understanding in the Choral Classroom
Marta McCarthy

A Tudor motet, an African-American spiritual, a Polynesian chant, a mass by Haydn—such rich diversity is now the province of the choral classroom. Yet the choral conductor-centred tradition in which I work apportions little time for students to reflect, internalize concepts, explore options, test choices, and transfer knowledge and skills to other contexts. When preoccupied by production goals, I tend to neglect engaging students in such activities, which Gardner (1999) identified as critical to genuine understanding of any subject. Yet the challenge of performing this wonderful range of repertoire—to feel "how the music goes," to interpret its style within the music's cultural and social context—offers us unique opportunities to foster musical understanding. Using gesture and imagery, we can help students to discover in their bodies and propel into the sound a sense of flow that captures the rhythmic essence of the musical tradition.

David Elliott (1995) associates the concept "musical understanding" with "a related network of knowings, not always linear or verbal, but weblike and procedural in essence" and involving "knowing anchored in the contexts and purposes of specific musical practices" (p. 68). One of my motivations for this study has been the desire to discover how we can *anchor* musical knowing "in the contexts and purposes of specific musical practices." That is, how can we help students really understand different musical styles, especially those to which they have had little exposure? My hypothesis is that giving students the opportunity to experience the particular quality of motion that drives a specific style of music will help them to feel its human impulse, share in the motivating force of that impulse, and thereby experience music in a more authentic, meaningful, and empowering way.

The Body's Role in Musical Understanding

Patricia Shehan (1987) noted that "as an approach to the conceptual understanding of music, movement has been successfully employed in the curriculum for at least one hundred years" and that movement "is at the heart of music and music learning" (p. 30). The words of composer Roger Sessions (1965) validate this experience: "If music consists in movement, or what I have called inner gesture, it is the performer who supplies the impulse and the energy through which the movement and gesture as conceived in the composer's imagination is given concrete form" (p. 80).

Susanne Cusick (cited in Stubley, 1998) describes performance as "a form of thinking through one's body...the music is experienced...as something done through and with the body." Rather than a thoughtless process, "the mind acts through the space carved out by the body as the symbiotic relationship between musician and instrument is forged and sustained" (p. 95). Eleanor Stubley (1999) reminds us that concepts such as repetition, contrast, open, closed, rounded binary, recapitulation, variation, etc., are grounded not only in formal perceptions but also, and perhaps more fundamentally, in bodily experience (p. 6).

> Concepts such as repetition, contrast, open, closed, rounded binary, recapitulation, variation, etc., are grounded not only in formal perceptions but also, and perhaps more fundamentally, in bodily experience.

According to evidence from EEG-studies (Atenmueller, Gruhn, Parlitz & Liebert, 2000, p. 48), music-making is typical of the highest level of sensory-motor integration. Auditory representation, also known as our inner hearing, is accompanied by a simultaneous feeling of the sound "as a kinesthetic representation." This research verifies the words of Jaques-Dalcroze (1921), who claimed that "the acuteness of our musical feeling will depend on the acuteness of our bodily sensations" (p. 60).

Dalcroze specialist, Frances Aronoff (1969) wrote that kinesthetic experience helps students "discover and come to understand musical ideas in terms of their potential expressive use" (p. 168). The musical elements can be appreciated in terms of aural and kinesthetic images, which in turn provide a repertoire of feelingful sensations to enrich performance, listening, improvisation, and composition.

David G. Woods (1987) observed, "the motor process serves an organizing function for perceiving, conceptualizing, and understanding music." Dalcroze, Orff, and Kodály approaches to music education provide effective opportunities for children to experience tangibly the qualities of movement shared by music, qualities such as light/heavy, smooth/jagged, rising/falling, and inward/outward (p. 36).

Vicki Lind (2001) recently confirmed that kinesthetic activities help students with learning disabilities to identify and reinforce concepts and to link these to notation. For example, for some students who have difficulty linking information from different parts of the brain or interpreting what is seen or heard, the connection between the notation and the performance of a whole note is clarified by moving their bodies through space for that duration (p. 29). The research of Mari Shiobara (1994) also provides compelling evidence that the comprehension of music is enhanced by the ability to "perceive its kinetic qualities in movement or motion, i.e., to understand musical gesture" (p. 115).

Dalcroze eurhythmics techniques increase musical understanding because, according to Irwin Spector (1990), they "establish intimate relations between the vitality of the body and of the mind by means of simultaneous education of the nervous system and of its controlling faculty" (p. 146). Among the objectives of Dalcroze eurhythmics detailed by Elsa Findlay (1971), the following directly refer to an increased ability to transfer knowledge from kinesthesia to cognition:

(1) use of the whole body, inviting larger muscle groups in order to achieve more "vivid realization of rhythmic experience";

(2) body movement as a reference for the interpretation of rhythm symbols;

(3) developing listening by relating what the child hears to what he does; and

(4) integrating body, mind, and emotion in rhythmic expression.

The most significant outcomes of the eurhythmics experience, according to Findlay, are *joy* and *meaning* (pp. 4–6).

Amidst all the stimulating discussion at the Victoria *Symposium*, there seemed to be a consensus that a recognition that the body is integral to understanding music: in other words, we need to make meaning out of our encounters with music. Gardner (1999) implies that education must be concerned with the process of meaning making and "understanding of, the broader themes of life—indeed, with the questions of why the world is as it is and how life can and should be lived" (p. 119).

These statements resonate with my most profound musical experiences as a member of the Westminster Symphonic Choir. Conductor Joseph Flummerfelt implored us to search for the "human gesture" of the art work. Flummerfelt taught us that tone quality, with all its subtleties of colour and intensity, is a reflection of human need, longing, understanding, and perspective. I think this expression, the *human gesture* aptly describes one of the deeper layers of meaning in any art form. Mark Johnson (1987) argues that meaning, imagination, and reason are rooted in bodily experience. Metaphors such as gesture provide bridges between the patterns of our physical experience and the appreciation of abstract concepts (p. xv).

According to Elias Canetti (1960/1962), physical postures are powerful projections of our status within a relationship, symbolizing meanings made in the context of that relationship (p. 449). I encourage young conductors and my own choir members to consider the implications of this concept to influence their tone production. First, we examine the poetry in terms of a conversation: Who is speaking to whom and what is their relationship? After setting the stage in this way, students decide how the speaker would express the "status" of that relationship in terms of posture and intensity of movement: How would we (singers, as representatives of the poet) approach this person/entity physically:

- from above/below/same level?
- from close/far?
- at what level and type of intensity: gentle, exuberant, forceful?
- from head on/sideways/backward?
- at what level of eye contact: direct/above/below?

In a first-year conducting class at the University of Toronto, we compared the symbolic postures in Aaron Copland's arrangement of "At the River," Handel's "And the Glory of the Lord" (from *Messiah*), and Fauré's *Cantique de Jean Racine*. After the discussion, the class decided that the following relationships could be expressed through posture and gesture:

Table 11.1. Relationships Expressed Through Posture and Gesture

Repertoire	"And the Glory"	"At the River"	"Cantique"
"Status" of poet	prophet	neighbour	child/childlike
Addressee	the people	friends/congregation	God
Posture	leading	invitation	kneeling/looking up
Key verb	revealed	gather	espère=hope

Another possible approach is to identify and explore the movement qualities of the key verbs appearing in or suggested by the text. For example, the verb "gather" in "At the River" contrasts with the momentum of the revelation of glory in "And the Glory." Students decide what physical intensity is suggested by these images; does glory break suddenly through the clouds or evolve slowly like a mist? Sometimes the tense of the verb, either literal or implied, is reflected in the quality of motion. For example, "shall be revealed" implies the future, projected "out-there," whereas "for the mouth of the Lord hath spoken it" suggests the past, rooted in known experience, its proclamatory style clearly defined by repeated notes.

We also consider the social or ritualized function associated with the music. Students can easily appreciate and experience the dance-like character of "And the Glory" (especially the opening) in contrast to the processional character of "At the River." A more subtle comparison can be felt between a Baroque menuet, with its stately sense of procession, and a Viennese waltz, also in a triple metre but with a completely different orientation. Body posture internalizes both the feeling of and the reason for the contrast. In the Baroque dance, the chest is always held aloft—the decorum of the court expressed by a sense of pulling away from the downbeat (which could be construed as a musical manifestation of a social convention: holding back from intimate contact). In contrast, the Viennese waltz invites leaning forward into the down-beat—a simple and very effective way for singers to experience the quality of motion in Brahms' *Liebeslieder Waltzer*.

Considering the evidence suggesting that many musical concepts are grounded in bodily experience, it follows that movement can enhance musical understanding by triggering our schematic memory of such experience. Gestures are particularly effective catalysts of musical understanding because they embody a concept or intention and convey meaning. Christopher Small (1998) explains that gestural language is a more adequate way than verbal languages to articulate and deal with the highly complex relationships in our world. Gesture has no grammar but instead relies on patterns (shapes, forms, and textures) which in turn consist of relationships: they are continuous and seamless. He stresses that

> Gestures are particularly effective catalysts of musical understanding because they embody a concept or intention and convey meaning.

> the relation between the shape or pattern of a gesture and its meaning is not arbitrary. Many gestures are fully iconic and carry within themselves the picture of their meaning.... This means not only that when we use this kind of communication we are using one set of relationships, one pattern, to signify another (the process that we call metaphor) but also that gesture and meaning are, at least to some degree, analogues one of the other. (pp. 59–60)

A natural way to introduce students to gesture is by teaching them to conduct. Since conducting requires a complex integration of mind, body, and spirit, it is an ideal vehicle to enhance musical understanding. Various studies (among them, Steven Kelly's 1997 research with beginning band students) attest to the effectiveness of conducting as a tool for teaching rhythm and phrasing in ensemble settings. Conducting is also practical because it is a means of easing into creative movement. As Jackie Wiggins remarked in the *Symposium* dialogue, we have to be sensitive to the vulnerable feelings of our students, especially adolescents who tend to be the most self-conscious about using their bodies. Fortunately, most students are willing and eager to conduct beat patterns, which they associate with a more "legitimate" or safe form of movement.

From simple patterns the movement can be expanded or mutated gradually as necessary to express the musical idea. Beat patterns were

developed to embody the organic logic of metre: the relationship between the beats in terms of weight (e.g., S-W-M-W), direction (down,
in, out, up) intensity (crusis/anacrusis) and speed of falling/rising. Experiencing these aspects of motion helps singers understand *viscerally*—by
engaging their kinesthetic intelligence—the rhythm, tempo, and phrasing. As singers develop confidence in this type of gesture, they can experiment with more subtle ways of connecting the beats and eventually
discover the expressivity of their entire body. Jacques-Dalcroze (1918)
emphasized the engagement of the whole body as critical to the transfer
from kinesthetic experience to musical understanding.

For an effective transfer of knowledge, singers are encouraged to reflect on the differences brought about by different qualities of motion in
both the sound and the feeling. During the warm-up segment of rehearsals, I encourage singers to make space for their low, supported
breath and then to release it in two contrasting styles. A completely fluid
line (surrendering the air as if you are a balloon suddenly released) precedes the singing of a Renaissance motet, while a thicker, sustained release (exhaling while wading through molasses) sets up the flow of a
Bruckner motet. In this way, the breathing warm-up serves as an effective model of the contrast in tone and intensity of the line.

Many choral conductors use images that engage the students physically and remind them of the origins of music in human experience and
collaborative understanding. Instead of "Breathe in, hold, exhale" students are encouraged to open themselves to receive the air, surrender to
the earth, give the air away. Warm-ups are sung with an acknowledge-
ment of attitude and quality. The head voice is accessed by sighing. The
soft palate is lifted by stifling a yawn or making an awesome discovery.
Facial resonance is awakened by smelling a richly scented rose.

Humming is a standard vocal technique to explore the resonance
space. To make a connection between sound and meaning, we imagine
searching for an idea while humming; when the sense of discovery is felt
(which tends to correspond to the moment the hum locks into an ideal
resonance space), we descend the scale to "aha!" In order that the singers
have time to consciously register the sensation, I encourage them to
"find" at their own pace. A rich tone cluster unfolds.

Since most of my students are unaccustomed to moving to music, I usually begin the process by inviting singers to move freely while listening to music. John Dickson (1992) suggests that this spontaneous movement enhances "the intuition and experience needed to effect a balance between the technical and expressive levels of music making" (p. 15).

After this exercise, I ask my choir members which elements or qualities of the music encouraged their bodies to move. "Lyric line, legato and fluidity, rise and fall of pitches, changes of timbre, the aggressive stuff, articulations" are characteristic responses. One singer described her own reaction to an avant-garde segment, "*I didn't feel that that part of the music was aggressive until I started moving to it. I think the moving made me more aware of the difference in the energies.*"

Having explored a range of motion and intensities in response to contrasting styles of music, we focus on finding an appropriate tone quality and sense of flow for particular repertoire. One of the main challenges of the Renaissance motet, "*Ascendit Deus,*" is to continually propel the line and find the distinct shape of the phrase in the individual voice parts, which are imitative but of different lengths and shapes. On one occasion I sent each section of the choir into a separate room for a few minutes and challenged them to all come back being able to spin their line convincingly. They began by extending the warm-up exercise so that they were moving through the room as if suspended from the ceiling while singing the phrase. Then they transferred this feeling into a circular motion in one or both arms while singing—a kinaesthetic representation of spinning the sound and shaping the phrase. An unexpected but important outcome was that the group began to function like a Renaissance ensemble: members of each section huddled together as if to form one voice, and began to rely much less on my cues but instead listen to the tapestry of the interweaving lines. Additionally, they were able to experience the relationship between the music and the text—the word painting of the rising line "*ascendit Deus*" and the transparent buoyancy of "jubilation."

Ramona Wis (1999) explores physical metaphor in her choral rehearsals in much the same way. She describes the process as "finding a gesture that seems to embody the essence of the musical idea and then applying it to the music." Wis suggests that choral directors especially rely on metaphor because we deal with both an abstract subject (music) and an abstract instrument (the voice). She argues that performing meaningful gestures can help singers "feel and understand the music at a deeper, more primal level. Singers can experience the structural elements or the expressive qualities of the music in their bodies...they can connect their kinesthetic awareness with the sound and its subtle or dramatic changes" (pp. 26–27).

Performing One's Musical Understandings

So far, I have described physical metaphors that I have presented to choirs based on my own understanding of the relationships between the music and the text. While I'm rather fond of my own interpretations, this process tends to replicate the traditional ensemble mode of instruction: obey and mimic the conductor. It seems critical, if students are to really understand, i.e., to transfer their knowledge to other situations and to affirm their understanding through creative artistry, that they have the opportunity to experiment with and choose movements reflecting *their* interpretation of the human gesture of the work.

Gardner (1999) states that in order to perceive the beauty of a work of art, one must "enter into the world of the work, and of the artist, to grasp what is being attempted, to familiarize oneself with the tools, and to try to 'perform' one's own understandings" (p. 175). Veronika Cohen (1998) trains students to perform their understandings of the form of musical works by designing and performing their own "movement analogues." In this creative choreography students embody the dynamic shape of the composition.

In our choral classes, we use a similar strategy to create gestural analogues of the pieces we sing. Movement helps us test options of colours, textures, and dynamic contouring and enriches our conception of the emotional character of the music. When these elements are in balance, the correct rhythms have an organic sense about them that seems to just "feel right," giving the music a life of its own, and in the case of choral music, illuminating the meaning of the text. The primary purpose of creating these analogues is to share in the embodied experience that inspired the music.

During the *Symposium* we were introduced to Wiggins' (2001) approach to teaching for musical understanding in which music students are offered a myriad of opportunities to solve engaging creative problems (see chapter 9). This approach resonates with the nature of Dalcroze's techniques as summarized by Farber and Parker (1987) in which the body is used to "solve" musical puzzles. Likewise, the purpose of the gesture-as-imagery approach is not to choreograph the music but instead to "enact particular musical meanings in physical space. The point of meeting that challenge…is to deepen understanding of, and ability to produce, music" (p. 45).

Recently, my chamber choir began to learn "Run Children Run." Although the composer provides a rich verbal description of the style, it proved to be very difficult for us to maintain a steady pulse because of the rests (someone always needed to fill in the silences!) and the syncopation. More difficult still seemed to be finding the "groove" of the music: Stephen Hatfield composed this piece, but it is based on a field yell—related to a spiritual—sung by African-American slaves. As soon as we were familiar with the music, we researched and discussed its context in order to appreciate the human impulse from which this genre evolved. Then we devised a set of gestures/movements that could have been the impetus for the music—in other words, instead of moving *to* the music, students sought movements that would have evoked this music.

Before this process began, I asked the students to consider: *Who was singing? When and where would they be singing? Remember to find movements that incorporate everything we know about the music instead of changing the music to justify your movements, but feel free to experiment. Don't discard an option until you've tried it!* The following is a transcript of their initial preparation. Students' names are used with their permission.

GESTURAL ANALOGUE of *"Run Children Run"* by Stephen Hatfield

Group 1
Text: "Run children run, Run children run, Run children run I say, Cuz I got a right to the tree of life."

Léna: *I think we're observers...we're sort of dictating to someone else to escape. I don't think we're moving forward because we can't run! Our feet are stuck* [she demonstrated by trying to surge forward with feet held down to the ground].
Erik: *Yeah, and it's like the Tree of Life is our freedom. We can't get to it, but our children are the future.*
Brynn: *But it's not necessarily really our children...*
Odiri: *It could be literally the parents urging the children...because parents live through their children even if they [the parents] don't survive.*
Erik: *Okay, so it's not the physical act of running but a spiritual symbiosis.*

They initially agree to each choose individual actions, but no one is happy with what they come up with because they can't feel the music in unison, especially the 2nd syncopated bar.

Brynn: *That part is the repression: we're being held back.*
Odiri: *I think we should try using the work image, because the reality is that we'd be working in a line, not doing our own thing...*[he demonstrates the swinging motion]
Léna: *Oh yeah. Did you see that movie* [I don't catch what she says here]*? They're chipping stone and they're all chained together in a line—but is that a stereotype?*
Odiri: *I think that's pretty much what they had to do. That part of it is probably realistic, and there might be a call-response thing, where the lead worker sings the first part solo and the rest echo.*

They decide to be chained together and they match their motion because "in real life" they would have to help each other move together in unison. Brynn suggests stopping, looking out over the field at "Cause I gotta right to the Tree of Life" to match the musical change and to reflect the hope of freedom, but Odiri argues that they wouldn't be able to stop working! I suggest that they incorporate both: they solve it by trying to look out—pulling the line forward but then being dragged back into the routine.

Group 2
Text: "I got a right, I got a right — I got a right to the tree of life — Everybody got the right — I got a right to the tree of life."

Daood: *I'm not sure how, but we all gravitated towards moving in a circle; it helps in our perception... We talked about the whole fact that there were two systems at work here: one is the pounding beat and we all ended up instinctively moving to that. And second, there is the work against the beat, the sort of syncopated resistance to the beat and that was the force, the power within this beat. There were two diverging patterns, so we either wanted to pull the power in* [he demonstrates with hands] *or sort of shout it out* [he flings his arms out in front of him]. *We sort of played with individual styles of moving within that.*

The groups also suggested these solutions to embodying the sound:

(1) chanting/whispering/yelling/moaning the words;

(2) extending the first slide right through the bar and dropping it into the next beat: the tone is the heavy object you're trying to move and the slide is the exertion; and

(3) connecting the stretch of beat 3 with the preparation to the clap on beat 4; add a grunt/pant on beat 1 of m. 2—the down stretch symbolizing pain and enslavement, the up-stretch projecting into the future—pushing the children forward with hope.

These motions helped us achieve rhythmic accuracy, vitality, and a more appropriate vocal style. Moreover, we began to walk in another person's shoes.

Conclusion

Wayne Bowman (1998) recently referred to the "utter neglect of corpo-reality and spirituality" in our validations of musical education (p. 14). Louise Steinman (1986) argues that as members of modern society, we have lost touch with our body as a source of understanding ourselves and others (p. 11). For many educators, these warnings are being heeded in terms of transformative education: schooling that values the qualitative experience, recognizes human values, nurtures spiritual growth, and considers the possibility of enchantment.

In "Run Children Run," students were able to make the connection between human suffering and communal singing, using movement as the metaphorical bridge. The process was made easier by our familiarity with gestures associated with the work of slaves, which we know to have been organically linked to their song. In addition, its style stems from the West African tradition described by Curtis and Cloud (1991) in which the world is viewed as consisting of "relationship between body, soul, and mind" (p. 16). The music of this culture is inherently linked to expressive dance. Song does not exist in isolation from bodily movement. Therefore it is more appropriate to learn the music while in motion.

All music is related to movement. Choral conductor Wilhelm Ehmann (1968) insisted that bodily movements both enliven and enhance choral singing because "singing and dancing belong together." Ehmann explained:

> artistic choral singing of the present must be regarded as a late cultural form, and should be understood, in a sense, as "dancing on the spot." This concept of "inner dancing" should continually be kept alive by the director.... Even a concert choir should regard itself as being fundamentally a choir in motion. (p. 78)

We need, therefore, to have experienced and been moved by the inner dance, the gesture that has evolved from the needs of a people and the shape of their communal experience, in order to comprehend their music.

Gesture and imagery nurture aesthetic discernment. Reflection on our body's perception is "the source of our connection to others and the basis upon which we are able to share understanding" (Walsh, 1999, p. 11). This awareness is particularly meaningful for the choral singer, whose instrument dwells within the body. When movement connects our voice to the collective song of the world community we become better integrated as human beings, more sensitive to other people, and more in touch with our universe.

References

Aronoff, F. W. (1969). *Music and young children*. New York: Holt, Rinehart & Winston.

Atenmueller, E., Gruhn, W., Parlitz, D., & Liebert, G. (2000). The impact of music education on brain networks: Evidence from EEG-studies. *International Journal of Music Education, 35,* 46–49.

Bowman, W. (1998). Universals, relativism, and music education. *Bulletin of the Council for Research in Music Education, 135,* 1–20.

Canetti, E. (1962). *Crowds and power* (C. Stewart, Trans.). London: Gollancz Press. (Original work published 1960)

Cohen, V. W. (1998). *Teaching for musical cognition*. Unpublished CD-Rom.

Curtis, M. V., & Cloud, L. V. (1991). The African-American spiritual: Traditions and performance practices. *Choral Journal, 32* (4), 15–22.

Dickson, J. H. (1992). The training of conductors through the methodology of kinesthetics. *Choral Journal, 32* (8), 15–20.

Ehmann, W. (1968). *Choral directing*. Minneapolis, MN: Ausberg Publishing House.

Elliott, D. (1995). *Music matters: A new philosophy of music education*. New York: Oxford University Press.

Farber, A., & Parker, L. (1987). Discovering music through Dalcroze eurhythmics. *Music Educators Journal, 73* (11), 43–45.

Findlay, E. (1971). *Rhythm and movement: Applications of Dalcroze eurhythmics.* Evanston, IL: Summy-Birchard Company.

Gardner, H. (1999). *The disciplined mind: What all students should understand.* New York: Simon & Schuster.

Jaques-Dalcroze, E. (1918). *The eurhythmics of Jaques-Dalcroze* (E. Ingham, Trans.) Boston, MA: Small, Maynard & Company.

Johnson, M. (1987). *The body in the mind: The bodily basis of meaning, imagination and reason.* Chicago, IL: University of Chicago Press.

Kelly, S. (1997). The effect of conducting practice on the rhythm and phrasing ability of beginning band students. *Journal of Research in Music Education, 45* (2), 295–305.

Lind, V. (2001). Adapting choral rehearsals for students with learning disabilities. *Choral Journal, 41* (7), 27–30.

Sessions, R. (1965). *The musical experience of composer, performer and listener.* New York: Athenium.

Shehan, P. K. (1987). Movement: The heart of music. *Music Educators Journal, 73* (11), 25–30.

Shiobara, M. (1994). Music and movement: The effect of movement on musical comprehension. *British Journal Music Education, 11,* 113-127.

Small, C. (1998). *Musicking: The meaning of performing and listening.* Hanover: University Press of New England.

Spector, I. (1990). *Rhythm and life: The work of Emile Jaques-Dalcroze.* Stuyvesant, NY: Pendragon Press.

Steinman, L. (1986). *The knowing body: Elements of contemporary performance and dance.* Boston, MA: Shambala Press.

Stubley, E. (1998). Being in the body, being in the sound. *Journal of Aesthetic Education, 32* (4), 93–105.

Stubley, E.(1999). Musical listening as bodily experience. *Canadian Journal of Research in Music Education, 40* (4), 5-7.

Walsh, A.-M. (1999). The body's full presence in arts education. *Canadian Journal of Research in Music Education, 40* (4), 9–11.

Woods, D. G. (1987). Movement and general music: Perfect partners. *Music Educators Journal, 73* (11), 35–42.

Wis, R. M. (1999). Physical metaphor in the choral rehearsal: A gesture-based approach to developing vocal skill and musical understanding. *Choral Journal, 40* (3), 25–33.

14

Nurturing Musical Understanding
Thinking Like an Assessor

Patricia Parai

"Just when we think we're doing really well, the bar gets raised." These words are from a recent conversation with twenty members of a high school vocal ensemble, who were preparing for a major challenge that would take them and their director to perform in Carnegie Hall. Their musical understanding had clearly deepened over the months of concentrated preparation for this exciting goal. They talked about the growth they had experienced through the singing of jazz and said it allowed them more freedom to explore and greater ownership over their learning. Though they valued their classical music training and would never be without it in their lives, they believed that it restricted their creativity and spontaneity. They noted that the small ensemble experience was allowing them more independence, challenged their mental abilities and gave them a lot of pride in their work. But they added that it also made them more aware and critical of voicing, pitch, unity, harmony, and stage presence. (Conversation with students from St. Mary's Vocal Ensemble, Calgary, Alberta.)

Introduction

During the past decade in Canada we have witnessed many advocacy groups coming together to articulate philosophies and to formulate action plans for maintaining fine arts programs in the schools. In the face of real and anticipated budget cuts, dedicated fine arts supporters have petitioned their governments, boards, and school administrators to retain and support the arts in education. While stepping back and reflecting on what the arts really do for our students and learning how to communicate the benefits in concrete terms has been a good exercise for arts teachers, the latter are usually fully engaged in teaching and celebrating the arts and have little time to discuss and justify what they do.

To a large extent, many of the advocacy initiatives have been successful. Some of the stakeholders have listened and are supporting our

229

arts programs. But it is not enough to advocate for strong fine arts programs. The challenge now must be to focus more of our energy on raising and maintaining the standards of the programs we already have. Now is the time to examine our common understandings about teaching and learning in the arts and to ensure that we are offering students the best possible music education we can. Canadian music educators have to be able to speak the language, walk the talk, and ensure that they know what best practice in music classes looks like and how they can help students achieve excellence.

In fostering a comprehensive music education for all students, teachers must nurture understanding in three major dimensions: performing, listening, and creating. Music educators have traditionally focussed on performance outcomes in their programs and they attach significant importance to the aim of achieving excellence in the music ensemble. There has been on-going discussion about whether or not too much emphasis has been placed on performance in our school music programs. Favaro (2000) reflected on the differing views of a public that expect concerts and of curriculum theorists, who criticize that practice. There is nothing wrong with accommodating public expectations, provided the latter are founded on sound educational practice. It is our job to share our passion for music while educating students and audiences about quality repertoire performed to a high standard. Performance should not, however, be seen as limited to public presentations. The less public (and less acknowledged) performing that takes place within the music classroom is of prime importance in developing musical understanding. Such performing includes singing and playing instruments—the skills through which students understand such musical concepts as melody, rhythm, harmony, range, form, and pitch.

Does the achievement of excellence in performance alone imply that all students have achieved musical understanding? Do we fail to teach our students the elements and concepts of music because we are too busy preparing them for performances? Are listening and creating receiving the emphasis they deserve? Though music teachers naturally focus on performance, true understanding can only be achieved when underlying musical concepts are linked to the outcome—musical understanding. If we intend to develop musicians who can take ownership for their own musical learning by thinking and responding critically and who can make musical decisions as individual learners—listeners, creators, and performers—we must be thorough and consistent in our planning and delivery of curriculum. In this paper, I will discuss the importance of teaching for understanding based on thoughtfully planned activities and ongoing assessment at all stages and in all aspects of the learning process.

Achieving musical understanding is part of a multi-faceted, ongoing process that includes not only the teaching and learning of elements and concepts but also the artistic application of that acquired knowledge. Musical understanding is demonstrated in the ability to communicate to an audience as a performer, to listen to a musical work and appreciate it, and to compose or improvise an original piece of music. How can we help our students develop musical understanding?

> Musical understanding is demonstrated in the ability to communicate to an audience as a performer, to listen to a musical work and appreciate it, and to compose or improvise an original piece of music.

The Six Facets of Understanding

In their book, *Understanding by Design*, Grant Wiggins and Jay McTighe (1998) identify six facets or views of understanding: explanation, interpretation, application, perspective, empathy, and self-knowledge. In *The Understanding by Design Handbook*, McTighe and Wiggins (1999) emphasize that, though all six facets are different components of understanding, "a complete mature understanding ideally involves the more or less full development of all six kinds of understanding" (p. 10). Their framework for nurturing understanding, though it unfortunately does not address the arts, does have implications for learning, teaching, and assessment in the arts just as for other subjects.

> "Teaching for understanding aims at having students explain, interpret, and apply, while showing insight from perspective, empathy, and self-knowledge" (Wiggins & McTighe, 1998, p. 64).

In order to understand the relevance of *Understanding by Design* to the music classroom, it will be necessary to examine the six facets of understanding identified by Wiggins and McTighe and reflect on their possible connections to best practice in music education. The following brief explanations of the six facets suggest some ideas for application to music instruction, though there are many other ways of approaching each facet, and examples will not always address all three ways of experiencing music (listening, creating, and performing).

Explanation

This facet assumes that students can show their understanding of a topic through dialoguing and justifying their choices. Students are able to "provide thorough, supported, and justifiable accounts of phenomena, facts, and data" (McTighe & Wiggins, 1999, p. 10), a goal that we should be striving to achieve in the music class. Explanation, when practised by students as an assessment strategy, teaches them how to monitor their own thinking and to assume ownership over their learning. Students need to be able to talk about a piece to help them make sense of it and interpret the composer's musical intentions. Perhaps we don't expect students to do enough of that in our music classes. Susan Farrell (1994) stated:

> If assessment is seen to be an ongoing learning process rather than simply a method of evaluation, then it must be used as an opportunity to develop complex understandings. Student musicians should all be allowed to develop the same understandings and habits of mind that professional musicians use to sustain and enhance their work. In doing so, they are also learning: to take responsibility for their work; about establishing a way of working, thinking and presenting their own ideas; about what it takes to pursue a project over time; and what continuous improvement requires. (p. 7)

Assessment and understanding go hand in hand. If students cannot talk about their work, they have difficulty making the necessary changes to bring it to a higher level. Because understanding does not happen when the conductor does all the talking and gives out all the orders, the diagnosing of problems and knowing what to do to improve the overall sound is a responsibility that all learners must assume, along with the conductor. When students are not expected to assess their own playing and that of the whole ensemble, their understanding of the work is bound to be limited and the resulting thoughtless performance may reflect that lack of understanding.

One way in which students can strive towards a deepening understanding through explanation is by regular use of rubrics that can then be employed to rate their progress. In the course of this type of practice, they are required to assess their own singing or playing, as well as that of their section and the whole ensemble, by writing down and sharing what students are hearing and what they should be hearing. Farrell (1994) gives several examples of individual performance assessment guides in which students are required to discuss specific performance elements. A scoring key is then used by the teacher to assess a student's critique or comments. On a scale from 1 to 4, a 4 might indicate that the student has consistently made specific and accurate references to musical elements, is able to make appropriate links to the score being studied, and has clearly articulated his own action plan for improved performance. A student might write, for example, "I need to enter more confidently in the 2nd movement and articulate the sixteenth notes more clearly" or "At B our section needs to feel the stress on the first note of each triplet so that we are exactly together in the rapid passages."

The facet of explanation is also clearly applicable in the listening dimension. Students begin to understand music at a different level when they are guided into making intelligent responses, verbal and written, to the music they are hearing. Expecting students to use descriptive words to explain what they are hearing is one way of helping them focus on listening for specific elements and styles. Students should be encouraged to describe short segments using the musical vocabulary with which they are familiar, including making references to such elements as dynamics, tempo, form, harmony, melodic and rhythmic patterns, and phrasing. While composing, students should be expected to talk about their writing and to explain the decisions they have made.

Interpretation

Interpretation, the object of which is "understanding, not explanation," is of special importance in the music classroom, though not in the same way as Wiggins and McTighe (1998) use the word. They speak about organising ideas through narrative "by telling a story of what something is about" (p. 48). Interpretation in music is usually linked to the way in which the player expresses the music.

The connection between explanation and interpretation is evident in a simple example of first graders responding to music through movement. During a series of listening lessons centered around excerpts from Camille Saint-Saens' *Carnival of the Animals* the children were asked to imagine which animals the composer might have been describing and to listen to the instruments he used for this purpose. They were then encouraged to interpret the music by moving freely about the floor space in a way that would be appropriate to the various animals.

In performance contexts we often tell our students to get the notes off the page and make meaning of the music. Within the ensemble, the conductor is responsible for shaping the music in a meaningful way. Having the students play or sing sections of the piece in different ways fosters understanding, provided students are engaged in analysing and critiquing their work. Developing that high level skill and sensitivity in students must be considered a major objective in nurturing understanding. Students should also be listening together to other interpretations of the works they are studying and comparing the different ways in which other performers play the same piece of music. Such a practice invites them to be active listeners and to recognise what constitutes an exemplary performance.

Wiggins and McTighe (1998) explain the importance of students' thinking for themselves:

> Learning cannot be primarily or exclusively the process of learning what someone else says is the meaning of something, except as a way to model meaning making or overcome basic decoding inability, or as a prelude to testing the interpretation so as to better understand the possibilities. (p. 51)

As music educators we would do well to consider the implications of this statement in our own curriculum design.

A strictly teacher-centered approach that does not encourage the input of students' ideas is counter-productive to the nurturing of understanding and will not lead to the accomplishment of all the curricular goals. Whether in the rehearsal setting, during the listening experience, or in the composition lesson, understanding is nurtured when the teacher guides the students to make informed choices and responses to music. Following a melody map of an instrumental piece or, at the next level, creating a melody map of a new piece calls on students to listen to the direction of the melody line, to the instruments playing it, and to the texture of the music.

Application

> *Application [is the] ability to use knowledge effectively in new situations and diverse contexts.... We show our understanding of something by using it, adapting it, and customizing it. When we must negotiate different constraints, social contexts, purposes, and audiences, understanding is revealed as performance know-how, the ability to accomplish tasks successfully, with grace under pressure, and with tact.* (Wiggins & McTighe, 1998, pp. 51–52)

Expecting students to apply their knowledge and understanding of musical vocabulary and elements to their music-making, listening and creating is an ongoing goal. My third grade classes were listening to "The Carnival of Venice" by Nicolo Paganini. Though most of the students understand the concept of theme and variations, they had difficulty applying music vocabulary to their written descriptions of each variation. Brainstorming for a list of descriptive words helped them understand how to find more appropriate words to reflect the differences and similarities in the variations. Many of the students are now beginning to use such words as staccato, legato, ascending, descending, bouncy, running, rather than just pretty, nice, and beautiful.

We know that significant learning occurs when students take part, as performers and listeners, in real life concerts that allow them to think like professional musicians. Nothing can be more authentic than the experience of being in the same role as professional musicians, following the same process they would use in concert preparation and performance. Likewise, being in the audience listening to a professional performance after meaningful classroom discussion about the repertoire to be performed allows students to move from being passive to active listeners, particularly when the learning experience is extended to the actual performance and students are asked to listen for specific elements. When local orchestra conductors and education coordinators collaborate with teachers in preparing appropriate curriculum materials, every participating student has a prime opportunity to apply knowledge in a new situation.

Performing musicians who really understand don't wait for the conductor to give all the instructions and signals but readily apply their knowledge of music to their playing or singing. They are active learners who, while making music, listen to the ensemble and make adjustments where necessary. In describing learning in the choral rehearsal, Hilary Apfelstadt (1989) wrote:

> Under the demands of public performance pressures, we seek the most efficient means of getting the music learned, or so we think. In the short term our students may fix the errors and produce an accurate performance in a relatively brief time. As for the long-term effects, however, we cannot be sure that the "quick fix" will have any lasting impact. The real test is whether the students can apply those learnings to new contexts or whether we must start all over again each time we introduce a new piece of music. (p. 73)

A few years ago I travelled to a festival in California with a high school band. At Disneyland we took part in an industry workshop led by a professional conductor who emphasised the importance of being able to sight read accurately on the first try. Taking the students through an exercise that involved them playing an unknown score, he gave them three chances to get it right. Removing his earphones after the second attempt, he signalled to a technician in the sound booth; at that point a video was shown on a large screen in front of the band. The students were in total shock when they discovered that they were part of the sound track of *Fantasia* and that every error they made negatively impacted on the production. The deepest understanding came at the end of the clip when Jimminy Cricket, who was drowning, suddenly rose back to the surface of the water accompanied by the precise burst of a bubble, followed by a few imprecise brass instruments from our band. From that point on, the students were fully aware that they had to think and play like professional musicians. This example highlights the importance of students taking ownership of their playing, while assessing, analysing, interpreting, and problem solving along with the conductor. Such an experience underlined the value of good sight-reading skills in an authentic assessment experience and describes a learning situation in which young musicians had to bring musical understanding to their work. While thinking as assessors, they practised what Wiggins and McTighe (1998) call "performance know-how, the ability to accomplish tasks successfully, with grace under pressure, and with tact" (p. 52).

Perspective

To understand in this sense is to see things from a dispassionate and disinterested perspective. This type of understanding is not about any student's particular point of view but about the mature recognition that any answer to a complex question typically involves a point of view; hence, an answer is often one of many possible plausible accounts. It is a mature achievement. (Wiggins & McTighe, 1998, p. 53)

Music students with perspective are those who listen to other choirs and bands and not only recognise the value in their work but are able to articulate in musical language what has contributed to an exemplary performance. Often in public performance settings young music students listen to another ensemble singing or playing the same selection as they are and then proceed to discuss the tempo, the balance, the articulation, or the style. These students are indeed responding from another point of view and making connections to their own work. Wiggins and McTighe (1998) state: "Novice learners, those just setting out on the road to mastery, may have a revealing point of view, even when they lack a thorough explanation of things" (p. 54).

With established guidelines, and using whatever tools they can to preserve their own ideas, young students are capable of creating quite unique and detailed compositions of their own when they are encouraged to do so. These tools do not have to include conventional notation and may be computer-assisted. Because there is no single right answer in this context, students are able to explore their own ideas and create a product at their level of understanding. This understanding is made evident in assessing and discussing the process and product.

Empathy

> *Empathy [is] the ability to get inside another person's feeling and worldview.... Empathy is a learned ability to grasp the world from someone else's point of view. This kind of understanding implies an existential or experiential prerequisite.* (Wiggins & McTighe, 1998, pp. 55–56)

Here again the point is made that "authentic learning experiences shift a student from the role of a passive knowledge receiver into a more active role as a constructor of meaning" (Wiggins & McTighe, 1998, p. 11). Analyzing a piece of music together gives students the opportunity to discuss in musical language what the composer has intended and achieved, what the style is, and to which era the piece belongs. Performing with an ensemble in a public performance requires a level of understanding similar to what is required of professional musicians.

In her guide to assessment strategies for music teachers, Susan Farrell (1994) stated: "Student musicians should all be allowed to develop the same understandings and habits of mind that professional musicians use to sustain and enhance their work" (p. 7). The following anecdote is about a small group of high school students whose musical understanding advanced significantly when they came together as the band accompanying a large scale musical.

During the preliminary rehearsal stages, when the musicians joined the actors, there were many territorial issues to resolve. The actors criticized the band and implied that they might not be up to the challenge because they didn't sound like the CD that the cast had been using. Not knowing how to respond and not being able to sound like a CD left the musicians somewhat humbled and uncertain, though they never let on. Their challenge was to go away and work harder, recognizing that they would each be accountable for supporting the singers. The biggest challenge for the actors was to understand and accept that a musical is not a play with music. During the course of the many rehearsals, evidence of understanding became more clear as both actors and musicians came to realize that they not only needed each other but that both roles with their implied understanding and responsibilities were critical to the success of the show.

Self-Knowledge

Self-knowledge [is] the wisdom to know one's ignorance and how one's patterns of thought and action inform as well as prejudice understanding. (Wiggins & McTighe, 1998, p. 57)

Musicians, like other learners, demonstrate self-knowledge by being aware of and acknowledging their strengths and weaknesses and then making the necessary improvements and corrections in their playing or singing. They engage in self-assessment and don't just wait to be told where they need to improve. In individual practice sessions, in rehearsal, and in performance, they contribute to the advancement of the whole group by monitoring their thinking and making any necessary adjustments. This is an aspect of understanding that occurs without correction or direction from a teacher, yet can be encouraged through reflection.

Through composing students learn to revise and edit their work, following an approach similar to that used in language arts, in which they are expected to take ownership over their work and figure out how to make it better. During this process, they engage in extensive editing and revising, hence discovering that it is not always easy to bring work up to the next level. On the contrary, persistent effort and determination are required if one is to become a better writer and to grow in understanding through creating.

Backward Design

One of the major factors necessary to foster understanding is the advance planning done by the teacher, beginning with the end in mind. Backward planning involves a teacher seeing beyond the skills students must acquire to come up with the end product first, then working backwards to set up the necessary lessons and activities to get to the end product. For musicians—teachers and students—that is a familiar concept. In fact it might be argued that the concept of backward design, though unnamed, has been borrowed from the arts. The outcome in music, however, as mentioned earlier, has been the performance rather than musical understanding. Backward design is important because it provides a framework for establishing the necessary steps through which teaching, learning, and assessment will occur.

Backward design may be thought of as purposeful task analysis. Given a task to be accomplished, how do we get there? What kinds of lessons and practices are needed to master key performances? This backward approach to curricular design also departs from another common practice: thinking about assessment as something we do at the end, once teaching is completed. It reminds us to ask what we would accept as evidence that students have attained the desired understanding and proficiencies—before beginning to plan teaching and learning experiences (Wiggins & McTighe, 1998, p. 8).

Before we move into the process we should have a solid understanding of what students should know, understand, and be able to do. Wiggins and McTighe (1998) use the term enduring to refer to "the big ideas" students should remember. Enduring understandings "go beyond discrete facts or skills to focus on larger concepts, principles, or processes" (p. 10). Teachers need to identify the enduring understandings that students will need to use beyond the classroom. In the music class, when students are studying different styles of music, they might be expected to know how specific styles were created, what melodic, harmonic or rhythmic features characterize these styles, and how a particular style evolved or was influenced by its genre. This kind of learning will serve students well after graduation.

How can we *cover* curriculum content and help students acquire skills within the context of a balanced music program in a way that makes it possible for every student to reach a reasonable degree of understanding and excellence? The concept of backward design implies that teachers will consider, in their long range planning, the importance not only of content but also of assessment and what is of enduring value. The process includes three stages: identifying the desired results, determining acceptable evidence, and then planning the learning experiences and instruction. How would the process look in long-range planning in music?

> The concept of backward design implies that teachers will consider, in their long range planning, the importance not only of content but also of assessment and of the value of enduring knowledge.

Stage One: Identify Desired Results

Toward what important understanding, knowledge, and skill does it aim?
(McTighe & Wiggins, 1999, p. 5)

The challenge we face as music teachers is quite the opposite of that encountered by core area teachers. For many of them, moving to backward design planning is a huge paradigm shift. We, on the contrary, know where we are going but aren't always sure about how to get there. Our vision of the outcome is often very clear in our minds but we don't always plan learning activities that link to the end product. Unlike teachers of core subjects whose curriculum planning is influenced primarily by content, standards, and achievement tests, music teachers are blessed with an unlimited array of repertoire, listening materials, activities, and methodologies. These may or may not, however, be related to the desired outcomes of provincial curricula and to students' prior knowledge. How often, for example, do we hear elementary choirs singing music that is pitched too low for their head voices, thus contributing to a less than desirable choral sound?

On the other hand, our idea of where we are going may be limited unless we include listening and composition in addition to performance and focus on musical understanding as the outcome. If the ultimate goal is to nurture musical understanding, all approaches, projects and resources must be selected with the class and the ensemble's knowledge, background, and growth in mind. What big ideas will contribute to musical understanding?

Stage Two: Determine Acceptable Evidence: Thinking Like an Assessor

Thinking like an assessor means that a teacher will ask key questions and peel off the layers, not only during the learning process but also during the planning of curriculum. Keeping the big idea at the center when planning helps the teacher identify, in advance, what concepts and skills students will find difficult. Singing in harmony, playing an instrumental accompaniment to a song, and notating a composition are all end products that don't happen without extensive practice and teacher guidance throughout the preparatory stages. Students need to be shown how to practice and how to figure out what they are doing that is detracting from their success.

To think like assessors, music teachers need to develop good ears and a mental model of the desired sound and then be committed to working consistently towards that result. In a band or choir rehearsal, as well as in the classroom, constant attention must be paid to intonation, balance, blend, articulation, phrasing, and expression. Teachers must help students come to terms with the musical ideas of the composition. Throughout the process of any performance preparation the same attention must be given to ongoing assessment as to the final evaluation. It is the continuous use of different assessment strategies that helps bring works to a higher level before the ensemble ever gets to the performance.

If important ideas, concepts, and processes are to be understood by students in all dimensions of music education, it is the teacher's job to lead them to that understanding through guided questioning and problem solving and by encouraging the use of an assortment of assessment strategies. These can include self- and peer-assessment, as well as sharing findings through teacher-student and student-student dialoguing or conferencing. Other valuable assessment strategies for music classes include written tests, rehearsal and concert critiques, videotaped performances, observation checklists, and journals.

Stage Three: Plan Learning Experiences and Instruction: Uncoverage

> At the heart of all uncoverage is the deliberate interrogation of the content to be learned, as opposed to just the teaching and learning of the material.
> (Wiggins & McTighe, 1998, p. 27)

When music teachers think like assessors they uncover in advance what it is that students will have difficulty understanding. For example, students in a choir or a band are often content to play or sing the notes on the page and nothing else. In these cases, it is the teacher who uncovers the meaning of the music and takes students beyond the stage of simple note reading. Choosing opening technical exercises that are linked to specific sections of a piece being studied is one way of assisting the students in mastering challenging passages, but understanding requires that students learn how to uncover meaning too.

The teacher must be able to identify the challenges students will encounter when learning to compose and perform their own works. Some of these challenges are not evident until we are actually engaged in the process with the students. Like the planning process, the compositional process is recursive. It circles around key ideas that aren't always easily transcribed and with which students need plenty of guided questioning as they learn to record their ideas. If the end result is to be the students' presentation of their written compositions, the process of getting there should include listening to examples from respected composers and exchanging their work with each other to find out whether or not other students can read and perform what they have written.

The work that teachers plan—repertoire, listening, reading, and writing activities—must challenge students, engage them in the learning process, teach critical thinking skills, and show them that the content they are learning in class is not just a collection of activities. Rather, it is knowledge and skills that they must then apply and interpret if they are to advance in musical understanding as performers, listeners, and creators.

Conclusions

How do we know when musical understanding has been achieved? While reflecting on the content of this paper, I informally asked several teachers for a spontaneous verbal answer to the questions, "When do you think your students have reached musical understanding? How do you plan your teaching to get them there?" All the teachers' answers clearly reflected their own personal philosophies of music and their visions for the music program in their respective schools. Here are a few of their responses:

- Literacy is important but communicating from the soul through performance has to be a major goal.
- It is better to teach young children by rote and have them sing expressively than to teach them to read music.
- Teachers have to let go of total ownership and control if they aim to further musical understanding in their students. They

need to allow for a lot more spontaneity and creativity in the classroom.

- Teaching my students to be literate allows me to accomplish more with them in the choir. I expect them to be able to sight read choral exercises in class and they do it!

- I know they understand when they listen to new music, recognize its genre and identify its musical characteristics by detailed and articulate descriptions, not just say "it sounds nice."

- I know they understand when they can sing the music meaningfully without me telling them everything.

- When I see my former band students in a concert hall, I am satisfied that they have acquired the musical understanding needed for music to be important in their lives.

Some of the teachers who responded consider the teaching of composition an important component of their programs, though none of them mentioned it. If the nurturing of musical understanding is a pedagogical priority, teachers must be given preparation and a framework for teaching composition. Many writers have discussed this topic and emphasized the importance of creativity, most recently Fiske (2000), Younker (2000), and Kennedy (2000). As music educators committed to excellence in music programs, our challenge is to develop young musicians who can compose music and make musical decisions, not just as performers and listeners, but also as creators.

The following current realities and concerns are key factors that have a profound influence on teaching and learning in school music programs:

- Though there are many outstanding master teachers in the field, there are many others whose own level of understanding limits their effectiveness in advancing student understanding.

- The lack of guidelines regarding the musical competencies of co-operating teachers who are actively engaged in modeling best practice and in coaching future teachers poses potential problems for the sound training and musical growth of some practicum students.

- The wide range in background, education, and experience of music teachers has a significant impact on the level of musical understanding that their students reach.
- There appears to be a large population of music teachers who have difficulty taking musical content and expressing it meaningfully and artistically.
- There is a general lack of awareness about the importance of thorough long range planning that connects skills to end products in performing, listening, and creating.
- When classroom management is an issue, musical understanding becomes a lost objective.
- Teachers today continue to deal with challenges that also extend into music programs and sometimes interfere with teaching and learning.

Musical understanding occurs at all levels of the learning process and encompasses performing, listening, and creating. Students construct their own meaning when they are engaged in authentic learning activities that allow them to experience playing music as professional musicians do, as well as listening and responding to the music of professional musicians in real life situations. They also make significant gains in understanding when they are engaged in the process of composing their own music, transcribing it, and then performing for their peers or another audience. In this instance, they have the opportunity to explain their work to an audience and to celebrate their own and the creativity of their peers. Through performance—that experience of advancing the work and bringing it to an exemplary level, of sharing it and celebrating it before an audience—young musicians develop enduring understanding. But, for performance to advance student learning, it must be supported by appropriate and well-planned activities that are linked to the end product and by the use of effective assessment strategies.

Competent and committed music teachers are key to nurturing musical understanding in our classrooms. The current lack of commitment to professional development in school districts invites us to look at other ways of supporting music teachers. As curriculum leaders we need to find out what teachers are doing now to nurture musical understanding in the classroom and then determine how we can move forward in leading and supporting pre-service and established teachers in their own journey to musical understanding. Should universities and school boards be working more closely together to mentor music teachers?

As we examine and renew our vision for excellence in school music programs, our challenge as music educators and as mentors of future teachers is to develop musicians and teachers who themselves have a deep musical understanding, who can think like assessors, and who are well prepared and qualified to nurture musical understanding in our schools.

References

Apfelstadt, H. (1989). Musical thinking in the choral rehearsal. In E. Boardman (Ed.), *Dimensions of musical thinking* (pp. 73-81). Reston, VA: Music Educators National Conference.

Farrell, S. (1994). *Tools for powerful student evaluation: A practical source of authentic assessment strategies for music teachers.* Calgary, AB: Farrell & Farrell Music Educators.

Favaro, E. (2000). Changing attitudes: Changing practice. In B. Hanley & B. A. Roberts (Eds.) *Looking forward: Challenges to Canadian music education* (pp. 41-53). Victoria, BC: The Canadian Music Educators Association.

Fiske, H. (2000). A 2020 vision of music education. In B. Hanley & B. A. Roberts (Eds.) *Looking forward: Challenges to Canadian music education* (pp. 273-299). The Canadian Music Educators Association.

Kennedy, M. (2000). Music for all Canadians: Dream or reality at the high school level. In B. Hanley & B. A. Roberts (Eds.) *Looking forward: Challenges to Canadian music education* (pp. 139-155). Victoria, BC: The Canadian Music Educators Association.

McTighe, J., & Wiggins, G. (1999). *The understanding by design handbook.* Alexandria, VA: Association for Supervision and Curriculum Development.

Wiggins, G., & McTighe, J. (1998). *Understanding by design.* Alexandria, VA: Association for Supervision and Curriculum Development.

Younker, B. (2000). The role of musical thinking in selected Canadian elementary music curricula: Evidence of success and ideas for consideration. In B. Hanley & B. A. Roberts (Eds.) *Looking forward: Challenges to Canadian music education* (pp. 169-192). Victoria, BC: The Canadian Music Educators Association.

Authors

Lee Bartel has been active as a choral conductor, singer, violinist, and adjudicator since he began as a music specialist in St. Boniface School Division in Winnipeg in 1969. He has been on the faculty of the University of Toronto, Faculty of Music since 1987, serving as Coordinator of the Music Education Division from 1996–2000 and teaching choral conducting, guitar, secondary general music, research, and social psychology. Dr. Bartel is known internationally for his work in music research and has presented papers at refereed conferences around the world. His special interest is the social psychology of music and response to music. He heads the Canadian Music Education Research Centre, is an Associate of the Centre for Health Promotion, and a Research Associate of the John Adaskin Project. He is currently editor of the *Canadian Music Educator*. Dr. Bartel has worked with neuropsychologists at the Bloorview MacMillan Centre researching the use of music in the therapy of head-injured children. He is the scientific designer of Solitudes' internationally best selling CD series, *Music for Your Health* with Juno award nominations for his work in 2000 and 2001. He is a trained EEG neurofeedback clinician and is particularly interested in the interaction of music and brain activity as related to health. His recent and current research focuses on the effect of people's positive and negative experiences with music teachers. He has contributed a chapter to *The New Handbook of Research on Music Teaching and Learning*, entitled, "Trends in Data Acquisition and Knowledge Development" and is working on a book for research advisors.

Brenda Bush Poelman teaches general music at the United Nations International School in New York City. She earned a B.Mus. in Music Education from Alverno College (Milwaukee, WI) and her M.A in Music Education with distinction from New York University. Brenda has taught music in Chester, England and was the recipient of the Wisconsin Association of Teacher Educators Beginning Practitioner Award in 1996 for her teaching in Wisconsin. She has been involved in the Kodály Summer Certification Program at New York University, where she served as Kodály Liaison for the past two years. Brenda is a singer and pianist whose current research involves the implementation of TfU in early elementary music education.

Darryl Coan joined the Southern Illinois University Edwardsville faculty in1996, where he is Director of Graduate Studies in Music and heads the Music Theory program. He is publishing editor of the Mayday Group's online journal *Action and Criticism in Music Education* (ACT), and editor for *Music and Society*, an online publication for research and discussion of seminal issues in music education. Coan holds a Bachelor of Music Education degree from Illinois State University and Master's and Doctoral degrees in Music Education from the University of Illinois at Urbana-Champaign.

Marian T. Dura is Assistant Professor and Coordinator of Music Education at the University of Massachusetts Lowell, where she teaches courses in music technology, general music methods, research in music education, multicultural music education, and foundations and principles of music education. Dr. Dura has written educational materials for the Hartford Symphony Orchestra's Discovery Concerts since 1998. Her work has also appeared in *The Sonneck Society for American Music Bulletin,* the *Bulletin of the Council for Research in Music Education,* and the *American String Teacher* journal, for whom she served as a member of the editorial board from 1995-2000. Dr. Dura holds a B.Mus. in Music Education from Arizona State University, a M.Mus. from the University of Arizona, and a Ph.D. from Northwestern University.

Ronald C. Gerhardstein received his Ph.D. in music education from Temple University in 2001. Currently, Dr. Gerhardstein is an instrumental and choral music instructor at West Valley Junior High School in Yakima, WA. Before relocating to his home state in the pacific-northwest, Dr. Gerhardstein served as Assistant Professor of Music Education at Ohio Wesleyan University where he taught elementary and secondary music methods, orchestration, music appreciation, and supervised student teachers. He has also taught instrumental music in Idaho, Pennsylvania, and Ohio, as well as early childhood music in Philadelphia.

Harold Fiske has been a member of the Music Education Department of the Faculty of Music at the University of Western Ontario since 1974, where he instructs courses in psychology of music and research methodology and also serves as a graduate thesis advisor. He holds B.Mus. and M.Mus. degrees from Boston University and a Ph.D. from the University of Connecticut. He has presented papers at many music education research conferences in Canada and elsewhere, most of which have been published. He is also the author of three books, *Music and Mind* (1990), *Music Cognition and Aesthetic Attitudes* (1993), and *Selected Theories of Music Perception* (1996), as well as a contributor to several multi-authored texts including the first edition of the 1992 *Handbook of Research on Music Teaching and Learning.* He has served as chair of the Research Commission of the International Society of Music Education, the chair of the Canadian Music Education Research Council, and is chair of the Research Alliance of Institutes for Music Education. Currently he is a member of the editorial boards of the *Psychomusicology* journal and the *Bulletin of the Council for Research in Music Education.* He is a former chair of the Music Education Department at Western. Prior to his university assignment, Harold Fiske taught instrumental music at the elementary, intermediate, and high school levels.

Thomas W. Goolsby is an Associate Professor in the Faculty of Education at the University of Victoria, British Columbia. Formerly on the School of Music faculties at University of Washington and Georgia State University, he completed his doctorate at the University of Illinois. Goolsby has co-authored *A Guide to Research in Music Education* (with Roger Phelps and Larry Ferrara) and *The Teaching of Instrumental Music* (with Richard Colwell). His publications have appeared in the *Journal of Research in Music Education, Music Perception, Psychomusicology, Journal of Aesthetic Education, Bulletin for the Council of Research in Music Education* (that awarded him Dissertation of the Year in 1987), and *Music Educators Journal.* His research interests are emerging teacher education, constructivist learning through multimedia, and measurement, assessment and evaluation. He was an author for the National Assessment of Education Progress in the Arts in 1997 in the United

States, and, as a Senior Fulbright Scholar, has lectured in 13 Indonesian provinces, Singapore, Hong Kong, Malaysia, Brazil, and Paris.

Betty Hanley teaches music education in the Faculty of Education at the University of Victoria. She earned a B.A. in Music from the University of Western Ontario, a M.Mus. from Wayne State University, and a Ph.D. from the University of Minnesota. She co-organized the 1989 symposium *Re-Thinking Music Education in British Columbia*, chaired the second National Symposium on Arts Education (NSAE), Victoria 1998; and has published articles in the *Canadian Music Educator*, the *Canadian Journal of Education*, the *Journal of Music Teacher Education*, and the *British Journal of Music Education*. She is a co-author of *Making Music Meaningful: A Source Book for Beginning Teachers* (1991) and *The State of the Art: Arts Literacy in Canada (1993)*, editor of *Leadership, Advocacy, Communication* (1999) and co-editor (with Brian A. Roberts) of *Looking Forward: Challenges to Canadian Music Education* (2000). She is the CMEA membership coordinator, a member of the steering committee for the National Symposium on Arts Education, and serves on the editorial board for *Music Education International*.

Marta McCarthy is a Ph.D. candidate at the University of Toronto and conductor of the University of Guelph Choir and Chamber Singers in Ontario. For six years, she also conducted the University of Waterloo Choir. A graduate of Westminster Choir College (Princeton, NJ) and of the University of Toronto, Marta was recently awarded a SSHRC grant and the 1999 Elmer Iseler Fellowship in Conducting. As a secondary school teacher, Marta directed music theatre and taught drama as well as strings and band classes. She has also conducted church choirs for 15 years and is active as an accompanist and vocal coach in Toronto. At the University of Guelph, Marta incorporates yoga, mime, and creative movement in her conducting course as a means of developing expressive gestural technique.

Amanda Montgomery is currently a professor in the Faculty of Education at the University of Alberta where she teaches undergraduate and graduate courses in music education. Dr. Montgomery also teaches music to the kindergarten–grade three children enrolled in the Department of Elementary Education's Child Study Centre. As past-president of the Canadian Music Educators Association and past-president of the Kodály Society of Canada, Dr. Montgomery provides leadership to many music educators across Canada. The author of *Teaching Towards Musical Understanding* (2002, Prentice Hall Canada), Dr. Montgomery received her graduate degrees with distinction from Indiana University. Her research includes studies in early childhood music, musical preference, and teacher education. Articles by Dr. Montgomery may be read in several national and international journals.

Patricia Parai has been active as a music educator in Alberta since 1965, where she has taught elementary music, as well as choral and instrumental music at the junior and senior high school levels. As a former music consultant and a member of a fine arts team in the Calgary Catholic School District, she has presented workshops and worked directly with music teachers in classroom and rehearsal settings. In addition, she has collaborated with administrators, colleagues, and arts organizations to establish and maintain innovative arts initiatives in support of teaching and learning. She holds a B.Ed. and a M.Ed. degrees from the University of Calgary and is an Associate of the Royal Conservatory of Music of Toronto. She is currently teaching music in the Calgary Catholic School District and conducting professional development sessions for music educators.

Carol P. Richardson is Associate Professor and Chair of Music Education at the School of Music, University of Michigan where she has been on faculty since 1997. In 1994 she won a National Academy of Education/Spencer Postdoctoral Fellowship which took her to the University of New South Wales in Sydney, Australia to study the music listening processes of Cambodian refugee children. In her most recent book project she served as co-editor with Richard J. Colwell for *The New Handbook of Research on Music Teaching and Learning*, to be published by Oxford in 2002. Her current research centers on the preservation, teaching, and learning of traditional music in Ghana, West Africa.

Matthew Royal was born in Amersham, England in 1967. He took his B.A. and M.Phil. degrees in Music at Emmanuel College, Cambridge. After a year teaching in Sarawak, Malaysia, he moved to Canada in 1990 to study for the Ph.D. in Systematic Musicology at the University of Western Ontario. He completed his Ph.D. in 1995 and since then has held sessional posts at the University of Waterloo and the University of Western Ontario. Dr. Royal's research interests include cross-cultural issues in music cognition, the relationship between music cognition and ear training, and music-theoretical issues in the psychology of music. He is married with two children.

Joseph Shively is an Assistant Professor in the School of Music at the University of North Carolina at Greensboro where his primary responsibilities are teaching instrumental music education and technology. His areas of interest include instrumental music, constructivist teacher education, and philosophy. He holds degrees from Limestone College and the University of Illinois. While at Illinois, Dr. Shively served as associate editor of the *Bulletin of the Council for Research in Music Education*. He is an active clinician, conductor, and adjudicator for public school bands and orchestras. He will be joining the Faculty at Kansas State University this summer.

Jackie Wiggins is Professor and Coordinator of Music Education and Graduate Studies in the Department of Music, Theater, and Dance at Oakland University, Michigan where she teaches general music methods, psychology of music learning, philosophy of music education, and research in music education. With more than twenty years of public school music teaching experience, she has been an active clinician, presenter, and author in local, state, national, and international settings. Among her publications are: *Teaching for Musical Understanding* (2001, McGraw-Hill), *Composition in the Classroom* (1990, MENC), *Synthesizers in the Elementary Music Classroom* (1991, MENC), and two books of lesson plans for the new Fm7 MIDI-Partner System (2000, Fm7; 2001, Fm7 for Silver Burdett Ginn). Her research involves qualitative study of children's musical cognitive processing, creative process, and the role of the music teacher in the development of these processes. She holds two degrees in music education from Queens College of the City University of New York and a doctorate in music education from the University of Illinois at Urbana-Champaign.

Renate Zenker is a private, in-home music educator, independent researcher, and educational consultant in Vancouver, British Columbia. Her research interests centre on the important conceptual issues concerning "understanding," appreciation, and "aesthetics" and their role in music education. With a background of 20 years of private teaching, she is also currently conducting a meta-survey of the literature on the mental, physical, and emotional benefits of music instruction. She is the 1995 and 1996 winner of the Canadian Music Educators Association's Franklin Churchley Graduate Essay Competition. She holds conjoint music and music education degrees from the Memorial University of Newfoundland School of Music and a master's and doctorate in education from the University of British Columbia.